INTRODUCTION TO SECURITY

HARVEY BURSTEIN

Prentice Hall Career & Technology
Englewood Cliffs, New Jersey 07632

Library of Congress Cataloging-in-Publication Date

BURSTEIN, HARVEY
    Introduction to security/ Harvey Burstein
        p. cm.
    Includes bibliographical references and index.
    ISBN 0-13-057051-6
    1. Private security services. 2. Security systems. I. Title.
HV8290.B873 1994   93-47229
363.2'89'068—dc20   CIP

Editorial/production supervision, interior design,
    and electronic production: *Barbara Marttine*
Cover design: *Ruta Kysilewskyj*
Director of production and manufacturing: *David Riccardi*
Production coordinator:: *Ed O'Dougherty*
Acquisitions editor: *Robin Baliszewski*
Editorial assistant: *Rosemary Florio*

 Prentice Hall Career & Technology
©1994, by Prentice-Hall, Inc.
A Paramount Communications Company
Englewood Cliffs, NJ 07632

Printed in the United States of America

10 9 8 7 6 5 4 3 2 1

ISBN   0-13-057051-6

PRENTICE-HALL INTERNATIONAL (UK) LIMITED, *London*
PRENTICE-HALL OF AUSTRALIA PTY. LIMITED, *Sydney*
PRENTICE-HALL CANADA INC., *Toronto*
PRENTICE-HALL HISPANOAMERICANA, S.A., *Mexico*
PRENTICE-HALL OF INDIA PRIVATE LIMITED, *New Delhi*
PRENTICE-HALL OF JAPAN, INC., *Tokyo*
SIMON & SCHUSTER ASIA PTE. LTD., *Singapore*
EDITORA PRENTICE-HALL DO BRASIL, LTDA., *Rio de Janeiro*

To my late wife, Ina,
and to the memory of my parents,
Morris and Rachel Burstein

CONTENTS

PREFACE

This book was prompted by the fact that far too many criminal justice and business administration students in particular, and business and police executives, as well as some academicians in general, do not seem to appreciate fully what security is. Some tend to think of it as a component of policing; others as little more than locks on doors, alarms, and guards monitoring access or shipping/receiving dock activities, or making periodic patrol rounds. In truth, security is a great deal more.

Like policing, security is concerned with crime prevention. However, in many respects it serves a bridge between our criminal justice system and the business community since its primary focus is on protecting and conserving all of an employer's assets, both tangible and intangible. To design and implement successful security programs there must be an understanding not only of how an employer's business or institution is organized and functions, but of how security must be integrated into all aspects of the organization's operations.

This book is intended to serve a dual purpose. First, it is hoped that it will provide its readers with a much better understanding of how security must be integrated and of the many types of organizations and activities that need effective loss prevention programs. Second, it attempts to give its readers a look at the variety of career opportunities available to students who seek careers that offer a challenge, mental stimulation, a chance to learn much about the operations of businesses and institutions, and no less important, the satisfaction of seeing their ideas for improved security implemented and the hoped for results achieved.

I have tried to give the reader at least some idea of how security is seen and how it functions in the real world. To do this I have drawn heavily upon my own experiences during thirty-eight years as either an active security director or a security management consultant. As a security director I have worked for both a major educational and a major financial institution, one of the largest international hotel chains, and a Fortune 500 multinational corporation. As a security management consultant my clients have ranged in size from a two-person retail business to several Fortune 500 multinational corporations.

Since one of the primary purposes of this book is to try to stimulate student interest in the opportunities open in the field of security, the use of photographs to illustrate rather than charts or graphs, was deliberate. The choice was based on the assumption that this would be more meaningful to those who may have little understanding of the variety of organizations that can offer rewarding career opportunities. In this regard I am indebted to those who graciously and willingly made illustrations available, and whose organizations have been given credit accordingly. I am also grateful to Jacob Frank, vice president and general counsel for Data General Corporation, for permission to use as appendices some forms I developed while employed as that company's corporate director safety security—staff attorney.

This preface would be incomplete if I failed to thank my late wife, Ina, for her patience and understanding during the period when I was preparing the book. I would be remiss if I did not acknowledge the support and encouragement that I have gotten from Robin Baliszewski, Senior Managing Editor, Criminal Justice, for Prentice Hall Career & Technology, since the inception of this project.

Harvey Burstein

Chapter 1

INTRODUCTION

THE HISTORICAL DEVELOPMENT OF SECURITY

The idea that people have a right to protect their property, whether real or personal, has existed since time immemorial. The exercise of this right long predates the notion that government help for that purpose might be forthcoming in the form of a public police or law enforcement agency. It was not until the time of the Roman Emperor Augustus (63 B.C.–A.D. 7) that what is described as the first large city police agency in the world was organized,[1] and it was not until some time between A.D. 1000 and 1300 that there appears to have been the development of a structured law enforcement system (in England). Only then was enforcing the law and maintaining the king's peace recognized as a public responsibility. While the primary purpose of the various guilds that flourished in Europe in medieval times was to promote the common interests of their members, the absence of formal policing also caused them to consider mutual aid and the protection of guild members as proper functions of membership.

The colonists who settled the United States and the early settlers who followed them came from England and the European continent. It is therefore not surprising that their thoughts about how best to protect their real and personal property in the New World were consistent with those to which they had become accustomed in Europe. Since for all practical purposes public policing was nonexistent, security was each person's responsibility. In fact, it was not until 1783 that New York City established its first, and rather rudimentary, police department. Seven more years passed before it had its first paid daytime police force.

With respect to private security, there is little or no evidence of such services being used in the United States until the railroads began their westward expansion. The railroads and those who used them became increasingly concerned with the need to protect both the goods and passengers being transported against attack, regardless of the source. Thus it appears that the first use of private security in the United States occurred in 1855 when Allan Pinkerton started the North West Police Agency. Its primary purpose was to provide contract services for the protection of the railroads as they expanded their routes across the western half of the country.

In 1857, Pinkerton founded the Pinkerton Protection Patrol, frequently referred to as the Pinkerton Agency, whose purpose it was to offer other businesses private watchman services, also on a contract basis. The William J. Burns Detective Agency was founded in 1909 to provide services similar to those offered by Pinkerton, and for many years these two firms were the country's principal providers of contract security personnel.

Initially, the railroads were the primary users of private security. However, during the latter part of the nineteenth and early part of the twentieth centuries an increase in the number of labor disputes began to plague both employers and employees, prompting larger companies to look for ways in which to protect their interests. While the problems were most noticeable in the coal mining and steel industries, manufacturers were not exempt. Such better known businesses as Carnegie Steel and the McCormick Harvester Company were among those affected. These labor disputes also provided an impetus for expansion of the contract security industry, with Pinkerton and Burns continuing to dominate the field for many years. Their principal stock in trade was the personnel they were able to provide for troubled clients.

Nevertheless, it is interesting to note the appearance of another type of security service on the American scene in 1858, when Edwin Holmes established the first central-station burglar alarm company. Holmes had little or no competition until the organization of the American District Telegraph Company (best known as ADT) in 1874.

By no means were contract security services the only form of protection used by the business community. Some businesses, notably retail stores and hotels, began hiring their own employees as "house detectives" for security purposes, and eventually, banks began to hire guards. All of these jobs were limited in scope. In retailing the object was to catch shoplifters, then considered the primary source of retail losses. Those working for hotels were expected to deal with fights in the saloons, occasional guest room burglaries, and prostitution for hotels concerned about their reputations. Banks felt that the mere presence of guards would discourage bank robbers from holding them up. This direct hiring of personnel by employers to protect their interests might be considered as the forerunner of proprietary security services.

Of course, the United States was not the only country where businesses felt a need for security. Nevertheless, it is interesting to note that despite Sir Robert Peel's 1829 reorganization of the London Metropolitan Police, considered to be the beginning of modern law enforcement, it was not until early in the twentieth century that England's highly industrialized society apparently began to consider the use of watchmen and guards on private property acceptable.[2]

In any event, American businesses seemed content to carry on with the use of watchmen, contract security services (which often functioned primarily as a private police force), the very limited use of proprietary security personnel, and alarm systems.

Regardless of the nature of a business or the circumstances, very few placed a high priority on the need to institute effective security programs that would help them reduce losses and prevent problems from arising.

This was particularly evident when two incidents, both attributed to German saboteurs, occurred before the United States entered World War I. Mysterious explosions at Black Tom Island in New York harbor in 1916 and at Kingsland, New Jersey, in January 1917 seem to have had little impact on the American business community. Many companies appeared satisfied with only their night watchmen, who provided largely a fire watch.

Nazi Germany's 1939 invasion of Poland and the start of World War II made the United States the principal supplier of materiel for the French and British forces fighting on the European continent. Recalling the two acts of sabotage that predated America's entry into World War I, the U.S. government was determined to avoid similar incidents even though it was not yet directly involved with the war effort. The government was also mindful of the existence of the German-American Bund, which publicly voiced its support for the Nazi Party, and the fact that its membership was located largely in major industrial areas.

These factors contributed to increased concern with the need to protect businesses doing work related to the French and British war effort. Security started to get far more attention than ever before. When the USSR and Germany signed a nonaggression pact, interest in industrial security was heightened even more. Fear of possible acts of sabotage by members of the Communist Party U.S.A. were now coupled with those already existing vis-à-vis the German-American Bund.

On December 7, 1941, Japanese forces attacked U.S. forces in Hawaii; within days the German and Italian governments also declared war on the United States. This meant that even more American businesses would become involved in what now became an Allied war effort to be fought in both Europe and the Pacific. The need to protect them against possible acts of sabotage and espionage would now rank next to production in terms of importance, a concern that understandably continued for the war's duration.

When German forces attacked the USSR, despite their nonaggression pact, the United States took on the added role of principal supplier of materiel to the Soviets. The war effort was then prosecuted by the so-called Big Four: the United States, Great Britain, France, and the USSR. While the May and August 1945 Allied victories in Europe and the Pacific, respectively, ended active military hostilities, political hostility among the former allies soon became evident. It was the United States, Britain, and France on one side and the USSR on the other. What soon would become known as the Cold War had started.

Fearful that it could become "hot," the Western Allies generally, and the United States particularly, agreed that they could not afford to decrease either the size of their armed forces or the supplies and materiel needed to support them. Insofar as the government's relations with the private business sector were concerned, the risks of sabotage and espionage remained. There was great concern with the need to protect both information considered vital to the production of such materiel, and the arms and equipment produced.

Consequently, the U.S. government, acting principally through its newly created Department of Defense, Atomic Energy Commission, and Central Intelligence Agency, felt that precautions had to be taken. Attention focused largely on possible acts of espionage by the USSR, in its behalf by any of its Eastern European allies, or by members of or sympathizers with the Communist Party U.S.A.

Therefore, to protect not only the development of information essential to both weapons production and political intelligence, but also the actual weapons or products produced, the government agencies most directly involved developed security guidelines for use by the affected businesses and academic institutions. An example was, and still is, the Department of Defense Industrial Security Manual. These guidelines were then incorporated by reference into contracts awarded to the private sector for manufacturing and into grants awarded to universities for research and development.

Since these requirements were mandatory, those who wanted to be awarded government contracts were obliged not only to institute security programs, but also to designate a "security officer" who would be responsible for the program's implementation and maintenance. However, inasmuch as these programs were mandated, their cost was deemed a justifiable part of the overhead for which contractors were entitled to be reimbursed by the government. Thus reimbursement might have been seen as a form of incentive for the initiation of security programs. Regardless, the post–World War II era may be considered the beginning of security as it exists today even though its genesis was primarily in defense-related activities.

Even with the Cold War, not all businesses that had been working on national defense matters continued to get government contracts. However, in many cases they had become so accustomed to having security programs that they elected to retain and in some instances even to expand them.

At the same time, other types of businesses and institutions were becoming increasingly aware of the need to do a better job of protecting their assets. No longer were those involved with national defense matters the only ones concerned. Retailers, hotels, financial institutions, and some manufacturers in industries where the protection of trade secrets or technology were important also saw a need for security. Although some executives still viewed security as little more than a "necessary evil," it was to be given a considerably higher priority in the scheme of things than even before.

Both defense and nondefense businesses and institutions in need of or wanting security programs were inclined initially to think of security as an aspect of policing. They saw security personnel as private police, and security directors or managers as private-sector police chiefs. It was this perception that resulted in their looking to the ranks of former law enforcement personnel, and in some cases to military or intelligence agencies, as logical sources from which to recruit security directors and managers. Academic credentials and exposure to the business world were unimportant. For all practical purposes women and minorities were not even considered.

With regard to academics, it should be noted that early in the twentieth century the University of California at Berkeley began offering summer courses in police administration.[3] Later a few other universities began to offer programs in police science and administration, but even these pioneers had no baccalaureate programs in security. However, in the 1950s, as some universities came to realize that there were differences between policing and security, they began to offer seminars dealing with various aspects of security. Even more time would pass before any of the nation's colleges and universities would offer students opportunities to earn degrees in security or with a security major.

Nevertheless, despite recognizing that differences existed, the academic community was still inclined to think of security as did many businesses; it was a form of private policing rather than something related to corporate management. Consequently, to a large extent faculty were recruited from the same sources as those used for hiring security managers—from among former law enforcement, military, and intelligence agency personnel.

Of course, even today there are some who fail to see any real distinctions between security and policing. To them the only important distinction is that security is private, policing is public. The latter function is performed by an agency of government while private security is policing by nongovernment entities. Of course, there is universal acceptance of the concept of "security" as used by the government to protect certain types of information.

Often overlooked is the fact that for years there has existed an agency of the U.S. government which, for all practical purposes, is charged with the protection and conservation of the government's assets, and which in many ways parallels the work of a modern corporate security department. That agency is the General Accounting Office. Furthermore, there are some departments of the federal government, and some states, which have inspectors general. In many respects their work is quite like that of a corporate security director.

Ideas as to just what security is, can, and should be are still evolving. Happily, there is a growing understanding of the differences between policing and security and of the contribution that security can make to the success of the businesses and institutions by which it is employed.

While security shares an interest in crime prevention with law enforcement, another aspect of security is the protection and conservation of all of an employer's assets, both tangible and intangible. As Norman Bottom and John Kostanoski point out, private security attempts to control five types of threats confronting businesses, of which crime is but one; the others are waste, accidents, errors, and unethical practices.[4]

The protection and conservation of assets, which frequently involves no criminal activity, is what enables security to make its greatest contribution to an employer. Thus increasing numbers of executives and academicians are now more inclined to see security not as policing but as having an important role to play in business administration. In many respects security as we know it today represents a bridge between our criminal justice system and the business community.

The latter's increased awareness of and concern with the need for protection has prompted the expanded use of proprietary personnel and the growth of contract security services in the form of guards, private investigators, and alarm systems. No longer are Pinkerton and Burns the only contract agencies, nor are Holmes and ADT the only central-station alarm companies. Today there are many firms, ranging in size from those doing business on a local or regional basis to some who operate internationally. The high-technology industry also has made and continues to make significant contributions to the security field.

As more and more employers have come to realize that security and policing are not the same, and that there is a genuine need for professional security directors and managers, academic institutions have made an effort to keep pace with their demands. As of 1990, 164 certificate or degree programs, the latter at both the undergraduate and graduate levels, were being offered by American colleges and universities.[5]

The acceptance by both business executives and academicians of security as a meaningful contributor to the economy and as an academic discipline has resulted in two developments. Along with the business community's demand for increased professionalism on the part of security directors and managers is the opportunity for variety and the challenges that security offers to those who are interested in careers that combine the best of the criminal justice system and the world of business.

Furthermore, the matter of security's contribution to the economy is by no means insignificant. As Louis M. Spadaro, an economist and former dean of the Martino Graduate School of Business Administration at Fordham University has pointed out, detection and punishment alone—the primary focus of policing—will not do since crime-related losses are not confined to the firms that incur them; they also result in increased costs to consumers.[6]

As for the variety and the challenges that are open to security directors and managers, virtually no business or institution is immune from problems, whether attributable to crimes or to other forms of questionable activity. Tangible assets in whatever form obviously need to be secured. No less important is the demand that intangibles, such as reputation, be protected. And while the need to prevent problems from arising initially is of paramount importance, logic suggests that some losses will be inevitable. In those cases the challenge is to keep the dollar amount of the losses to an absolute minimum.

THE MAGNITUDE OF LOSSES

Thus logical questions are posed. How great are the losses, and in view of the relationship between security and the economy, how does the absence of the former affect the latter? Those responsible for managing any business or institution that suffers losses, whether due to crime or other forms of questionable activity, are faced with the need to increase their operating and profit margins. To do this they must examine their few options, knowing that regardless of the one chosen, the community will be affected adversely.

The first choice usually will be an increase in the cost of goods sold or services rendered. Even if successful in terms of saving the organization, this undeniably affects consumers. However, if unsuccessful, a second choice may be downsizing. This has an even greater impact on the community since it means a loss of at least some jobs. The least desirable choice, and the one involving the greatest hardship for the community, is to go out of business. In this case the increased unemployment usually affects the remaining businesses and institutions. Since this also decreases the city's tax base, a tax increase may be needed to provide additional revenue to cover unemployment compensation, and possibly even food and shelter for the less fortunate.

Therefore, that losses exist is a forgone conclusion. To what extent is another matter. Although it is impossible to project figures with any degree of accuracy, it is nevertheless worth looking at what data are available to at least try to appreciate the magnitude of those losses that may be security related.

The figures and sources vary. Although the sources themselves may be reliable, the fact remains that without knowing from where or under what circumstances they obtained their data, one cannot realistically attest to the information's reliability. Still, it is worth looking at some examples if only to get an idea of what may be involved.

For instance, one source has projected a loss of $114 billion or more a year by American businesses due to crime,[7] a figure reportedly equal to what American corporations spend in a year on business travel and entertainment.[8] To help illustrate the extent to which losses have increased over time, compare the $114 billion currently projected with the estimated cost of crime against business for the period 1967–1976, made by such organizations as the Small Business Administration, U.S. Chamber of Commerce, American Management Association, and Joint Economic Committee of the U.S. Congress, which ranged from a low of a little over $3 to a high of over $44 billion a year.[9] A look at other sources is no less illustrative of the disparity among them. However, the data may also be useful in terms of getting an idea as to the types of losses on which some of the projections are made.

In 1977 the American Management Association reported that the business community's losses ranged from $3.5 to $10 billion a year in kickbacks alone.[10] Employee theft cost businesses from $15 to $25 billion a year according to a 1988 estimate from the Bureau of National Affairs.[11] The November 14, 1988, edition of *Forbes* reported that retail theft amounted to $30 billion a year.[12] The *Lipman Report* released the following day indicated that "some experts" put the losses from computer crime at $200 billion a year, a figure that exceeds the latest projection for all losses. According to the International Trade Commission, the estimated value of stolen intellectual property has been placed at $40 billion a year.[13] In 1989 business property theft was estimated to cost $100 billion a year,[14] and the International Trade Commission estimated losses due to the counterfeiting of American-made products at from $8 to $20 billion a year.[15]

The Uniform Crime Report published annually by the Federal Bureau of Investigation is another source frequently referred to by those interested in estimating business losses. However, before looking at the figures for any given year, one must remember that there are factors that affect even their accuracy.

First, the FBI is entirely dependent on the submission of accurate data by participating police departments. Consequently, if in any year not all departments submit reports, or their submissions are inaccurate, the data will be incomplete or inaccurate. Second, of necessity the police can only submit data based on the crimes reported to them. Therefore, if victimized businesses or institutions do not report crimes to appropriate law enforcement agencies, they obviously cannot be incorporated in the information submitted to the FBI.

Turning then to the *Uniform Crime Report* for 1990, released by the FBI on August 11, 1991, almost 22 percent of all robberies perpetrated involved some form of commercial enterprise, including commercial houses, gas or service stations, convenience stores, and banks, with the average convenience store loss placed at $341 and the average bank loss at $3244. A little over 30 percent of all larcenies or thefts consisted of either shoplifting (16.2 percent) or thefts from buildings, with the average shoplifting loss being $115 and the average loss due to a larceny from a building being $791. There were 735 cases of arson involving industrial or manufacturing premises, with a highest average loss of $73,703, and 5106 acts of arson against other commercial properties, with a highest average loss of $37,572. In addition, the average loss from burglaries of nonresidential properties amounted to $1110.

The Surety Association of America, which compiles data on fidelity or honesty insurance, is yet another source. It has statistical information on both the dollar value of premiums paid to insurers and on claims paid by them to the insured parties once claims have been submitted and processed. Figures available in 1990 for calendar year 1989 indicate that the total premiums paid to the carriers amounted to more than $825 million, while the claims paid in the some period exceeded $309 million.[16] Thus over 37 percent of the premiums received by the bonding companies were paid out in claims. Once again, however, without questioning the accuracy of the data, the Association itself recognizes that the figures are incomplete, so that a true picture is unavailable. As pointed out by Robin Weldy, the association's director-legal, information with regard to the total dollar amount of loss caused by dishonesty in the United States is "quite elusive" since not all fidelity bonds respond to all employee dishonesty, claims are not submitted when losses are below the bond's deductible amount, if the loss exceeds the limits covered the additional amount is not reflected in insurance statistics, a majority of businesses do not have employee dishonesty insurance, and Lloyd's (of London), a large writer of fidelity bonds in the United States, does not report its statistics to the Surety Association of America.[17]

MANAGEMENT'S NEED TO PROTECT AND CONSERVE ASSETS

While the need to prevent crime is as important to businesses and institutions as it is to the communities in which they are situated, crime prevention alone is but one of senior management's worries. However, from an administrative or operational point of view a greater need is to protect and conserve all assets. Many incidents can adversely affect a business or institution. True, technically, some may even be crimes, but of a sort rarely prosecuted. For example, careless hotel or hospital kitchen employees who cause unreasonable amounts of food to spoil or go to waste are responsible for decreased profits or operating margins, but their negligence is not a crime. On the other hand, those who steal time in reality are guilty of stealing their employer's money, yet seldom are they charged with a crime and prosecuted.

There actually are many compelling reasons for management's need to protect and conserve assets. One is legal, since the law holds that the board of directors and officers of a corporation have a fiduciary, or special, relationship of trust to its stockholders. This obliges them to adhere to sound business practices so as to ensure the efficient and effective management of the particular business or institution for the benefit of those stockholders, a responsibility that includes protecting and conserving all assets in whatever form they may be.

Of course, these same sound business practices allow them to delegate authority for discharging their obligations to key employees. Among the latter are their security directors or managers whose direct role in the area of asset protection is especially critical since, unlike many other key personnel, their job responsibilities are company- or institution-wide. However, before they, or anyone else for that matter, can participate in the process, there obviously is a need to know just what comprises *all* assets, and why they need protection. To merely say "all" without further explanation is not enough. Everyone would tend to think of tangible property, but how many would be prepared to include employees, or intangibles that may be of value? It also may be that if security's role in the world of business is to be better understood by those who still tend to think of it as a form of policing, some explanation is needed for the "why" as well, even though the answer should be self-evident.

Since tangible assets can easily be recognized, it is easy to convince people of the need to protect them. When one speaks of tangible assets, people can readily appreciate the value of such things as buildings, money, documents, products, office equipment, and even raw materials: things that can be seen or felt. It is not hard for management to understand why they need to be protected against theft, or why land needs to be protected against acts of trespass and buildings against arson.

By the same token, management does not always understand, and too often tends to overlook, the equal importance of protecting employees and intangible assets as well. Property rights, business information transmitted orally or by electronic means, time, and indeed employees and reputation are also assets. Their loss may have as great or greater impact on a business or institution as would the loss of tangible assets. Nevertheless, it is precisely because of their nature that assets in these categories are much more difficult to appreciate and thus to protect.

It is interesting to note that while intelligence agencies representing various governments often refer to their personnel and informants as "assets," the private sector rarely uses that term and may not even think along those lines. Yet employees, especially those whose many years of experience or relatively unique roles in the organization make them invaluable contributors to its success, definitely are an asset. Consequently, with the increase in terrorism, multinational corporations, and even some domestic ones, have become increasingly conscious of the need to protect their personnel as well as their facilities. In addition, certain types of local crime have highlighted the need to think in terms of protecting domestic employees and facilities as well. Even as fundamental a question as whether groups of key employees should be allowed to travel together has caused some companies to rethink their policies because they are so valuable an asset.

Information in hard copy is a tangible asset accorded protection; transmitted verbally, whether in person or by telephone, or electronically, it is an intangible. Making both employers and employees aware of the need to protect information in the latter category is much more difficult, even though in some cases it is precisely the information's sensitivity that has prompted the decision not to transmit it in hard copy.

For example, since the early 1980s U.S. intelligence agencies have suspected the French government of being actively involved in acts of industrial espionage against U.S. companies. Although the French government has denied this, in September 1991, Pierre Marion, who once was the head of France's equivalent of the U.S. Central Intelligence Agency, confirmed his government's role in such activities as a way to keep current in the fields of international commerce and technology.[18]

Similarly, too often ignored is an organization's reputation. It is not uncommon for a business being sold to have both the sellers and buyers attach a dollar value to its "goodwill," or reputation. Despite this, in the ordinary course of doing business things may occur that can adversely affect not only reputation, but also profits and operating margins. Consumers frequently are much less inclined to want to do business with a corporation or institution whose reputation is questionable.

A statement by Warren Buffett, who in the summer of 1991 became interim chairman of the board of Salomon Brothers, Inc. when this old and large private banking firm first came under investigation for questionable practices, helps illustrate a reputation's importance. He reportedly told Salomon employees worldwide: "If you lose money for the firm by bad decisions, I will be very understanding. If you lose reputation for the firm, I will be ruthless."[19]

From the foregoing it is evident that no business or institution can afford not to protect and conserve its assets, in whatever form they may be. Failure to do so can have serious consequences for it. If losses of any magnitude are allowed to go unchecked, they can have both a social and an economic impact on the business or institution itself and its employees. No less important is the socioeconomic impact on the communities in which they are located. Neither can one ignore the fact that if the particular organization is big enough, it can even have an impact on the nation's economy and social problems.

SECURITY'S REAL AND POTENTIAL IMPACT ON SAVINGS AND OPERATING EFFICIENCY

While the need to protect and conserve assets may be more easily understood now, a discussion of security's impact on an employer's savings and operating efficiency may seem futile. This is true since so much of what security programs do is not easily measured in terms of their contribution. This problem is not unlike one that confronts law enforcement agencies. For example, good records enable either a police or a security department to show differences in activity from year to year or over a period of time. The number of incidents reported, and the number of cases solved, may go up or down from one year to the next. An increase will be cause for concern, and probably some criticism. A decrease will suggest that the police or security department, as the case may be, has done a better job than it did the year before.

Truthfully, although statistical data can be used to reflect levels of departmental activity, they do not, and in fact cannot, show the extent to which incidents have been prevented. Theoretically, one might argue that if a community has no crime, or if a business or institution has no security-related incidents, the need for either a police department or a security department no longer exists. However, logic tells us otherwise. Thus for all practical purposes trying to measure the true effectiveness of either a police or a security department is impossible.

Therefore, one is tempted to ask just how security has an impact on real and potential savings. Again, logic tells us that effective security programs, by virtue of incidents prevented even though not easily measured, help employers save money. Preventing the loss, theft, or destruction of assets obviously eliminates the need to buy or make replacements, some of which may be more costly at this time than they were originally. This, then, represents both real and potential savings for the employer. Furthermore, prevention also reduces the need to file insurance claims for losses, with the attendant risk of increased premiums. Of course, this assumes that the value of the affected assets does not fall under the policy's deductible clause to begin with, in which case the victim organization absorbs the entire loss.

Then, too, since effective security programs emphasize prevention, the amount of otherwise productive time lost by employees who are affected by the loss, theft, or destruction of assets is reduced. Also reduced is the amount of time spent by security personnel trying to locate the assets and to learn what happened, how it happened, and who is responsible. Bear in mind that in all likelihood whatever insurance coverage exists, regardless of the policy's deductible clause, will not compensate the victim organization for any of this time. Therefore, that real and potential savings can be realized by using a preventive approach in security programs becomes increasingly clear.

Accepting this premise, what role does security play in terms of affecting operating efficiency? One facet of successful security programs is their emphasis on good accountability. This, in turn, reduces the gaps that otherwise might exist among operating functions and makes it apparent to employees that if a loss of any kind occurs, the employer has the ability to localize the problem's source. This very reduction in such gaps also helps to increase the organization's operating efficiency. These principles apply whether organizations operate for a profit or are nonprofit, as often is the case with medical centers and some schools.

For example, good accountability can help prevent the loss of raw materials in a manufacturing environment. This permits them to flow to production areas without interruption. It also helps to eliminate the disruption that occurs whenever losses do happen and otherwise productive time has to be spent by all affected employees assisting investigators. Production schedules and finished goods inventories can be planned with a degree of confidence, shipping can better assess its needs, and transportation can be arranged to ensure timely delivery to customers. Other by-products are a sales staff confident of the company's ability to fill customers' orders on time, and the employer's enhanced reputation, which increases the likelihood of more sales, which translates into more profit.

In a similar vein, since a major part of a sound security program involves helping to protect and conserve assets, security has a legitimate interest in having a hotel kitchen use a first in–first out method to reduce waste and spoilage. This, in turn, gives the kitchen staff more time for preparation, cooking, and presentation since less time needs to be spent examining perishables for possible spoilage and then having to dispose of them. The fact that the quality of the food and the way in which it is served gives guests a favorable impression of the entire hotel, not just its dining room, not only will encourage them to return, but it will also lead them to recommend the hotel and its facilities to others. The result will mean new and additional guests, increased sales, and increased profits.

These illustrations show how security can help prevent problems and have a positive affect on savings and operating efficiency. Ultimately, both will be reflected as profits on the organization's balance sheet. Preventing the loss of raw materials, or reducing the risk of spoilage, is a saving.

PHILOSOPHICAL DIFFERENCES BETWEEN POLICING AND SECURITY

Despite logical reasons for security to be viewed as part of the criminal justice system, of which policing is also a segment, there are certain underlying philosophical differences between the two in terms of their respective objectives and what each can hope to accomplish. Those differences should not be minimized. The contributions of public and private policing to their communities or institutions are of inestimable value, but no matter how effective, they still are considerably different from what effective security departments can contribute to the businesses by which employed.

As noted earlier, public and private policing and security admittedly share the common goal of crime prevention. However, without minimizing law enforcement's importance, security's contribution to the overall protection and conservation of an employer's assets, as well as to its success, is much broader and more meaningful than what a police agency can do for its community or institution. This is true even among select private police forces, such as those found on a number of university campuses, which do provide a limited form of security for their employers. A number of factors contribute to these differences.

For example, the principal assets of a community protected by its police are its inhabitants and reputation. If those who live, work in, or visit a city, are victimized in any way by crime, they and the community's reputation suffer. A bad reputation may cause both people and businesses to move. This, in turn, will affect the city's tax base, and the lost income often will cause further deterioration.

In an effort to prevent this, the police historically have tended to follow two theories. One, of deterrence, is based on the idea that the speedy detection of criminals followed by their trial and punishment will discourage other criminals. The second, making a police presence known through high visibility, consists of getting an optimal number of both uniformed and undercover officers on the streets. Equally noteworthy is the fact that when crime in a community increases, a typical reaction is to increase the size of the police department. This approach, reminiscent of a military organization's reliance on superior numbers and armament to win battles, is not surprising in view of the quasimilitary nature of police departments. In any event, crime prevention, even among public police agencies, or private ones for that matter, that either have adopted or reverted to neighborhood policing is largely an approach based on reaction.

Then, too, even the most progressive and effective police agencies can operate only within imposed legal and budgetary limitations. Although security departments must also operate within the law, there nevertheless are legal constraints imposed on public law enforcement, such as the Fourth and Fifth Amendments to the Constitution, which do not apply to private citizens, security personnel included. As for budgetary limitations, security directors are no less mindful than police chiefs of the need to operate within their budgets, but they also know that if they can present sound reasons for exceeding the budget, their employer will make the necessary funds available.

The police have no control over social or economic problems that may contribute to the causes of crime, or losses to the city. Rarely, if ever, do they even have any input to government agencies designated to deal with those issues. As an example, they will be asked for their thoughts on eradicating drug problems in the community, but not for ideas about ways to deal with the problems of homelessness or unemployment. Similarly, despite the fact that the quality of operating systems and procedures is crucial to loss prevention, a police chief would not consider it proper to meet with the head of the city's purchasing department to offer suggestions about ways in which the potential for kickbacks could be reduced.

On the other hand, security directors are responsible for protecting all of the employer's assets, both tangible and intangible. Unlike police chiefs, they must realize that providing their employers with effective prevention programs requires them to be proactive, not just reactive. Relying solely on detection, apprehension, and punishment as the best ways to prevent future problems from arising is shortsighted. Detection, apprehension, and punishment, on the one hand, and loss prevention on the other, are not mutually exclusive concepts, but prudent security directors know that by putting their emphasis on prevention they are offering their employers the most cost-effective and least troublesome way in which best to serve their organizations.

To do this they must seek contact with other department heads, not avoid it; they need to learn how operating departments function. They can have significant input into what goes on in the organization, and as long as what they advocate is lawful, operationally feasible, and cost-effective, security directors only need senior management's approval to proceed to implement new programs. They need not await the introduction and passage of legislation.

Thus it can be much easier for security directors, and their departments, to operate and see the results of their efforts. These are the reasons why well-managed security departments can do more for their constituents than even the finest police departments can for theirs.

SUMMARY

With the passage of time the theory that persons have a right to protect their property has progressed to a point which recognizes that business entities, as well as individuals, have that same right, and that in fact they may be legally obligated to do so. However, this concept has evolved slowly. Despite the first known use of security personnel in the United States in 1855, it really was not until after World War II that security as we know it today started to become an integral part of the American business scene.

Even with the development of security programs, that businesses and institutions have suffered and continue to suffer losses is undeniable. Equally undeniable is the fact that determining their magnitude is a practical impossibility. When losses for any business dictate economies in order to survive, both the business and the community in which it is located are affected. Knowing this, management will seek additional ways in which to protect and conserve assets.

Properly designed, fully integrated security programs that emphasize prevention and use lawful, operationally feasible, and cost-effective means to protect and conserve an employer's assets can have a significant impact on both savings and operating efficiency. For this there is a need to recognize that despite a common interest in preventing crime, there are philosophical differences between policing and security, with security being able to do more for an employer than policing can for a community, and that security directors are members of a management team, not private-sector chiefs of police.

REVIEW QUESTIONS

1. When was the first large city police department organized?
2. How did members of the medieval merchant guilds in Europe protect their assets?
3. What was the first use of private security in the United States?
4. When did security as we now know it develop in the United States?
5. What is the primary mission of a security program?
6. Why is it impossible to know with any degree of accuracy what U.S. losses amount to?

7. Why must management be concerned with protecting and conserving assets?

8. How can an effective security program have both a real and a potential impact on the savings and operating efficiency of a business or institution? What about its impact on society and the economic stability of the area in which it is located?

9. What are some of the principal differences between policing and security?

10. Why is it essential for security directors to understand the ways in which various departments other than their own function?

NOTES

[1]Martin A. Kelly, "The First Urban Policeman," *Journal of Police Science and Administration*, vol. 1, no. 1 (March 1973), p. 56.

[2]F. Oughton, *Ten Guineas a Day: A Portrait of the Private Detective* (London: John Long, 1961); R. B. Fosdick, *European Police Systems* (Montclair, NJ: Patterson Smith, 1969).

[3]Gene Edward Carte, "August Vollmer and the Origins of Police Professionalism," *Journal of Police Science and Administration*, vol. 1, no. 3 (September 1973), p. 274.

[4]Norman Bottom, Jr., and John Kostanoski, "An Informational Theory of Security," *Journal of Security Administration*, vol. 4, no. 1 (Spring 1981), p. 1.

[5]*Security Letter Sourcebook 1990–91*, pp. 305–310; *Journal of Security Administration*, December 1989, pp. 85–96.

[6]Harvey Burstein, *Industrial Security Management* (New York: Praeger Publishers, 1977), foreword.

[7]William C. Cunningham, John J. Strauchs, and Clifford W. Van Meter, *The Hallcrest Report II* (Stoneham, MA: Butterworth-Heinemann, 1990), p. 17.

[8]"Business Travel Management in the Nineties," *Fortune*, March 26, 1990, p. 196.

[9]Cunningham, Strauchs, and Van Meter, *The Hallcreast Report II*, p. 24.

[10]*Crimes against Business: Background, Findings, and Recommendations*, American Management Association, October 1977, p. 3.

[11]*The Wall Street Journal*, August 30, 1988, p. 1.

[12]*Forbes*, November 14, 1988, p. 258.

[13]*The Wall Street Journal*, March 16, 1989, p. 1.

[14]*Forbes*, August 7, 1989, p. 106.

[15]*The Washington Post*, December 30, 1989, sec. B, p. 8.

[16]Memorandum from Robert G. Hepburn, Jr., vice president, actuarial department of the Surety Association of America, dated November 15, 1990, addressed "To All Companies" and captioned "Distribution of Loss Experience Data Fidelity, Forgery and Surety Statewide Classification Experience Summaries Calendar Year 1989."

[17]Letter from Robin V. Weldy to the author dated July 19, 1991.

[18]*Newsweek*, September 23, 1991, p. 40.

[19]*Newsweek*, September 9, 1991, p. 62.

Chapter 2

CAREER OPPORTUNITIES IN SECURITY

To the uninitiated the idea of a career in the field of security may be unappealing. The tendency is to think only in terms of patrolling security officers or of those given the task of monitoring alarms or access to a facility. Those who are mindful of the fact that a good deal more is involved, and who may be interested in careers as security professionals, know that security departments must be managed and have as a goal the job of a *security manager* or *director*, terms used interchangeably throughout the book. This is understandable, and since most students ultimately aspire to become security managers, that is the subject on which we focus initially in this chapter.

However, it is also worth noting that other career opportunities in security do exist. They are discussed later in the chapter. Among them are teaching security courses at the college or university level, selling security-related products or services, being a consultant to businesses and institutions on matters related to the protection and conservation of assets, and being an inspector general for a civilian agency of government.

THE SECURITY DIRECTOR OR MANAGER

Qualifications

The underlying inability or refusal of so many senior executives to distinguish between policing and security, as noted in Chapter 1, is shown by what they have viewed as the principal qualifications for employment as a security manager or director. Initially, it was thought that to be successful as a security director one needed extensive law enforcement experience. However, with the end of World War II and the government's mandated security programs for companies doing defense-related work, prior service in the military or with a government intelligence agency became an equally acceptable qualification.

A study by James S. Kakalik and Sorrel Wildhorn of the Rand Corporation, published in 1972, reported that over 43 percent of security executives employed by firms with 500 or more total employees, and almost 40 percent of those employed by firms with 100 to 500 total employees, had backgrounds in either local or state police agencies, the military (provost marshal, intelligence, or investigations), or with federal investigative agencies.[1] They also noted that in 1960 the American Society for Industrial Security estimated that of all in-house or contract security executives who were society members, 10 percent were former special agents of the Federal Bureau of Investigation, and another 25 percent had been trained by either the FBI or some other federal law enforcement agency.[2] Management and human relations skills appeared to be of secondary importance.

Another factor that made their recruitment attractive to many employers, but which the latter undoubtedly would deny, was a matter of economics. For those who considered security as a necessary evil contributing only to expenses and not to profits, it made little or no sense to pay a security director a salary on a par with others of comparable rank in the organization. Therefore, businesses and institutions rationalized that persons who had the qualifications in which they were most interested, but who also received pensions as a result of their prior government service, represented a fertile field from which to recruit.

Thus it was a failure to understand the importance of both the security director's role and of paying what the job itself really was worth, which helps explain why so many security managers or directors came from the ranks of retired police officers, military personnel, or intelligence agency employees. Employers simply assumed that by holding responsible positions in their former assignments they must have acquired at least some managerial and human relations skills. Whether those skills were transferable to a business or institutional environment was a question rarely asked. Furthermore, it was felt that by drawing pensions, salary would not necessarily be a major consideration in terms of their accepting private-sector employment.

At the same time, as supervisory and lower-level managerial positions became available within a security department, whether established or in the process of being organized, the natural tendency on the part of the department head was to fill them with people with whom he would feel comfortable. Not only did this mean hiring people whose backgrounds basically were the same as his own, but it also helped to perpetuate the notion that government experience of one sort or another was the primary qualification for security management positions.

With the passage of time and the slow but certain evolution of security as a profession, with demands upon security managers previously unheard of, the qualifications began to change. Those for which employers now look are different from what they were. Today's applicants for security management positions are evaluated on the basis of education, experience in jobs which also have given them opportunities for increasing responsibility, and personal traits or characteristics.

Display advertisements for security directors or managers in newspapers and professional journals more often than not now indicate that at the very least, baccalaureate degrees, preferably in criminal justice with a security major or concentration, or possibly in business administration, are essential. In some cases, depending on the size of the prospective employer and nature of its business, there may even be a preference for someone with a graduate degree. As for experience, with the possible exception of jobs as entry-level supervisors, applicants almost invariably are required to have a minimum number of years in security positions of increasing responsibility. Employers now are more interested in applicants who have been exposed to the management side of security operations than they are in those with police or military experience, even if in supervisory assignments.

This is not to say that persons with appropriate academic degrees and some police or military management experience are not serious candidates; it merely indicates that for many of today's employers, police, military, or intelligence agency experience no longer is the principal qualifier. Such experience now is considered neither a plus nor a minus, and it should neither automatically qualify nor eliminate a candidate.

Knowledgeable employers, recognizing the importance of human relations skills if a security department is to succeed, also are inclined to pay much more attention to the personal traits or characteristics of applicants for the position of security director or manager than has been customary. They have come to appreciate the fact that security directors who cannot easily relate to their subordinates and peers, as well as to their superiors, will find it extremely difficult to implement even the best of programs, regardless of their education or experience.

What, then, are the traits for which employers look when considering applicants for jobs as security managers or directors, and why are they important? The most significant characteristics are patience, self-control, wisdom, empathy, a sense of humor, credibility, and the ability to speak and write clearly, easily, and concisely. Equally important is the need to be well organized and to have analytical skills. It is also possible that in some cases even foreign language skills may be helpful.

Patience and self-control are essential in terms of doing the job well. This is true with regard to both some aspects of the job and dealings with people. For example, security managers occasionally find themselves either personally conducting or overseeing complex investigations. Unlike what appears on television or in the movies, even relatively simple investigations, let alone complex ones, are not completed within one to two hours with time out for commercials. Even the most skilled, experienced investigators will often encounter obstacles that are frustrating, but they know that they need to be patient if they are to bring matters to a logical conclusion. They know that impatient investigators rarely are successful ones.

Self-control means being able to control one's feelings, not just one's temper. This, too, is critically important for the security director's or manager's success. The hallmark of the true professional is the ability to be objective in all aspects of one's work. For instance, no investigation should be undertaken with preconceived ideas of a suspect's guilt or a determination to prove him or her guilty. When the inquiry has been completed, guilt or innocence should be established solely on the basis of the evidence developed. If the results are inconclusive, so be it, but only the objectively written investigative report setting forth the facts should determine what action, if any, will be taken with regard to the suspect. The security director's personal opinion or feelings must neither dictate the outcome nor influence the decision about what is to be done.

To illustrate further the importance of controlling one's feelings, there is the need to be completely objective in managing the security department. Like all human beings, security directors have personal likes and dislikes. In all probability there will be some members of the department whom they will like more than others. This is perfectly natural, and to be expected. Nevertheless, the fact remains that where work assignments, performance reviews, salary increases, and providing opportunities for members of the staff to better themselves are concerned, security directors must perform their duties relative to security personnel in a wholly even-handed way. If they do otherwise by failing to control their personal likes and dislikes toward members of the department, they are inviting disaster in the form of morale problems that can adversely affect their ability to manage. No less important is the fact that should this happen, those very morale problems conceivably can destroy the entire security program.

As noted before, security directors must be able to control their tempers in addition to their feelings. Again, this relates to their ability to work with people both within and without the security department. While every person responsible for managing a department or a function of any size operates under varying degrees of stress and pressure, security directors are particularly susceptible because of the very nature of their jobs. This is not to say that they are constantly under pressure or stress; it merely recognizes the fact that on occasion the work itself may create some rather unique pressures.

For instance, production managers in a manufacturing environment are under pressure to keep the line running smoothly and without interruption so that customers' orders can be filled and deliveries made on time. They manage their work on the basis of schedules given to them by production planners, and unless they encounter things over which they have no control, such as an order that must be produced for a customer in less than normal time, or problems with labor, equipment, or late deliveries by suppliers, stress or pressure ordinarily are minimal.

On the other hand, while security directors have days that are quite normal, they also will have more than their share of days when the opposite is true. For example, a security director is called to the president's office. Upon arrival he is told that employees are parking in spaces reserved for visitors. The president, who feels strongly on this subject, is adamant about wanting all such employee cars towed. The security director, well aware of the president's feelings on the subject and wanting to ensure continued compliance with policy, has contacted a towing company that has been used before only to be informed that they no longer will tow vehicles off private property. Other towing companies within a 15-mile radius of corporate headquarters also are contacted and take the same position. The president is unwilling to accept either this information or alternative solutions offered by the security director. He clearly indicates his displeasure to both the security director and the latter's immediate superior. The fact that the president's unexpected displeasure has been incurred, coupled with the fact that there apparently is no solution other than towing which will please the president and which obviously cannot be done, is a form of stress and pressure to which most other managers are not subjected.

Under ordinary circumstances the security director might well be excused for a loss of temper since the president is demanding the impossible. However, that would be imprudent to say the least. At the same time the security director must not take out his anger and frustration with the president on members of the security department. This is another case of having to exercise self-control.

To be wise and educated are not necessarily one and the same thing. One definition of *wisdom*, in *Webster's New World Dictionary*, is "the power of judging rightly and following the soundest course of action, based on knowledge, experience, understanding, etc.; good judgment; discretion." Good judgment and discretion are inseparable as qualities that successful security directors must possess in abundance.

Although the exercise of sound judgment is a prerequisite for security directors, their greatest test comes when they must make decisions under pressure. There will be times when they must act in an emergency without any opportunity to reflect on all of the circumstances, consult with their superiors, or take the time to examine in detail information that otherwise might influence their decisions. Deciding on a course of action under such conditions is never easy, yet they know that indecision could prove to be far more damaging.

Discretion also requires the exercise of good judgment. For example, the need to have good relations and communications with one's peers is essential. Consequently, a security manager investigating allegations about an employee's misconduct, whether criminal or otherwise, should as a matter of courtesy inform that person's manager that an investigation has been initiated, but without disclosing any of the details. In this particular case, however, assume that the security director knows that this employee's manager, although honest and hard working, nevertheless cannot keep a confidence. Thus the prudent thing to do under these circumstances is to say nothing at all about the inquiry to the manager.

Security managers who can empathize with others will find it much easier to develop good relationships and communications with their peers, without whose cooperation they cannot hope to succeed. Trying to understand why and be sympathetic to a department manager's concerns about the possible impact on operations if a particular security recommendation is implemented often can lead to a solution which is acceptable to both that manager and the security director. On the other hand, security directors who find it difficult to put themselves in another person's position will also find that their efforts to implement security measures will meet increasing resistance, frequently in subtle ways. Should this happen, it can lead eventually to the program's failure with both the employer and security director the losers.

Security directors must have credibility. Persons who cannot be believed or trusted to keep their word should not consider the possibility of careers as security directors or managers. Once a security director has given an assurance, the person to whom it was given should have no doubt about the fact that the promise will be kept. If it is not, the security director will have caused himself or herself irreparable harm.

As an example, security directors must rely on people for information, especially in cases involving thefts by employees. Since it is not uncommon for the sources of such information to be wary about having their names disclosed, it is not unusual for them to ask that their identity be kept confidential. Although such a request will not prevent a security director from proceeding, it may make the investigation more difficult and time consuming. However, if the source is told that the confidence will be kept, that promise must be honored. If it is not, word will soon get out that the security manager cannot be trusted. If that happens, other employees will avoid reporting even the most serious offenses of which they have knowledge for fear that they, too, will be betrayed. The fact that more time and effort must be devoted to the inquiry to corroborate independently the information provided by the source does not excuse such a breach of confidence. When employees feel that they no longer can trust their security director, the latter's usefulness has been outlived.

One might ask why security directors should have a sense of humor. Most persons who hold such positions probably would reply that having one can make the job much easier; not having one can make it much more difficult. A security director who cannot take a joke soon will earn a reputation as someone who is impressed with his or her own importance. That, in turn, often tends to make people not only less friendly but also less cooperative when their help is needed. They may react by letting that type of security manager proceed through the mine field of corporate politics to his or her own detriment to teach them a lesson in humility.

For instance, if an employee, as a gesture of friendship, jokingly asks a security director whether he or she has caught any thieves lately—and gets a very chilly reaction—that employee will probably hesitate to initiate any communication with the director in the future. Such a response from a security director may well cause the person rebuffed to hesitate about having any contact with the former even when a matter of which the security director should be informed comes to that person's attention.

Although such behavior admittedly can make life more difficult for a security director in a business setting, it may pale by comparison with a situation where college students decide to play a harmless prank on some of their classmates. The security director who fails to see any humor in what was done, and instead decides to refer the matter to the dean's office for some form of disciplinary action, will be seen by the student body as throwing down the gauntlet. They, in turn, will challenge the security director by becoming involved with a range of other pranks on campus for the sole purpose of annoying him or her. This can become both very time consuming and unproductive for a security director who is determined to identify the students involved so that they, too, can be disciplined. It creates another problem, and an unnecessary one at that, with which the security manager must deal.

With respect to communications skills, security directors must communicate with people both within and without the organization by which they are employed. In doing so they find that their communications, both written and oral, will be directed to persons whose positions and levels of education may vary. As a result, the ability to speak and write easily, clearly, and concisely cannot be overemphasized. This is especially true when one considers that the ways in which people express themselves often convey an impression not only of the person, but also of that person as a manager.

For security directors speech is a means of communication not confined to conversation or the issuing of instructions to subordinates. There will be times when security directors may be asked to make oral presentations to groups of new employees or to meetings of other managers or executives. There may also be occasions when one is invited to address a local chapter of the American Society for Industrial Security or Rotary Club, or even to appear before a seminar of a national organization.

Wise speakers always keep several things in mind. First, they need to be clear in their own minds about what they are going to say. Waiting until called upon to speak before deciding what to say can be embarrassing even for the most experienced public speaker. Second, they will make certain that whatever they say is said in the most interesting way. Third, they never lose sight of the nature of the audience being spoken to in terms of their choice of language. However, this does not excuse the use of poor grammar under any circumstance. Fourth, just as they keep eye contact with the audience, they also keep one eye on the clock. The most fatal error that any speaker can make is to be boring or to speak too long. Security directors who follow these few simple rules cannot help but impress their audiences with their professionalism.

In many respects the same basic approach applies to written communications whether sent electronically or in hard copy, or in the form of letters, memoranda, policies and procedures, or instructions to security personnel. A cardinal principle to be remembered before putting anything in writing is for the writer to think about what he or she really wants to say. Clarity in written communications, as with oral ones, is of the utmost importance. Documents sent by security directors that raise questions in a recipient's mind about what the author intended to say are not clearly written.

Closely related to the matter of clarity is the importance of keeping in mind the nature of the audience for which the document is intended. When employers consider qualifications and a security manager's ability to write, they want someone who can communicate easily with persons both outside and inside the organization. Thus they are interested in how one uses language in relation to the educational levels of those to whom any given communication is directed. For example, one might logically expect that a memorandum to the company president will contain language that he or she will easily understand. At the same time, using some of the same words in a memorandum to security officers might result in their misunderstanding just what the document means.

The security director who can write clearly also should be able to write concisely, another important qualification. In a business environment the overwhelming majority of either hard copy or electronically sent documents are intended for people who do not have an unlimited amount of time to spend reading regardless of an item's importance. This is no less true of security officers, to whom post orders are sent than it is of the company president to whom a proposal for a new access control system is submitted. Therefore, being able to present ideas clearly and coherently, using the fewest possible number of words, can be a significant qualifier for a security director.

Since the ability to communicate effectively is essential for any security director, there are some cases where being able to speak a foreign language may also be an important qualification. This might be true of a business or institution that employs a significant number of people who are not particularly fluent in English or of a multinational corporation. Although fluency may not always be necessary, security directors who can understand what an employee speaking a foreign language has to say, and who in turn can manage to be understood by persons for whom English is not a native language, will find doing their jobs much easier and their communication problems far fewer.

Like other efficient and effective managers, security directors find that they are often called upon to deal with multiple tasks at the same time. While it is true that each different task will have its own priority in the scheme of things, the fact remains that each item must be attended to in due course. This is no less important for the security manager who is responsible for a single site than it is for one who has corporate-wide responsibility. Consequently, the inherent nature of the job requires security directors to be well organized to ensure that each task, whether handled by themselves personally or assigned to a staff member, is carried out in timely fashion. They must also have analytical skills so that they can quickly and easily analyze any situation with which they are confronted, whether it involves a matter under investigation or something that comes to their attention during the course of a site visit or security audit.

Thus it is evident that the qualifications for security directors not only have changed considerably over the years, but also that they still are undergoing change. As more and more security directors find themselves increasingly involved, whether directly or indirectly, with their employers' safety and environmental protection programs, no doubt greater familiarity with the Occupational Safety and Health Act, and the various enactments at both the federal and state level dealing with clean air, clean water, and the handling and disposal of hazardous or toxic materials, will be added to the qualifications for the position.

Duties and Responsibilities

To approach the job of a security director or manager with preconceived ideas of just what the positions' duties and responsibilities are can be either a meaningful or a disappointing experience. While the purpose of a sound security program is to protect and conserve all of an employer's assets, the fact remains that one might expect to find some variations in security directors' duties and responsibilities among different types of businesses or institutions but with a degree of uniformity among a specific category. For instance, one would expect differences between manufacturing and retailing, yet at least a degree of similarity for all those in retailing. However, even then there is no uniformity. The reason is a simple one; in the final analysis a security director's duties and responsibilities depend entirely on what his or her employer wants them to be.

Perhaps this is best illustrated in two ways. A large financial organization hired a corporate director of safety and security whose duties and responsibilities were expanded almost constantly. Before long, security was fully integrated into virtually all aspects of operations. This resulted in increased efficiency and savings. However, on one occasion the security director, working closely with the local authorities, prevented what could have been a $2 million loss. His internal investigation also showed that the theft almost succeeded because two departments, each headed by a vice president, had not been as attentive to their respective functions as they should have been, something that both vice presidents admitted. Nevertheless, neither vice president was penalized, whereas the security director's duties and responsibilities were reduced to the point where he had little to do other than supervise a small group of security officers and administer the company's parking program.

By way of contrast, a corporate manager of safety and security for a multinational company reported to the vice president for manufacturing. His duties and responsibilities were limited to that division during the entire course of his employment. Upon his departure, his successor, who was also a lawyer, reported to the vice president and general counsel. He was given responsibility not only for all aspects of the company's safety and security activities worldwide, but also for environmental matters. In addition, he was responsible for making recommendations regarding the advisability of filing criminal complaints, civil suits, or both against employees who were found to have acted against the employer's best interests.

The only sameness in terms of duties and responsibilities seems to occur when distinguishing between security directors for multisite operations and those in charge of a single facility. As a rule those employed by organizations with more than one site function only, or at least primarily, in a staff capacity; security managers at individual locations serve in a line capacity. Of course, security directors or managers who work for companies with but a single site almost invariably function in a combined staff and line capacity.

In any event, it is not unusual for the scope of a security director's duties and responsibilities to be influenced by his or her job performance. The question, then, is: What should those duties and responsibilities be under ideal conditions? The answer is best given by considering the role of a security director who performs in a staff capacity, and that of one who functions in a line capacity.

Security directors, particularly those assigned to corporate headquarters and serving in a staff capacity, find that they function primarily as in-house consultants, who with senior management's support, are also expected to provide direction and leadership for the security program. This means developing and writing appropriate security policies and procedures and overseeing their implementation, providing guidance in matters of security orientation and education for all employees, preparing a departmental budget, and keeping abreast of new security-related technologies that will help line security managers provide more cost-effective protection for their respective locations. Even in organizations that are largely decentralized, they are responsible for exercising general oversight of security managers employed at individual facilities. Neither is it unusual for them to be the corporate headquarters liaison with law enforcement agencies, especially those at the federal level. In some cases they may also be expected personally to conduct investigations that either are very sensitive or involve a high degree of sophistication. Their only line duties and responsibilities consist of supervising security personnel assigned to the corporate security office.

On the other hand, line security managers, usually assigned to single-site operations, are responsible primarily for the actual security operations that are necessary for the implementation of corporate security policies and procedures and the protection of the employer's assets at the particular facility to which they are assigned. Based on the corporate policies and procedures, they write local procedures to help achieve corporate goals, hire and train site security personnel, schedule their work, help conduct general employee security orientation and education programs, conduct investigations when necessary, and prepare the site security budget. Like the staff-level director or manager, they must also keep abreast of developments in the field of security technology that will help provide cost-effective ways of protecting assets. They provide guidance to local management on security issues, maintain appropriate relationships with local public safety officials, keep records pertaining to site security activities, and inform the corporate security director of all incidents and other significant occurrences that take place at the facility.

Of course, not all corporate security directors are employed by multinational, or even multisite, companies. It is entirely possible for a person in such a position to work for a sizable business or institution which nevertheless operates from but a single location. When this occurs the person to whom the job is given, regardless of his or her title, assumes all of the duties and responsibilities normally associated with a combined staff and line function.

It also is worth noting that on occasion businesses and institutions will assign the responsibility for safety, and possibly even for environmental protection matters, to security. When this is the case the basic duties and responsibilities normally associated with staff and line functions must obviously be modified to reflect the inclusion of these all-important management concerns. Among other things this requires staff personnel constantly to be aware of changes in safety and environmental protection laws and standards, or insurance company requirements, so that they can write and oversee the implementation of policies and procedures that will provide employees with a safe and healthful workplace. In addition, at the staff level the security director is expected to keep abreast of new safety- or environmentally related products. This is so that he or she can provide guidance to line security managers who also are involved with safety and environmental matters, but who may not always have access to the same sources of information, despite the fact that they are responsible for implementing safety and environmental protection policies and procedures at their facilities.

In any event, from what has been said it is clear that the duties and responsibilities of security directors or managers, whether serving in a staff, line, or combined capacity, are subject to change. More often than not, they may be expanded by an employer who fully understands the vital role that security can play and who appreciates what a security director's professionalism can contribute to the financial health of the business or institution. This is not to say that the duties and responsibilities may not be contracted. However, on those rare occasions when this does happen, there usually are political reasons for the reduction in scope, as distinguished from a lack of ability on the security director's part.

Relations with Co-workers

"No man is an island, entire of itself; every man is a piece of the continent."[3] This quotation from John Donne is one that all security directors or managers should always keep in mind if they hope to be successful. There often are times when matters affecting security either have happened or are about to happen. For instance, if a theft has occurred or is being planned, the security director must have access to information that can help solve or prevent the crime. In either case, unless a knowledgeable employee comes forward willingly to provide useful information, the former may be extremely hard to do, and the latter almost impossible. Consequently, like the police, security directors know that good sources of information are invaluable. However, they also know that unlike the police, they rarely have either the authority or the resources required to get a job done. Therefore, they must depend on the relationships they have established with their co-workers to benefit from the cooperation and goodwill needed to succeed. This is true whether it involves preventing security-related incidents or identifying the persons responsible for those that have occurred.

By the same token, security directors and managers often are seen by their co-workers as authority figures who must be obeyed. In fact, some encourage their fellow employees to think of them in this way. Others try to avoid giving this impression of themselves. Regardless, if this is what their co-workers believe, even when it may be unjustified, the feeling is one that will not endear them to the very people whose cooperation they must have if they are to serve the employer's best interests. If the relationship is not a good one, and there is a lack of cooperation and understanding, both they and others who directly or indirectly depend on the employer, such as its employees, stockholders, and consumers ultimately suffer.

Remember that among a security director's qualifications discussed earlier in this chapter were the personal traits that employers now trend to consider. Included were patience, empathy, self-control, credibility, and a sense of humor. The degree to which security directors possess these characteristics can be crucial in terms of their relationships with their co-workers. Humility, a willingness to admit that they do not know everything, and readiness to admit mistakes, can also contribute in this respect. Perhaps this is best illustrated.

A manager allegedly was giving business to a company and getting kickbacks; an investigation was initiated. It proved the allegations untrue and showed them to have been made by a subordinate whose job performance was such that he got no salary increases on two successive reviews. The cleared manager went out of his way not only to thank the security manager, but also to tell others that the security manager's objectivity had saved his job. Thereafter there was a noticeable difference in how the security manager was viewed by employees at that location.

In another case, an incident at a manufacturing plant prompted the plant manager to call the new security director, whom he had not yet met, to report what happened and how it had been handled. During the conversation the plant manager asked if the security director would be visiting the site and if he would let him know when he was coming. The security director said that he would visit, but before doing so he would ask if the proposed time was all right. He said no purpose would be served by his coming if the plant manager and his staff would not be able to meet and work with him. The plant manager, recalling his unhappy experiences with the former security director, who believed in making surprise visits, replied, "You mean we don't have another *** inspector general in your job?" The resulting relationship between the two was close, and the plant manager was completely supportive of the security director and his efforts to protect their employer.

Security directors who work in isolation, or who fail to develop and maintain good relationships with their co-workers, cannot hope to succeed. True professionals can have the best of relationships with their co-workers without any loss of personal dignity, or running the risk of compromising their integrity or work or that of their departments.

Relations with Other Security Directors and Law Enforcement

Just as having good relations with one's co-workers is crucial to a security director's success, so is it important to develop and maintain good relations with other security directors and law enforcement personnel. Important as these relationships are, however, they should not be entered into blindly by assuming that no risks are involved, and no precautions need be taken, since every security director or police official necessarily is honest and of the highest integrity. Remember, too, asking someone for a favor, or their help, opens the door for them to make a similar request in return, no matter how ethical and honest they may be. Consequently, one security director should not ask another, or a law enforcement contact, for a favor or assistance unless he or she is willing to reciprocate.

For relationships with other security directors and law enforcement to be good, they also must be ethically, morally, and legally correct. As examples, exchanging information among security directors regarding the current activities of a known shoplifter, or for law enforcement to disseminate information about possible terrorist activity, would be perfectly proper. On the other hand, to ask another security director for information about a person working at his or her company or institution, or a police officer for someone's criminal history in a state where the law prohibits making such information available to private parties, would be wrong. If such questionable behavior by an erring security director should become known, at the very least it could lead to a good deal of embarrassment. Of even greater significance, it could also result in possible litigation for the employer.

There may also be times when law enforcement contacts will be the ones asking a security director for some help. The need for a security director to behave correctly is no less important under these circumstances. To illustrate, in two different investigations the investigators, looking for leads, wanted to review numerous personnel files. Each of the security directors at the two companies was given a list of over 100 names and asked that they be made available for examination.

Each company's security director handled the request differently. In one the security director, aware of the possible risks involved if he merely complied with the request, told the investigators that he would assemble all of the pertinent files for them, but that he would not release them for examination until the investigators first served him with a subpoena. He wanted to avoid even the slightest hint of impropriety should any employee whose file was to be examined ever learn of what happened. The investigators, understanding the reasons for the request, did not object to it, easily obtained a subpoena, and in no way was the relationship between them and the security director damaged.

In the other case the security director, who liked to think of himself as a member of the law enforcement fraternity and who always did things to try to ingratiate himself with the police, gladly made all the files available. Subsequently, employees whose files were among those examined heard about this. They threatened to bring a class-action lawsuit against both their employer and the security director for violating their privacy. To avoid embarrassment, damage to its reputation, the cost of defending against such an action and the amount of possible damages it would have to pay if the plaintiffs won, the employer reached an out-of-court settlement with the complaining employees. The employer's criticism of its security director made it clear that a repetition could lead to his termination. This, in turn, caused him to be overly cautious in his dealings with his police contacts. The result was that his behavior in this case ended up hurting rather than helping his relations with the local law enforcement community.

It is human nature to want to be liked by those with whom one works and associates. Security directors are no exception; if they can do their jobs and be liked at the same time, so much the better. This does not necessarily pose insurmountable obstacles for them, but it does mean that professionalism must take precedence over personal relationships. It also means that given a choice between being well liked by other security directors and police contacts, or respected for their honesty and integrity, the respect is far more important. In only the very rarest of instances will respected security directors find that their relationships have suffered. On the contrary, they are often enhanced.

Managing the Security Department

To understand the duties and responsibilities of a security director or manager is one thing; to be able to manage a security department is another. Just as some students do well in their daily classes but test poorly, so is it possible for a person to know what is involved in being a security director, yet find it difficult to put that knowledge into practice.

Basically, managing a security department requires the security director to be able to carry out the duties and responsibilities delegated to the position by the organization's senior management. To discharge those duties and responsibilities in ways that will be of greatest benefit to their employers, security directors must be able to make decisions and set priorities with respect to three interdependent elements: the human, financial, and physical resources over which they are given control.

If denied adequate financial resources, security directors obviously cannot have either the human or physical resources that may be needed for them to do their jobs. However, unless and until both they and the organization's executive management fully understand security's role in the organization, and what they collectively envision as the security program's objectives, thinking in terms of what human and physical resources they need will be difficult. One thing is certain, there are limits on the resources to which security directors have or can expect to have access. Therefore, being able to do more with less is the real test for which security directors must be prepared.

Among a security manager's duties is budget preparation. Regardless of the employer's approach to this subject, or the extent to which a security manger has attempted to justify every item, it is doubtful that the entire budget submission will be approved. When this happens security managers must be able to compensate for those line items that have either been reduced or completely discarded. In other words, they must be able to manage what financial resources are available to them by deciding how to spend them wisely in view of their priorities.

Since the cost of salaries and fringe benefits for human resources often are the largest item in a budget, limited funds may require close examination of the department's personnel requirements to see whether better management can help reduce expenses without in any way jeopardizing the security program. For instance, are personnel needs determined by following the old formula, which states that covering a post 24 hours a day calls for 4.3 security officers, or is time taken realistically to graph what is necessary to provide adequate coverage? Is the number of security officers such as to permit them to handle all possible emergencies without paying overtime? If so, it may mean that there are times when some are physically present but with little or nothing for them to do. Perhaps a wiser and less costly approach would be to reduce the size of the staff and pay a limited amount of overtime on those occasions when specific coverage is needed.

On the other hand, what about the physical resources that are available? Is it possible that by using modern technology in some way the size of the staff could be reduced so that the substitution would prove to be both more efficient and cost-effective? In a multisite organization, does each facility's security department need its own training film library or closed-circuit television camera with a pinhole lens for surveillance purposes? In such a situation a corporate security director who is a good manager would find it more economical and realistic to maintain a training film library at corporate headquarters for distribution to the facilities as needed. Also, instead of each site having its own pinhole lens camera, he or she would have an inventory of all physical resources available company-wide so that equipment could be borrowed by one facility from another when necessary rather than having each spend money for items whose use might be needed only occasionally.

Of course, managing the security department means making decisions, not all of which are easily made. Those that affect personnel or which have to be made under stress of any kind, although difficult at best, nevertheless are inescapable if one hopes to manage a security department successfully. Security directors whose superiors recognize their professionalism will find that by and large they are expected to make most decisions affecting both their departments and the protection and conservation of the employer's assets. This does not mean that there will not be times when they must have senior management's approval for something, but those occasions will be relatively rare. Security directors who, no matter how familiar with the duties and responsibilities of the job, feel a constant need to get a superior's approval to do what obviously needs to be done really are not managing their security departments.

OTHER CAREER OPPORTUNITIES

As noted at the outset of this chapter, while most students interested in security careers tend to think in terms of ultimately becoming security directors, other satisfying and rewarding career opportunities are open to them in teaching, sales, consulting, and government. By and large the security director's qualifications would serve them well should they choose to enter another aspect of the security profession.

Teaching

While a security director's qualifications would be useful, those interested in teaching careers would also have to have the appropriate academic qualifications. An advanced degree might be acceptable, but a terminal degree would be preferred. However, just as medical students get part of their training from clinical professors, and law students find it helpful when teachers either have practiced law or can accept select cases even as faculty members, so does it help those interested in becoming security professionals if they can learn from the experiences of faculty who have worked in a corporate or institutional security environment. Theories are important, but theory alone is not enough. Students must be able to apply theories to practice starting with their first job interviews. This poses a real challenge for their instructors. It is precisely because of this that at least some practical experience can be as important to faculty members as their academic qualifications.

Even those who are interested in research in addition to their teaching cannot ignore the benefits of at least a measure of practical experience if their research itself is to be meaningful. Opportunities exist for making a significant contribution to security as both an academic discipline and a profession. Although a fair amount of research has been done to date, it has tended to focus on either security industry shortcomings, especially in terms of salaries, levels of education, prior experience, and types of crimes most often encountered by security directors, or on comparing security with policing and studying their relationship. Too little has been done regarding other types of problems with which security must cope. Questions regarding their root causes, of how security is perceived by executives and employees generally, and of how it is perceived by the public in retailing or the lodging industry, where contact may be relatively frequent, remain unanswered. One who has worked as a practicing security administrator would be mindful of the areas in need of research and the contribution that such research could make to both the protection and conservation of assets and the effective management of a security department.

Academic qualifications obviously are not the only significant difference between security directors and teachers; the duties and responsibilities are also different. Among those of a teacher is the need to help prepare students so that they can be gainfully employed upon graduation, whether as security directors, academicians, salespersons, or consultants. Teachers must impart knowledge and stimulate their students so that the latter will both want to be and will be educated people, not merely technicians. Since in so many ways a good security education involves an interdisciplinary approach, teachers themselves must fully understand the nature of security as it is seen by today's employers if they are to be capable of directing students realistically in terms of proper course selection. Thus experience can once again become an important factor.

Without doubt a career teaching security and security-related courses at a college or university can be challenging, stimulating, and satisfying. The challenge and stimulation come largely from students who are genuinely interested in learning, as well as from one's association with other faculty members. Teaching admittedly is not the most financially rewarding career, yet the satisfaction of having students graduate and go on to become successful is in itself a most satisfying experience.

Sales

A person with an outgoing personality can sell security equipment or services. Like teaching, selling can be stimulating and challenging, but it is different since it can also be financially rewarding. Thanks to the high-technology industry, over the years new security-related products have been developed while at the same time the number of companies offering various security services has grown tremendously. However, no matter how good the products or services, for vendors to be successful they must be able to sell consumers. Thus another career opportunity is available to those interested in the security field.

A baccalaureate degree may be all that is needed for a sales position. Since many companies offering products or services have their own training programs for sales personnel, particularly those selling products which are technical in nature, the initial lack of technical training need not be an obstacle to success. Sales trainees are given what training is needed with regard to the product's technical capabilities and its selling points.

Nevertheless, a person with a background in security has a decided advantage over one who has not. Someone selling a security-related product or service is expected to be thoroughly familiar with whatever he or she is selling. At the same time, however, such familiarity does not always mean that the sales representative is equally familiar with the best application of what is being sold. The salesperson without prior exposure to security may know all of the technical details of the product or service offered, yet he or she may have difficulty closing a sale because of the inability to translate that particular product or service into something that will satisfy the customer's need. On the other hand, the salesperson who has had some security experience can bridge the gap between the product or service. This helps the customer understand, and the salesperson sell. It is this ability that can contribute significantly to the physical or general protection of businesses and institutions.

Consulting

Regrettably, the word *consultant* has on occasion been abused by some of those who work in the security field. Although *Webster's New World Dictionary* defines a consultant as "a person who gives professional or technical advice," there are people who are private detectives or investigators, not consultants, who nevertheless call themselves security consultants. For the uninformed this misuse of the word can be misleading.

However, for someone who has been a security director and is looking for something even more mentally stimulating, consulting as defined in the dictionary offers the greatest challenge for a security professional. As with sales or working as an inspector general in government, a baccalaureate degree generally is sufficient, but to be a security consultant in the truest sense of the word makes a person's hands-on experience critically important. Although clients do not expect consultants to be experienced in every possible type of business or institutional environment, they do expect them to be generally well versed in the fundamental principles of good security and business management. Otherwise, they will have little confidence in what consultants can do or recommend.

In addition to experience, successful consultants must possess three other characteristics. One is the ability to work well and communicate easily with people without instilling fear. Another is credibility. Finally, the consultant must be able to learn as much as possible about the client's business both easily and in the shortest possible time. The latter is true not only in terms of learning about different types of businesses and institutions, but also with regard to variations among multiple locations operated by the same organization.

To illustrate, a company operating a chain of over 50 retail speciality stores, all of which were located in either shopping plazas or malls, retained a consultant who expected to find differences between corporate headquarters and its adjoining warehouse on one hand, and stores themselves on the other. However, once engaged it soon became apparent that there also were differences among the individual stores. Although some differences in physical security had been anticipated, operating procedures were also different, despite a corporate operations manual. That store managers' manual interpretations and the need to make adjustments to satisfy purely local considerations were largely responsible did not alter the fact that differences did exist. Before realistic recommendations for better security could be made, the consultant had to be able to detect and make allowance for those differences.

The same consultant was also retained by an international hotel company. Again, variations in physical security from one property to another were expected, but would this be equally true of operating procedures? The answer soon became obvious; it was "yes." In one country additional security officers had to be recommended because the government prohibited private organizations from owning or operating any form of two-way communication system, such as hand-held radios. This denied the hotel the flexibility that it otherwise would have in terms of staff utilization. For another of the chain's properties, located on an island, virtually everything needed to operate the hotel, including foodstuffs, had to be shipped in. This often caused a congested receiving area. Possible theft aside, it posed a problem since the risk of excessive spoilage of perishables was a factor that had to be considered. As with the retailing client, simply because corporate headquarters had developed and issued an operations manual did not mean that the consultant could afford to assume that studying operations at one property would provide a true picture of operations at all. Before submitting individualized reports for each site visited, and writing a new security policies and procedures manual, the consultant had to be able to note the variables and take them into account when recommending steps to protect and conserve the company's assets.

Truly professional security consultants generally offer their clients only their experience and reputations; they do not sell products or other services. They can be of help to organizations that have no security directors or formal security programs yet are looking for ways in which to improve asset protection. This was true of both examples cited above. It is also true of those which do have security managers and programs but who want to have their programs evaluated objectively. In fact, some security directors feel sufficiently secure in their jobs to suggest the retention of a consultant to their employers. They theorize that if the consultant finds few if any faults with the existing program, it confirms their own professionalism and ability as security directors. If, on the other hand, a consultant recommends improvements, the chances of getting approval to implement the recommendations will be better because of the consultant's objectivity and experience.

Inspector General

Private organizations are not alone in their need to protect and conserve assets. Government agencies are equally susceptible to many of the same problems that confront the private sector. In many ways the inspector general's role in government parallels that of the private-sector security director, and it offers yet another career opportunity for students interested in security.

Inspectors general have long been part of the military services, but the creation of such a position for civilian agencies of government, to be held by civilians, is a relatively recent development at both the state and federal levels. The Inspector General Act of 1978, passed by the Congress of the United States, created an Office of Inspector and Auditor General in seven executive departments and six executive agencies to more effectively combat "fraud, abuse, waste and mismanagement in the programs and operations of those departments and agencies."[4]

When the 1978 act was amended in 1988, it stated that part of its purpose was "to provide leadership and coordination and recommend policies for activities designed (1) to promote economy, efficiency, and effectiveness in the administration of, and (2) to prevent and detect fraud and abuse in, such programs and operations; and (3) to provide a means of keeping the head of the establishment and the Congress fully and currently informed about problems and deficiencies relating to the administration of such programs and operations and the necessity for and progress of corrective action."[5]

The federal government is not alone in using the idea of an inspector general to help protect and conserve assets. Some states have also created such an office. In Massachusetts, for example, the purpose and duties of the office of inspector general include action "to prevent and detect fraud, waste and abuse in the expenditure of public funds, whether state, federal, or local, or relating to programs and operations involving the procurement of any supplies, services, or construction, by agencies, bureaus, divisions, sections, departments, offices, commissions, institutions and activities of the commonwealth, including those districts, authorities, instrumentalities or political subdivisions created by the general court and including the cities and towns."[6]

In examining the "purpose" of an office of inspector general, whether at the federal or state level, the similarities between it and the duties and responsibilities of private-sector security directors become clear. Therefore, for inspectors general to be effective, they need to have qualifications not unlike those in which private-sector employers are most interested. Equally noteworthy is the fact that inspectors general in government and security directors in the private sector face many of the same challenges.

Despite the many similarities, there also are differences between working for government and working in the private sector. For instance, inspectors general cannot develop and implement new safeguards for their employers as quickly as security directors can for theirs. This is due primarily to the fact that their activities are governed by the laws that created the position, whereas security directors are limited only by the extent to which executive management approves their recommendations. Then, too, although security directors about to implement newly authorized programs need not wait for legislatures to appropriate funds as do inspectors general, neither do they have access to the same resources as those available to inspectors general. This is particularly true where investigative matters are concerned.

SUMMARY

Contrary to what many people think, even though being a security director may be the first choice of those interested in security careers, it is by no means the only possible opportunity open to students interested in the security field. Neither are they necessarily limited to private-sector employment, as evidenced by the fact that the roles of security director and inspector general are very alike. And, of course, other security-related careers such as teaching, sales, and consulting can be equally challenging, stimulating, and rewarding.

Except for an academic career, where an advanced or terminal degree is required, and sales, where experience may not be as critical a factor as for other types of employment, the qualifications in terms of education and personal traits or characteristics are basically the same. It is immaterial which option one chooses. The ability to get along and be able to communicate effectively with co-workers is essential to success not only for the individual, but also for the person's employer. Furthermore, just as security directors and inspectors general must have good relationships with their peers and law enforcement, so must academicians have good relations with other faculty, staff, and students, salespersons with customers, and consultants with clients.

The duties and responsibilities associated with the different career opportunities necessarily vary, although once again there is a similarity between those of security directors and inspectors general. Naturally, a teacher's duties and responsibilities involve teaching and being available to students. Salespersons' duties involve selling, and consultant have as their primary duty rendering a specific service to a client.

Security directors and inspectors general obviously manage their departments and offices in every sense of the word. Aside from those responsibilities normally associated with the day-to-day management of their departments, they may also be involved with such other employer concerns as risk management, legal and insurance factors that can affect operations, a wide range of physical and personnel security issues, and security's role in safety and environmental matters. While each of these topics will be developed more fully from a security director's perspective in the chapters that follow, it should be noted that all of the other security-related positions also have some managerial involvement.

Whether fully realized or not, faculty members, salespersons, and consultants also perform some degree of management activity. Although the scope may be considerably narrower than for security directors or inspectors general, the fact is that faculty members are expected to manage their classes, office hours, research, and writing, while salespersons have their schedules and sales calls to manage, and consultants their client contacts and work. Of course, a consultant who works either independently or as the head of an organization is involved with all aspects of managing the business. Consequently, for those who thrive on challenges and diversity, careers in security have much to offer.

REVIEW QUESTIONS

1. What career opportunities are available to persons interested in working in the security field?

2. Which two are most alike, and in what ways?

3. What are the principal differences between working in a staff capacity and working in a line capacity?

4. Under what circumstances is it possible for a security manager to function in a staff capacity and a line capacity simultaneously?

5. Of all of the personal traits in which employers are now interested, which might be considered most important in terms of contributing to a security director's success? Why?

6. A security manager has two applications for an opening for supervisor. One applicant has an associate's degree and has been employed for three years as a police officer; the other just received a baccalaureate degree in criminal justice with a security major and business administration minor. Of the two, which appears to be the better candidate?

7. Why are co-worker relationships important?

8. Are all relationships with other security directors and law enforcement personnel necessarily good? If not, why not?

9. A police officer investigating a case asks a security director with whom he or she has a good working relationship for access to a number of personnel files. Should the request be honored without question? If not, what should be the security director's position?

10. To be a good manager, why is it necessary for a security director to be familiar with an employer's total business operation?

REFERENCES

[1] JAMES S. KAKALIK and SORREL WILDHORN, *The Private Police Industry: Its Nature and Extent*, Vol. II; R-870/DOJ (Washington, DC: Law Enforcement Assistance Administration, National Institute of Law Enforcement and Criminal Justice, U.S. Department of Justice, 1972), p. 76.

[2] Ibid., p. 74.

[3] JOHN DONNE, *Devotions* (1624), p. 17.

[4] Inspector General Act of 1978, Pub. L. No. 95-452.

[5] Inspector General Act of 1978 as amended by the Inspector General Act Amendments of 1988, Pub. L. No. 100-504; 102 Stat. 2515.

[6] M.G.L.A., ch. 12A, Office of the Inspector General.

Chapter 3

THE SECURITY DEPARTMENT

In the same way that every rural area, village, town, and city suffers from crime, so every business or institution, regardless of its size, location, or the nature of its activity, has to be concerned about security problems. Just as a community's size will influence the size of its police department, so does the size of a business or institution have a bearing on its security department's size. For example, while a rural area may find it impractical to have its own police department, so may a small business, such as a neighborhood hardware store, market, or pharmacy, find it unrealistic to have its own security department, although it still has security concerns.

Rural areas without their own police departments rely on either a county sheriff or the state police to help fight crime. Since the most cost-effective approach to solving security problems lies in prevention, businesses and institutions without security departments must look for other ways to protect and conserve their assets. Since no business or institution can hope to operate successfully unless someone at least acts in a role comparable to that of a security manager, with or without a security department, one of those ways is to assign the responsibility for the security function to a specific person in the organization. This may be no less true of a large business, where for whatever reason senior management is not convinced that a security department is necessary, than it is of a small one, where the need for and economics of having a formal security department militate against taking such action.

These situations aside, understanding security departments is important not only to those who want to become security directors or managers, but also to those whose interest lies in teaching, sales, or consulting. Therefore, some of the fundamentals involved with managing a security department need to be examined and understood.

THE SECURITY DEPARTMENT STAFF

Once a decision has been made to have a formally organized security department, it must be staffed. This involves more than deciding on the number of people to be employed. While the department's size certainly is a major consideration, other questions, such as the qualifications of personnel, how they should be dressed and equipped, and whether the staff should consist of proprietary or contract personnel, or perhaps a combination of the two, will have to be answered.

However, before addressing these issues it is important for students of security to understand certain developments that have, and will continue to have, an impact on security department staffing. With the approach of the twentieth century's last decade, and as it began, businesses in the United States were confronted with a recession. A number of them, both large and small, including such stalwarts as Pan American World Airways and Eastern Airlines, ceased to exist. Others were forced to examine their positions to see if economies could be effected, and if they could reduce the scope and magnitude of their operations. Some Fortune 500 companies, proud of the fact that historically they had never been obliged to lay people off, found themselves closing plants and doing precisely that. By no means were these reductions in force limited to hourly personnel; salaried and managerial employees were also terminated. Even such industrial giants as IBM and General Motors were obliged to close or consolidate operations and find ways in which to reduce their work forces. The consensus was that to be profitable, and in some cases simply to survive, leaner organizations were necessary. Equally noteworthy was the fact that while American businesses had gone through recessions before, it now appeared that the survival measures being adopted at this time were permanent, not temporary.

As senior management looked for ways to save money, it became apparent that despite their value to their employers, security departments would not be immune. The realization that salaries and fringe benefits could constitute the greatest part of a security department's budget suggested that they, too, would have to lose personnel, often at both security officer and supervisory levels. As an illustration, salaries and fringe benefits for the security department at a Fortune 500 company's corporate headquarters represented approximately 85 percent of the department's total budget.

This was not a unique situation; personnel historically have been the mainstay of security operations. Nevertheless, as a result of the state of the economy generally, security directors and managers found themselves having to do more with less and to reexamine the ways in which they could provide protection. Greater reliance would have to be placed on the use of high technology instead of people. In many cases, capital expenditures for hardware were found to be less expensive than the continued payment of wages, especially when allowance was made for fringe benefits and periodic salary increases.

These considerations make it obligatory for security directors and others interested in security management and administration to avoid shortcuts in trying to calculate the number of people needed to staff a department adequately. Theories on how "ideal" security departments should be staffed were made to give way to what employers would accept as a practical mater. Bloated bureaucracies such as one supervisor for every three to five security officers,[1] specialists for every conceivable function, and private secretaries for directors and managers became the exception.

Size

In trying to staff a security department, the security director or manager must first carefully evaluate the employer's physical and operational security needs and see to what extent they can be satisfied by using technology or hardware. However, the manager must also understand that while technology can be used very effectively, it is not a panacea nor will it necessarily entirely eliminate the use of security officers. For instance, no purpose is served by installing alarm or closed-circuit television systems if they are not monitored.

Having done this, the next step is to determine exactly what functions can be performed only by security officers. Such functions include fixed posts that must be covered, patrol rounds that must be made by personnel, and the number of hours it will take for each function to be performed since, as a general rule, not all posts will require full-time coverage. By way of illustration, security officers might be assigned to a shipping or receiving dock for only 8 or 12 hours a day five days a week, to patrol functions 16 hours a day plus 24 hours a day on weekends, and to a control room monitoring alarms and closed-circuit television, around the clock, seven days a week.

Once the total number of hours has been calculated, the number of persons required has to be determined. It is an axiom among security managers that it takes 4.3 security officers to cover any given post 24 hours a day, seven days a week. Consequently, there are some security mangers who on occasion will make their staffing decisions on nothing more than that formula instead of actually taking the time to chart or graph their needs to make certain that they are neither over- nor understaffed. Use of the formula can save time; it also can create problems. It does not always take into account such things as the need for security officers to have a minimum of 16 hours off between shifts and a minimum of 48 consecutive hours for their days off, considerations that are important since they affect the morale and health of the staff.

Therefore, prudent managers will take the time to graph or chart their personnel requirements. Aside from making certain that the department is properly staffed and that the needs of the staff also are satisfied, this approach will allow security mangers to see if there are some posts whose hours of operation are so limited that using part-time security officers should be considered. For instance, suppose that a corporate headquarter's main entrance is kept open from 7:00 A.M. to 8:00 P.M., five days a week, for the convenience of the executives. Since controlling overtime is an important managerial obligation, should a security manager be willing to pay 25 hours of overtime a week and have a security officer work a 13-hour day, which is too long for one person in any case? Or would it be preferable to hire and pay another full-time security officer for 40 hours when only an additional 25 hours are needed? In this case would not a part-time employee be worth considering?

No less important is the need to consider carefully to what extent supervisory personnel are necessary, or if there may be other ways in which to provide for supervision. Of course, the number of security officers assigned to any given shift will be a factor in reaching such a decision. As an example, since security managers in many if not most businesses normally work during the day, Monday through Friday, they must ask themselves whether they really can justify paying a salary for a supervisor who will be working the same hours.

There is no simple answer. A corporate security director functioning entirely in a staff position may well have less need for supervisory personnel than would be true of a security manager functioning in a line position. This is due to the fact that the very nature of a staff job usually does not involve the direct supervision of large numbers of people, whereas the line function may. Consequently, a great deal will depend on the scope of a line security manager's duties. If, for example, the latter's responsibilities involve participation in numerous meetings and a host of other business-related activities in addition to normal management duties, and the number of security officers working the day shift is sizable, it is possible that a supervisor may be needed. On the other hand, the mere fact that there also are security personnel assigned to second and third shifts does not mean automatically that supervisory personnel are needed. Once again, the security manager's decision would have to be based largely on the number of people assigned to each of those shifts, and how, in his or her opinion, their work can best be supervised.

To illustrate some different possibilities, the security manager for an institution with more than 200 security officers working three shifts in widely scattered buildings needed supervisors to make certain that personnel performed all of their duties properly. In the case of a site security manager at a corporate headquarters complex, with coverage required for all three shifts in two connected buildings and most security officers working days, the security manager was assisted by a supervisor during the day. Senior security officers, who were designated as lead guards and given some additional compensation, handled the minimal supervisory duties required for the second and third shifts. In yet another situation, with six members of the security department on duty during the day, including a receptionist and an elevator starter, and only three on each of the other two shifts, the security manager used different types of high technology instead of supervisory personnel, with excellent results.

In Chapter 2 mention was made of the need for security directors and managers to be both creative and imaginative. The responsibility for suitably protecting and conserving an employer's assets in the least expensive way is but one of the many challenges that security directors and managers can meet by using their creativity and imaginations.

Qualifications

Having finally decided on how best to provide protection through the combined use of hardware, technology, and personnel, and having fully evaluated staffing requirements in terms of numbers, security managers need to determine what the qualifications should be for whatever supervisory personnel and security officers are to be employed. In making this determination it is important to remember that in the final analysis the quality of the staff may prove to be far more important to the security program's success—or failure— than will the size of the department itself.

Certain qualifying standards should apply to all departmental personnel. Without question, honesty, integrity, and reliability are of paramount importance. However, security managers must remember that security department employees are not law enforcement personnel. For the latter there may well be certain standards of behavior that apply even when they are off duty, but the private lives of security personnel are exactly that, "private." Therefore, although security managers may show an interest in their employees, under no circumstances should they try to control their after-hours activities, or even participate in them, unless they are invited to do so by individual members of the staff. There could be an exception to this if an employee's private activities were such that they either prevented or interfered with the person's ability to do the job for which hired, or if their activities reflected adversely on the employer's reputation. Then the security manager might have no choice but to intervene to protect the department's interests.

Appearance and courtesy are legitimate qualifications. Since in many cases a security department representative may be the first person encountered by visitors, whether customers, guests, vendors, or applicants, all members of the department should make a good appearance. This is especially true in terms of their personal neatness and cleanliness. They should also be courteous, considerate, and helpful, but not to the degree that in their eagerness to be of assistance, they neglect their primary duties as members of the security department.

The importance of physical qualifications should not be minimized. Regrettably, many people think security officers have little or nothing to do but sit behind a desk or make occasional patrol rounds. Consequently, the tendency is to underestimate this factor. For security managers to expect security officers of either sex to be perfect physical specimens, including 20/20 vision, would be unrealistic, but they do have a right to expect staff members to be in reasonably good condition. A security officers's ability to stand for long periods of time, to walk up and down long flights of stairs, or to perform arduous duties could be important. Those who feel that physical qualifications are unimportant ignore the fact that in emergencies the first people to respond will usually be security personnel.

Good eyesight, even if correctable through the use of glasses, can be significant. This is especially true if something occurs and a security officer has to identify a person or an object. Security officers whose defective hearing would prevent understanding any form of verbal communication, or promptly responding to an alarm, can be a source of concern. Perhaps of even greater importance would be security officers whose physical condition would make them incapable of handling a full-sized fully charged fire extinguisher, or of helping to remove an injured or unconscious person from a potentially dangerous scene. Neither can security managers afford to ignore the direct and indirect costs involved when security officers in poor physical condition suffer injuries on the job or aggravate preexisting injuries.

Physical standards are not the only concern; if possible, security managers should also try to determine their employees' emotional stability. The security manager for a major academic institution, already responsible for over 200 security officers protecting government classified research projects, given the task of setting up the institution's first campus police force had all likely candidates interviewed by the school's psychiatrist as part of their preemployment physical examinations. This was to minimize the risk of hiring campus police officers whose real motivation for wanting the job was a chance to wear a badge and carry a gun and who could cause needless confrontations with faculty, staff, students, and the general public.

Conceivably, failure to at least try to determine an applicant's or employee's emotional stability can lead to problems. For example, an emotionally disturbed security officer might say something that adversely affects both the department's and the employer's labor or public relations, and also displeases the security manager and employer. However, the results of such an incident pale by comparison with a situation where an emotionally unstable security officer fails to react properly in an emergency and as a result, liability attaches to the employer.

Educational standards must also be established. Since those hired for supervisory positions will have to deal with employees at various levels, including managers, and occasionally may even have to appear in behalf of the security manager, it is not unreasonable to expect them to be able to satisfy the same requirements, other than experience, as are set for employment as a security manager. Neither is there any reason why the educational level for other departmental personnel should be anything less than a high school diploma. All members of the security department, regardless of position, certainly should be able to express themselves clearly in both oral and written English.

Although not necessarily qualifications in the true sense of the word, there are other factors that security managers should keep in mind in staffing their departments. Of necessity, all departmental personnel should be able to read English. At the same time, however, if there are employees, or visitors to the site, who are more comfortable speaking a foreign language, a prudent security manger will make an effort to have someone on the staff who can establish a relationship with those people. It is not uncommon to find retailers, hotels, and even some medical centers where the availability of multilingual personnel is made known to the public. Since security personnel are more likely than many other employees to have a need to communicate with non-English-speaking people, be they other employees, customers, guests, patients, or visitors, there is good reason to try to staff security departments in like manner, keeping in mind the foreign languages most often encountered.

The same can be said with regard to having both racial and sexual representation. Even if there were no equal employment opportunity laws, the security department's composition should reflect the composition not only of the employer's work force but also of the people with whom the employer does most of its business. Security departments should be made up of the best qualified people for the job. No security manager should be influenced by any personal prejudices with regard to race, creed, color, sex, or religious beliefs in terms of hiring, retaining, or promoting departmental personnel.

Uniforms and Equipment

The subject of equipment is considered under the broad heading of staffing inasmuch as security personnel need to be identified and properly equipped if they are to do their jobs properly. As with so many other things, the final decision about the types of uniforms they will wear, and the equipment with which they will be provided, will be made by an organization's senior management staff. Nevertheless, since the executive staff most often will look to the security director or manager for guidance, and the latter can influence the final outcome, it is important to give some thought to the options available.

Nameplates should be used for identification, but they are not the primary means used for security departments; uniforms are. Of course, it is entirely possible that under certain conditions security personnel will wear neither uniforms nor nameplates, but since most will be in some type of uniform, the question that needs to be answered is, what type? Basically, there are two choices: either a police type of uniform or blazers, slacks, or skirts. In some cases the answer may depend largely on the nature of the employer's business. In others, management's perception of security's role, or its thinking about the kind of image it wants security to project, may be factors.

Courtesy of First Security Services Corp.

In an environment where it is important for people to be aware of security's presence, such as a hotel, a medical center, or even in certain retail businesses, but in ways which are neither threatening nor overly authoritarian, blazers with slacks or skirts are quite appropriate. This is especially true if the word "security," possibly along with the organization's logo or name, are on the left breast pocket. Security officers dressed this way tend to make people feel more comfortable than they would if the security staff dresses like police officers. The blazer uniform also has been found acceptable in what is primarily an office environment, such as a corporate headquarters.

However, there may be times when it is felt that security personnel should project a more authoritarian image, whether for the benefit of employees, others having access to the site, or both. This might be the case with an industrial or manufacturing facility, or possibly even for certain medical centers or retail stores if located in or near relatively high crime areas.

Of course, under certain circumstances it is possible that a combination of the blazer and the police or military type of uniforms may be worth considering. A good example would be a large university complex obliged to provide security for certain research activities housed in academic buildings, where they might choose blazers for security personnel assigned there at the same time that the campus police force, also part of the school's security department, wears a more traditional police uniform. Another illustration of how a combination can work well would be a manufacturing plant. Here security officers whose contact is largely with employees and visitors might wear blazers; those on duty in shipping and receiving areas could wear police uniforms.

Rarely will security managers encounter problems with regard to such basic items of equipment as notebooks and pens, foul-weather gear, flashlights where useful, whatever is used for ensuring that patrol rounds are made, and possibly even some form of transportation, depending on the facility's size and configuration. Neither should it be difficult to justify equipping the staff with two-way radios. The ability to have direct communication between security officers and the security office, and among security officers, is a form of technology that can enhance a department's performance in ways that additional personnel cannot.

However, equipping them with what might be any form of weaponry may well prove to be controversial. Although this will be especially true if firearms are involved, it may also be true if such items as handcuffs or batons are being considered. Aside from the fact that as a rule security personnel rarely have need for equipment of this sort, security managers dare not overlook other critical factors before recommending the issuance of such equipment to departmental personnel. Perhaps the most important issues are those related to an employee's emotional stability (a subject discussed earlier in this chapter), licensing, training, liability, and public relations.

Certainly, no security manager can risk providing an emotionally unstable employee with any sort of weapon, defensive or otherwise, since even a defensive weapon may be used offensively. Like members of the general public, security officers must satisfy the licensing requirements of the jurisdiction in which they are employed before being issued firearms. By the same token, being able to get a license does not guarantee that the licensee is properly trained or otherwise qualified to use a gun. Consequently, if personnel are to be armed, it is mandatory that security managers make certain not only that they are properly trained in the weapon's use, but also that they maintain their proficiency. Firearms are not the only forms of weaponry for which training is needed and for which some form of ongoing qualification should be required. Training in the proper use of handcuffs and batons is equally important and must be provided by security managers whose departmental personnel are to be equipped in this way.

Courtesy of Wackenhut Corp.

Since security mangers have the protection and conservation of all the employer's assets, reputation included, as one of their primary duties, they also need to be fully aware of the risks of liability and adverse publicity that can arise if members of their departments are equipped with any form of weaponry. In the event that firearms, handcuffs, or batons are used improperly, particularly if that use results in injury or death, almost certainly litigation will follow, often accompanied by adverse publicity in the news media. The fact that the employing organization has adequate insurance coverage and has little or no real out-of-pocket loss, or even is found not liable, will not necessarily void the bad publicity that has been generated and its impact on company reputation, with the possible attendant loss of sales of its products or services. Therefore, prudent security directors and managers should not rush to recommend that their employers allow them to equip the security staff with weapons.

Proprietary or Contract Personnel

Another staffing decision with which security managers may find themselves involved is whether to use proprietary or contract personnel as security officers. This will necessitate considering the pros and cons on both sides of the issue. Although some security managers prefer an all-proprietary staff, others prefer contract security personnel and still others feel that combining the two is best.

Those who want proprietary security officers will say that this arrangement allows an employer to have a better security staff since it can do its own screening and training. They will also argue that a proprietary staff's loyalty is to their employer rather than to a third party, and that it is better disciplined since employees know that salary increases and promotions depend entirely on satisfying the employer.

On the other hand, security managers who favor the use of contract personnel will claim, among other things, that this can save the employer time and money since it need not train or directly supervise security officers, therefore, overhead expenses for fringe benefits, uniforms, and general administration are eliminated. They will also say that contract agencies are better prepared to provide coverage in emergencies, something that is not necessarily the case.

Although there is general agreement among security managers that having proprietary security officers is advantageous, it is only fair to say that this may not always be true. Despite the fact that the advantages of hiring a proprietary staff more often than not outweigh the advantages of using agency personnel, there may be times when a contract staff might be better for the employer. Consequently, all of the variables need to be taken into account before making a final decision. This leads to three principal questions that have to be answered. First, what is the quality of people in the area who are available for security officer positions? Second, what are the comparative costs? Third, if, in fact, contract services are less expensive, what is the quality of the agencies offering such services?

Very often, the general state of the economy will have a bearing on the answer to the first question. If a particular geographic area is suffering from high unemployment, the likelihood of finding qualified people is good. Of course, this can be advantageous to both prospective private employers and to agencies that do business in the area. At the same time, the former need to remember that if the local economy improves and security officers leave for more lucrative jobs, there could be a relatively high rate of turnover, accompanied by all the expenses that may be involved in terms of recruiting, screening, hiring, and training replacements. The impact on private employers might be greater than the impact on contract security agencies since the latter have come to accept a rather high turnover rate almost as a fact of life to which they have become accustomed.

If qualified people are available to both parties, the matter of comparative costs, always important, tends to become even more important. In other words, which will be less expensive for the employer: to hire its own security officers or to use personnel provided by a contract agency? Geography may be a factor in answering this question. For example, in some parts of the country a company's pay scale might be such that the starting hourly wage for the grade under which security officers would fall, plus the additional cost of fringe benefits, might prove to be higher than the hourly rate that would be charged by a contract agency. In other areas it might be possible that an agency's hourly rate for its security officers equals, or is even slightly higher than, the rate the company would have to pay its own employees, fringe benefits included.

Should the employer be a multisited business, its security director would find it useful to study this issue in terms of the costs corporate-wide. This was what one corporate security director did when asked if any savings could be realized within the framework of the security department since the company was looking for ways in which to cut costs. At the time there were 12 facilities located in different parts of the United States, each with its own security department. Some were using a combination of proprietary and contract personnel; others used only contract services. The security director's study indicated that because of hourly wage variables, changing to an all-proprietary staff would cost several facilities more than they were paying for contract security officers. However, these same variables showed that a change to an all-proprietary department at other locations would mean considerable savings. In fact, converting to an all-proprietary staff at the 12 domestic facilities would result in a projected net annual saving to the employer of over $250,000, despite the fact that a few sites would be adding to their security costs.

Nevertheless, in the event that a decision is made to use contract personnel, whether in whole or in part, it is of the utmost importance that those involved with the decision-making process not base their decision on cost alone. The selection of a contract security agency should be based on more than what it will cost the business or institution by which retained. The agency's quality, not merely its fee structure, must be evaluated with great care since failure to do so can be both costly and a source of embarrassment to the client.

Several things need to be taken into account as part of an agency's evaluation process. Of course, its reputation with existing clients is one factor, although a good reputation alone may not be a good indicator of the agency's ability to service the organization in question. As an illustration, if its existing client base consists of businesses or institutions all of which are relatively small and require only a limited number of guard hours, will it have the capacity to provide the coverage and supervision needed for a new, much larger and more demanding client? The answer obviously can be critically important in deciding whether to award the contract.

Two other factors that can help influence a decision with regard to a particular agency are the length of time that it has been in business and its financial stability. A new firm may not have the experience required by a new large client. One that is not financially stable may be unable to offer its personnel a reasonable salary and benefits package, or even if it can, it may have difficulty in meeting its payroll if on occasion payments from other clients are slow to arrive. Consequently, the matter of financial stability can affect the quality of its staff, and if it ever has problems paying its employees, its clients conceivably might find themselves without coverage.

Still another matter that warrants careful evaluation is the composition and experience of the agency's managerial and supervisory staff. Are its executives qualified to provide the guidance and direction necessary to satisfy clients' security needs? Do they really know and understand just what security is, or do they see themselves as merely providing a form of police service? With regard to its line managers and supervisors, are they men and women who have the academic backgrounds and practical experience to be able to provide proper guidance and direction to the security officers for whom they are responsible, or were they promoted simply by virtue of their seniority with the agency? Regrettably, this is the case with some contract organizations. The answers to these questions must satisfy prospective clients if they are to feel comfortable with the relationship and if the agency wants to avoid constant problems.

Assume that the agency's managerial and supervisory personnel impress the client favorably. The fact remains that it will be the individual security officers assigned to the account with whom the client ultimately must be satisfied. Therefore, as part of the evaluation, it is quite proper to ask the agency not only what it actually pays its personnel and what it provides in the way of fringe benefits and uniforms, but also from what sources it recruits, what the educational and physical standards are for employment, and to what extent they are screened and by whom. These are not inconsequential questions. Certainly, the client wants reliable, honest, educationally and physically qualified security officers assigned to its facility, and it knows that to get persons of this sort they must be paid decently and provided with some benefits.

The matter of uniforms is also a legitimate concern. Will the agency dress its personnel in a uniform that is acceptable to the client? Does the agency provide uniforms, or do its employees have to buy their own? Do they get an allowance toward uniform maintenance? Since it is not uncommon for visitors to a client's place of business to have contact with security officers, it is important for those visitors to have a favorable impression of the staff. Many of them will consider the security department's appearance and manner a reflection of the client's entire organization. Furthermore, they are unlikely to distinguish, or care for that matter, whether security personnel are proprietary or contract; they are simply aware of the fact that there is a security department. Consequently, because of this association it is the way in which contract security officers are dressed and behave that should be of concern to the client's security manager.

TRAINING

Making certain that security personnel are properly trained is one of the duties and responsibilities of security directors and managers, regardless of the department's size. Whether the staff is composed of proprietary or contract security officers, or a combination of the two, the fact remains that the importance of training cannot be either overemphasized or limited to the one-time training of new members of the department.

In planning a suitable training program it helps to remember that there are times when instructing security personnel in what *not to do* may be very bit as important as telling them what *to do*. Security managers must appreciate the fact that personnel who lack training, or who are trained inadequately or poorly, can be more than a source of embarrassment to the employer and to themselves. Errors by the staff, whether of omission or of commission, can be costly. Sometimes a security officer who simply says the wrong thing may find that he or she has added to the risk of liability on the part of the business or institution by which he or she is employed.

Training raises questions for which answers are needed. They are: who needs to be trained, when and how often do they need to be trained, and how and by whom should they be trained? The first question is answered easily: Everyone needs to be trained. The best time to offer any form of initial training is when people start the job. While a person's experience may have some bearing on the scope of the training required, experience alone does not justify a failure to insist on training for all new employees regardless of the level at which they are hired.

Even the most experienced manager, supervisor, or security officer, if new to an organization, needs both an orientation to the business or institution and information about how the new employer wants things done. For instance, a seasoned manager or supervisor who is new to a job does not know all of the employer's policies and procedures and what they may require of him or her. A newly employed but experienced investigator still does not know the exact format or style in which the new employer wants reports written, nor does a newly hired security officer who has had experience in making patrol rounds necessarily know how the new employer wants rounds made.

Of course, it goes without saying that inexperienced security officers need more than an orientation to the business or institution and information about how management wants things done; they also need training in how to do the job. Those who feel that training is unnecessary because the work of security officers appears to be relatively uncomplicated are shortsighted. This being the case, what should training consist of in terms of subject matter?

There are some generic or basic subjects in which all security personnel should be trained. There are also other more specialized subjects in which training is necessary depending on the particular type of organization. As an example, although all security departments have a great deal in common, there are differences between those in hotels and those in hospitals. In addition, even though there is a considerable difference between policing and security, there are some law enforcement-related topics with which security personnel should at least be familiar.

The core subjects in which all security personnel should be either trained or to which they should be exposed consist of the following: criminal law and the laws of arrest; the laws of search and seizure; how to make patrol rounds; investigations and investigative techniques; first aid and cardiopulmonary resuscitation (CPR); crime scene searches and the preservation of evidence; report writing; how to conduct interviews of complainants, witnesses, and suspects; self-defense; human relations, and how to respond to various types of emergencies. Each of these topics lends itself to instruction in terms of both *what to do* and *what not to do*.

Courtesy of First Security Services Corp.

Courtesy of First Security Services Corp.

Then, depending on the nature of the business or institution by which employed, additional training based on the environment in which the security officer will work should be provided. For instance, hotel security officers need training in such subjects as guest and public relations; protecting guests and their property; and problems caused by guests who have had too much to drink, prostitutes, and those who leave without paying their bills. Additional topics unique to a hospital environment, such as patient and visitor relations; the trauma suffered by relatives and friends when a patient is seriously ill, dying, or dies; how to deal with hazardous waste and radiation; and the different ways in which such institutions need to respond to fire emergencies need to be part of the training experience of those employed by medical centers.

Once again, however, it is important to remember that training should not be a one-time thing. Truly professional security managers not only are aware of the need for their staffs to undergo refresher training periodically but will find new and different ways in which to provide that training. Refresher or in-service training can be offered using different techniques. Among the ways in which this can be done are formal classroom instruction with lectures on various topics of interest and importance to security; the use of training films made in-house or bought or rented from companies or organizations such as the National Fire Protection Association which specialize in making materials of this sort; or for businesses and institutions where security officers have access to computer terminals, by developing their own form of computerized training so that the staff can be both trained and tested on certain subjects stored in the computer's memory.

Regarding the question of by whom security personnel should be trained, it obviously is important that all training be provided by persons knowledgeable with respect to the subjects on which they will provide instruction. Although most of the training should be provided by the security director or manager, keep in mind the advisability of inviting the participation of qualified people who are not necessarily members of the security department. Doing this can be of immeasurable value to a security department's public relations. Instead of the security manger attempting to discuss the employer's personnel practices, why not ask the personnel director to speak on the subject, or if the topic is fire prevention, why not invite someone from the fire department to do it? Providing training in this way enhances both the professional reputation and the skills of the security staff.

SUPERVISION

Although the word *discipline* has various meanings, the tendency is to associate its use with military organizations or police agencies. However, one of the word's several meanings is to have self-control, be orderly, and be efficient. Thus it is obvious that discipline applies equally to both individuals and organizations, whether small or large. Individuals must exercise self-discipline to achieve their personal goals, whether as students, in the business world, or socially. Organizations of any size need discipline if they are to reach their objectives. Self-discipline is what makes students study when they might prefer to party, it makes athletes train despite possible distractions, and it makes working people go to work and do their jobs even on the first sunny day after a long, hard winter. No business or institution, military or police organization, or sports team, amateur or professional, can succeed unless it is disciplined.

A result of orderliness is efficiency. In any organization, security or otherwise, the mere fact that more than one person is involved calls for supervision to make certain that the work that has to be done is performed in a way that is both orderly and provides for optimum efficiency. Supervision prevents needless wasted effort and duplication on the one hand while ensuring that all tasks are executed in a timely and cost-effective fashion.

Although the size of the security department will dictate what may be necessary in the way of supervision, the fact remains that everyone in the department, from the director or manager downward, needs to be supervised. How closely they need to be supervised is another matter. The same may be said of the extent to which they, in turn, must supervise their subordinates.

Security directors and managers are hired because of their professional skills and competence. In most cases the person to whom they report has little, if any, real or direct knowledge of security operations. Consequently, it is not at all unusual to find that as the two become more familiar with each other, the superior will rely on the subordinate for guidance and advice on security-related matters with increasing frequency. Neither is it unusual for truly professional security directors to have a good deal of leeway in discharging their duties and responsibilities. The number of times when they must get prior approval before they can make a decision should be relatively rare. In fact, security directors who constantly seek clearance before making any significant decisions, and who hesitate to act without it, may find that before long their superiors and other senior managers will begin to question their ability.

Courtesy of First Security Services Corp.

Despite this, however, security directors and managers dare not assume that because they enjoy a good deal of freedom in operating their departments, they are not subject to supervision. They are. Superiors rightly expect that any major action to be taken by security will first be discussed with and cleared by them unless it is already clearly covered by an existing policy, or there is an emergency. For instance, any activity that might have a significant impact on operations generally, on labor, or on public relations; which might risk incurring liability on the part of the employer; or which might become the basis for a news media "headline" should not be undertaken unilaterally by a security director or manager.

To illustrate how such a situation might arise and how it could be handled, suppose that in the interest of employee morale a company had a policy stating that as a rule employees leaving any facility with parcels of any kind, pursues, briefcases, and attaché cases included, will not be searched by security personnel unless the security director has prior permission to do so from his or her superior or from the company president in the superior's absence. However, the policy also says that if neither person is available, the security director can make the decision but must report it to the superior as soon as possible. A plant manager calls the security director, reports that employees know that a decision has been made to close the facility, several telephones are missing from the site, and the plant and human resources managers feel that a parcel search should be instituted before more losses occur. The security director agrees, but knowing that his superior is absent, calls the president's office only to learn that he, too, is unavailable. The security director authorizes the search, but tells his superior what was done and why immediately upon the latter's return to the office.

Another aspect of the supervision of the security director, which interestingly enough requires the latter to take the initiative, lies in the need to keep one's superior informed of unusual security activities. This is to be distinguished from seeking clearance for every action to be taken by the department. No one likes to be embarrassed. It does security directors or managers no good if out of-the-ordinary incidents are reported to them, but they, in turn, fail to advise their superiors.

Suppose that the security director gets a call at home from an outlying manufacturing facility at 2:30 A.M. on a Sunday morning to the effect that there has been a fire. Although it is unlikely that there will be an immediate call to the person to whom he or she reports, neither should the matter be deferred until the security director and his or her superior arrive at the office on Monday morning. Instead, in such a situation a call should be placed some time later that morning to both the superior and the corporate-level person in charge of manufacturing operations. Otherwise, there is a risk that before the security director can inform his or her superior, the president or person in charge of manufacturing may ask that person for information about the fire. To have to say that one has not even heard about a fire but that the security director will be asked for details is not the kind of admission that one likes to make to either peers or superiors. Neither does it do anything for the kind of relationship that must exist between a superior and a security director if the latter is to be successful. Therefore, in this regard the need to keep one's superiors informed is an element of supervision notwithstanding the fact that it requires communication upward rather than downward.

The same basic principles apply to the relationship between security directors and their subordinates. At the same time, there will usually be a greater degree of supervision downward since security directors, unlike their superiors, do have an intimate knowledge of just what security is and what it can do. Of course, this very knowledge may also lead to a pitfall best avoided. Napoleon once remarked that "If you want a thing done well, do it yourself."[2] Security directors who follow this maxim soon realize that it not only increases their own work, but also that it can be damaging to morale and the confidence their immediate subordinates have in themselves.

Just as security directors should be prepared to advise and guide subordinates and provide general oversight for all of the department's activities, they must also be ready to allow subordinates to do their jobs with minimal interference. They are charged with making certain that all of the duties and responsibilities of their departments are carried out in ways that serve the employer's best interests; they are not expected to perform each and every one themselves, or to become immersed in their execution. The dangers to be avoided are one of either becoming so involved with details as actually to interfere with the work of subordinates, or exercising so little supervision as to give an impression of disinterest in what is going on. In other words, a balance must be struck. Of course, subordinates must also understand that because their superiors want to be kept informed of other-than-routine activities does not mean that they are taking over the subordinate's duties. Just as security directors need to keep their superiors informed, so must they be kept advised by their subordinates. Good communications both upward and downward are essential to effective supervision.

This principle must be accepted and implemented throughout the security organization; it does not apply only to management and supervisory personnel. As corporate-level security directors provide advice, guidance, and general oversight to security managers who report to them, so do security managers advise, guide, and generally oversee the activities of supervisors for whom they are responsible. However, as one descends through the ranks of the organization, the need for closer supervision increases. This should not be taken to mean that security officers are less trustworthy than supervisors, supervisors less trustworthy than managers, and so on. The extent to which it is necessary to supervise personnel tends to be more a matter of their experience. As employees, properly trained through the efforts of effective managers and supervisors, gain experience and become more familiar with their duties and responsibilities, they also become more capable of doing their jobs with only a minimum amount of direct supervision. This heightens their morale and everyone benefits. It is also indicative of the quality of the training and supervision given employees and brings credit to the entire organization.

The basic characteristics of supervision discussed above will not by themselves necessarily assure security directors and managers of success. No matter how well they may know the fundamentals of supervision, the personal traits or characteristics described in Chapter 2, for which employers now tend to look when hiring security directors, will to a large extent determine their effectiveness as supervisors. In many respects being a good supervisor is much the same as being a good teacher. It means helping subordinates learn; it may also mean disciplining them on occasion.

In furtherance of the idea of the supervisor as teacher, it is important to remember that some subordinates, if not all, inevitably will make mistakes. When they do, supervisors have to deal with them in ways that relate to both the offending security officer and those offended. Not infrequently, the employee who makes a mistake is also one who ordinarily does a better than average job, one who is willing to make a decision, whether good or bad, under conditions when making even a bad decision may be far better than not making any. As the famous author and playwright George Bernard Shaw once said: "A life spent making mistakes is not only more honorable but more useful than a life spent doing nothing."[3]

When a mistake is made, no matter how good the employee's intentions, that person's supervisor is obliged to take some form of disciplinary action. While the type of action to be taken is, or should be, influenced by the error's seriousness, some mistakes may be serious enough to leave the supervisor with little choice other than to discharge the person. However, when this is not the case, the supervisor as teacher should use the incident not to embarrass the employee or cause that person to lose interest in continuing to do a good job, but rather, as a learning experience. In other words, the errant employee should be given a chance to learn from his or her mistake. Naturally, if the same mistake is repeated, the supervisor is justified in assuming that the subordinate either is incompetent or simply is not interested in doing a good job. Then the only alternative may be to terminate the person's employment.

Thus it is evident that being a good supervisor also means being able to make decisions, sometimes very difficult and painful ones, which directly affect subordinates. Consequently, the most effective supervisors are those who have good human relations skills. It is very difficult to be either a good teacher or a good supervisor unless one has more than a little patience, a lot of self-control, an abundance of wisdom, and the ability to empathize with subordinates, who in reality are the superior's students. In the last analysis it is these traits, good communications skills, and an understanding of the fundamentals of supervision which, when combined, make for an efficient, effective security department.

RESPONSIBILITY AND AUTHORITY

Responsibility and authority are not the same. However, for security personnel at any level to try to discharge their responsibilities without having the authority they need to do so can doom the program to failure. It must also be clearly understood that while all employees, regardless of position, have responsibilities, they are limited in scope and so is the authority they have to carry them out. As far as senior management is concerned, the security director or manager ultimately has total responsibility for the successes and failures of the department.

In policing, responsibility and authority are creatures of the law. However, security departments find that while their authority to carry out their responsibilities may be based on legal principles, by and large it is derived more from the employer's executive management than it is from legislation. Even when conditions permit security officers to be commissioned as special police officers or deputy sheriffs with full police powers, geographic limitations usually are imposed by the granting authority. The purpose is to restrict their actions so as to allow them to discharge only those responsibilities assigned to them by their employers.

What, then, are the responsibilities of security personnel, and what authority must they have to carry them out? One could list a number of different responsibilities which in theory would be entirely proper, but it would be misleading to give the impression that they are universally acceptable to employers. In reality, as with job titles, responsibilities will consist of only those which senior management feels are proper for its security personnel: nothing more, nothing less. Therefore, since employers make the ultimate decisions with regard to responsibilities, it is not surprising that the authority which they will grant usually will be only that which in their opinion is needed for the security staff to do its work. Nevertheless, there are some responsibilities that might best be described as generic since they are assigned to virtually all security departments regardless of the type of business or institution by which employed. Among them are the following:

- ❏ To prevent the theft or loss of any of the employer's assets through the commission of a crime
- ❏ To prevent the loss of assets as a result of a preventable fire or a human-made disaster
- ❏ To prevent unauthorized persons from gaining access to the premises
- ❏ To protect all persons lawfully on the premises against criminal or other forms of activity that could result in injury or death
- ❏ To investigate questionable activities that might result or have resulted in the loss of assets
- ❏ To identify those persons responsible for the theft or other loss of assets
- ❏ To maintain liaison with local law enforcement agencies

Of course, other responsibilities may be assigned, but they will depend on the given set of circumstances. Even those listed above may be expanded or reduced depending on what an employer wants done. Since the duties and responsibilities of security directors and managers generally are a good indication of those that will fall to their departments, several instances illustrating how they are subject to being expanded or limited were discussed in Chapter 2.

To further illustrate various possibilities for expanding or limiting security department responsibilities, if security is defined as the protection and conservation of assets, does senior management see security's role as reactive or proactive? In other words, is security expected to wait for incidents to occur and do nothing more than quickly identify and apprehend those responsible so that they may be punished, or is it encouraged to work closely with all departments to find and develop ways in which to prevent problems from arising in the first place? Knowing that injuries to employees represent losses to employers, is security to have a role in a company's safety program? Realizing that the criminal and civil penalties for violating environmental laws and standards can prove costly in a number of ways, to what extent, if any, should the security department be involved with efforts to prevent them? If there is parking for employees and visitors, is controlling access and monitoring the facilities a proper security department function, or should this be handled by some other department? Who should provide receptionists: security or another department?

Regardless of the answers to any of these questions, or whether an employer elects to have its security department in a proactive or reactive role, merely delegating responsibility without authority to act becomes self-defeating. Assume that a proactive stance emphasizing prevention is preferred. To expect security directors to find and develop ways in which to reduce risks and losses affecting the entire organization without all other department heads being told that they have the authority to ask questions about all aspects of their respective operations will, in effect, prevent security directors from doing precisely what executive management expects them to do. Expecting security personnel to control access to and monitor company parking facilities without the authority to stop unauthorized vehicles from entering or to tow those illegally parked makes a mockery of the organization's parking program and security department. If security is to be involved with the employer's safety program but a security officer seeing an unsafe condition such as a wet floor lacks the authority to call maintenance and ask them to take corrective action, the risk of both injury to persons and possible loss to the employer remains.

Employers have a legal right to protect their assets. By virtue of that right, or authority, they also are empowered to delegate that authority and exercise it through their employees or other representatives. The legal aspects of this issue are considered at greater length in Chapter 6. Of course, in some jurisdictions it is permissible for employers to have security personnel commissioned as either special police officers or deputy sheriffs. If employers choose to avail themselves of such opportunities, the question of authority for certain actions may also be based on the terminology used in both the statute or ordinance that grants a police or sheriff's department the right to commission security personnel and in the commissioning document itself. Usually, the latter will also define the geographic limits within which those who are commissioned can exercise their police powers. Nevertheless, the source of the authority is secondary to the fact that without it a security department will find itself operating in a vacuum, thus being of little or no real value to the employing organization.

Recognizing the importance of and need for authority, the fact remains that the very issue of authority is a matter of grave concern to all security professionals. That concern is based on the reality that some members of the staff, and occasionally even some employers, may be inclined to abuse their authority. This may be attributed in part to those employers and security personnel who either fail or refuse to accept the fact that security is not policing, and security officers are not police officers. On the occasions when this does happen it can lead to a host of legal problems, which are examined at greater length in Chapter 6.

Some examples of how authority can be abused by security personnel and employers may lead to a better understanding of this serious problem. *The Boston Globe* of August 16, 1991, carried a story in which a security officer for a retail grocery chain alleged that under pressure from his employer, he and other security officers were expected to get employees to confess to stealing from stores despite the fact that in his own experience there was no evidence against employees in 75 percent of the cases.[4] The October 19, 1990, edition of the same paper reported that a major retail department store and its security officers were being investigated by the Federal Bureau of Investigation and the U.S. Department of Justice because members of the security staff allegedly had impersonated federal officers while attempting to carry out their responsibilities to their employer.[5]

The New York Times reported on August 29, 1991, that a grand jury had indicted four Washington, D.C., area college security officers on charges of involuntary manslaughter in the death of a deaf student through the use of excessive force in making an arrest.[6] Less then a month later, *The New York Times* carried a story to the effect that a special Bergen County, New Jersey, grand jury's five-month investigation of security at a major sports complex documented the fact that between 1987 and 1990 there had been 20 cases in which security guards had either beaten or otherwise abused patrons.[7]

Thus it is of the utmost importance that all security personnel clearly understand the limitations imposed on their authority, while security directors and managers must insist that subordinates act properly. That responsibilities cannot be discharged without the authority to do so does not excuse the abuse of that authority. Neither can security directors and their employers afford to overlook the direct and indirect costs of such misconduct when it occurs in the exercise of authority. The ethical issues that confront security directors and managers when their superiors ask them or other security personnel to exercise authority in ways that are morally and ethically objectionable are explored more fully in Chapter 6.

RECORDS AND COMMUNICATIONS

While some types of records are clearly distinguishable from communications, the fact remains that for the most part, all communications eventually become part of a records system. Furthermore, whether computerized or otherwise, the maintenance of good records and the proper use of written, oral, and electronic communications are essential to the operation of an effective security department. Therefore, it seems only logical to acquaint those who may not be familiar with security with the existence and use of both records and communications.

Records

Although virtually all security departments maintain records of one sort or another, too often they are of little real use. In many cases they represent nothing more than a sort of departmental history that takes up valuable filing space instead of helping the department satisfy its daily operating needs, or they are a compilation of statistics. This may well be due to the way in which they are kept rather than of what they consist, or because statistics, important as they are, represent but one aspect of good record keeping. To be of optimum value and benefit to security departments, records must be effective working tools rather than mere historical documents or statistics.

Some of the records most commonly found in security department files are the following:

❑ Personnel records of departmental employees
❑ Data on identification badges issued by all employees and on the disposition of those recovered from terminated employees
❑ Key records, including to whom keys have been issued and from whom they have been recovered
❑ Employee vehicle registration data
❑ Security incident reports
❑ Pending and closed investigative reports
❑ Budget data
❑ Information on all losses and recoveries
❑ Records of accidents involving company-owned or company-leased motor vehicles
❑ Copies of internal memoranda between security and other departments
❑ Copies of correspondence between security and outside organizations or persons

❑ Copies of general and special instructions to security personnel regarding such matters as duties, post assignments, and uniform regulations
❑ Records of patrol rounds

Others, depending on the duties or operations of any given department, might include:

❑ Security audit reports
❑ The location and an inventory of all security equipment, supplies, and training materials corporate-wide
❑ Records of the issuance and recovery of all truck seals
❑ Tables of comparative data based on annual losses and recoveries
❑ Personal information on those employees and their families who are covered by the employer's executive protection program
❑ Inspection reports related to safety and environmental matters
❑ Incident reports related to safety and environmental matters

Although departmental records should be available for use as needed, whether in hard copy or computerized, some obviously may be of more value than others. Good examples of some in the latter category are records on keys, security incident reports, and investigative reports. For instance, an inventory shortage from a locked storeroom is discovered; an investigation is opened. It helps to know who has keys and if any keys to that room were ever reported lost or stolen. Security incident reports should indicate if there have been other losses from the room, and if so, of what items. Closed investigative files might contain information about other problems relating to this storeroom, and conceivably the names of persons who either were involved or were suspected of involvement.

If all keys can be accounted for, the possibility exists that someone who is authorized access may be involved; if they cannot be, a logical investigative lead would be to review the circumstances under which a key was reported lost or stolen, and who made the report. In the event that there have been other problems with this storeroom, the nature of those problems may well indicate a pattern which, in turn, will suggest additional investigative leads. Certainly, if previously closed investigative reports reflect problems with this particular storeroom, and they contain the name or names of persons who either were known to be involved or whose involvement was suspected, whoever is handling the current investigation will want to consider the probability that they may have had something to do with the latest loss. At the same time, if key control records are incomplete or inaccurate, security incident reports lack details, and there is no system to or cross-referencing of closed investigative reports, the investigator will be seriously hampered. It will require him or her to spend much time and effort that might be used to much better advantage in trying to solve the problem and identify the party responsible.

Since this is only an introduction to the subject of security in its broadest sense, not a text on records management, we do not consider in detail the best ways in which to keep records. However, security directors and managers need to remember that the key to a good records system lies in the ease and rapidity with which data can be retrieved. This should be taken into account when planning and organizing a records system regardless of whether the system is in hard copy or maintained electronically. That is why progressive security directors and managers recognize and welcome the introduction of electronic data processing as a management tool which they can use to advantage.

One question that invariably arises is for how long a period security department records should be kept. The answer should be based on the value of a given type of record. However, the employer's general records retention policy also needs to be taken into consideration. Many companies assign responsibility for the development and implementation of their records retention policies to their law departments; their security directors may be involved, either directly or indirectly. The likelihood of this happening is greatest in organizations where they report to the vice president and general counsel or to whomever is in charge of the law department. Of course, even if this were not the case, they should help decide what a logical time would be for the retention of the various records in the custody and control of the security department.

For instance, since occupied space can be costly, there ordinarily is no valid reason for automobile registration data, records of patrol rounds made by security officers, or the personnel files of terminated security staff members to be retained in any form of storage beyond a predetermined number of years. On the other hand, all incident reports and investigative files, whether pending or closed, should be kept in the security office indefinitely.

Communications

The types of communications with which security departments are involved may be written, electronic, or verbal. In hard copy they may consist of memoranda, letters, post or other instructions, and reports, among other things. Electronic communications may be used for the same purposes, with the exception of those that are being sent outside the employer's organization. Verbal communications are often used for temporary or emergency instructions of one sort or another, when time is of the essence. Thus it is by no means unusual for security personnel to provide information orally that otherwise might be in writing, and which will subsequently be reduced to either hard copy or electronic media.

In Chapter 2 we discussed the importance of good communications skills for successful security directors and managers. These skills, with the likelihood of fewer refinements, are no less important for other departmental personnel if the department itself is to succeed. This, of course, does not alter the fact that while all members of the staff need at the very least to have acceptable communications skills, communications themselves must be handled through the appropriate channels. This applies to all internal communications, whether upward or downward. It must also apply to all security department communications being sent to persons outside the employer's business.

It has been pointed out that an important aspect of training involves instructing the security staff about what not to do as well as about what they should do. The same principle applies to communications. Brevity and clarity are essential insofar as all communications are concerned, regardless of the form of media used. However, bearing in mind the litigious society in which we live, an imprudent remark, whether in writing or made orally, may cause an employer untold grief; the security manager, endless embarrassment; and the offending security officer, unemployment.

Courtesy of Wackenhut Corp.

In trying to reduce the risk of any communications causing an employer problems, the need to go through proper channels must be incorporated as another part of training so that it is fully understood and obeyed by all departmental personnel. This does not necessarily mean that the security director is or should be the employer's sole spokesperson. There may be other managerial employees who have an equal right to communicate, but not without following established guidelines.

As an illustration, a corporate security director would be the logical person to handle communications between the employer and the Federal Bureau of Investigation or Department of State on matters concerning terrorist activities, but it would be perfectly proper for the site security manager to be the principal channel of communication between the company and local police department if it appears that a crime may have been committed. Neither would it be improper for a site security supervisor who has just completed an investigation of an errant employee to discuss the results with the latter's personnel representative or superior, or to speak with the local police if a security incident occurs on his or her after-hours shift. On the other hand, it would be improper for a site security manager to discuss corporate security issues with the company's president unless the latter specifically requested such a discussion, or to communicate with anyone, either inside or outside the company or institution, on matters of corporate security policy. Therefore, where communications are concerned, all departmental personnel need to be made aware of the fact that there is but one "boss," and that person is the one who speaks for the department.

The same channeling of communications either upward or outward must apply to those directed downward. The security manager who has fault to find with a security officer should discuss the matter with the person's supervisor instead of taking it up directly with the offender. To do otherwise will only serve to create a problem in the relationship that exists between the manager and the supervisor. At the same time it will make it more difficult for the supervisor to discipline the employee for another offense committed at a later date.

Another important aspect of communications has to deal with the protection of information. Regardless of the nature of any communication, be it a letter, memorandum, or report, or whether it is in hard copy or electronic form, the fact remains that it contains information. Information is an asset, and as such must be protected. Of course, the degree of protection required will depend mainly on its sensitivity. In this respect security personnel in particular need to remember that at least some security communications may contain information which, if exposed either in writing or orally, regardless of whether the exposure was deliberate or inadvertent, could cause irreparable harm not only to the employer but also to others.

Consequently, while good records and communications play a vital role in the administration of an effective security department, employees also need to be mindful of more than their importance. They also need to understand how and why records are maintained, and how communications have to be channeled, controlled, and protected for a department to operate efficiently and in the employer's best interests.

LAW ENFORCEMENT LIAISON

Although considerable space has already been devoted to the differences between security and law enforcement, particularly policing, no security department can hope to do its job, and do it well, without effective liaison with law enforcement. It is also important for students of security to realize that the very term *law enforcement* means more than just policing. The term includes prosecutors as well, as evidenced by the fact that one will hear an attorney general, whether federal or state, referred to as that entity's "chief law enforcement officer." Understanding this is particularly important when security personnel become involved directly with prosecuting offenders, as so often happens to those in retailing, who frequently appear in court in shoplifting cases.

The critical issue, then, is not good liaison. Rather, it is a question of its development and maintenance in ways that are legally, morally, and ethically correct. It is also a question of what each side, security on one and law enforcement on the other, has a right to expect of the other, and under what circumstances. Although we would like to believe that all law enforcement and security personnel are above reproach, the fact is that in many respects their behavior is a reflection of the society in which they live and work. Consequently, not all are going to be completely ethical and moral in performing their duties. Since both law enforcement, particularly those in policing, and security personnel work under varying degrees of stress and pressure, there are times when one might be tempted to bypass proper procedures by taking advantage of personal contacts.

Two illustrations may prove helpful. One concerns a questionable if not altogether improper request of a police agency; the other is an example of how security and law enforcement can cooperate in a legitimate and beneficial way. A large corporation and major influence in the city in which its corporate headquarters was located, concerned about the apparent unauthorized disclosure of proprietary information and wanting to identify the employees responsible, asked the police department to conduct an electronic search of all telephone records in that city's metropolitan area. The police department conducted the search.[8] In the other, a security force and the police department of a major east coast city cooperated with the private group, making regular patrols of a 53-block area. The agreed-upon result was a reduction of crime in the area.[9]

Despite the first example, where a business asked the police to do something, it is often easier for someone in law enforcement to take advantage of security than it is for security to take advantage of the police. This is not because security mangers necessarily have more scruples than police officers; it simply means that some security officers are more vulnerable when approached. This is largely due to several factors, and security personnel must be made aware of them to avoid not only questionable activities, but also to avoid embarrassing themselves and their employers.

First is the matter of ego; everyone has an ego. As a result, if a law enforcement officer asks a security manager for help with something, it may inflate that manager's ego to a point where ego outweighs logic. The manager rationalizes that there either are no moral, ethical, or legal problems in complying, or else that they are less important than providing assistance to the police.

Dangerous as the ego factor is by itself, the problem may be compounded by those security directors, managers, and security officers who think of themselves as members of the police fraternity—which they are not. Whether they are former police personnel, merely frustrated law enforcement officers, or security officers who have been commissioned as special police officers or deputy sheriffs, the fact remains that they are not members of the law enforcement community in the true sense of that phrase. Nevertheless, those who fail to see or understand this may be prepared to do things with or without a request for help from someone who is actively engaged in a law enforcement function.

For security directors to ask for police assistance and work closely with the police on investigations involving the loss or theft of an employer's assets is perfectly proper. The same is true when an employer is involved with a special event that may result in a traffic control problem. In contrast, for security managers to ask for criminal history information, which by state law is not to be made available to private persons, or for the police to ask for access to any of the employer's records without first getting a subpoena, is improper.

Since district or prosecuting attorneys are also an integral part of law enforcement, the question of liaison with their offices warrants consideration. Important though it is, the fact remains that the need is less. What need does exist will be more limited since many businesses and institutions rarely have contact with the prosecution of a criminal case. When an occasion does arise, it usually is as a result of an investigation by the police, with security's help. Both security and the police will then coordinate their efforts to satisfy the prosecution's requests in preparation for and at the time of trial. Perhaps the greatest need for liaison in these cases will develop during any possible pretrial negotiations with defense counsel to reach an agreement, or plea bargain, that will be acceptable to the victim and court as well as to the defendant.

Businesses that are inclined to prosecute on a more or less regular basis, as happens with retailers and shoplifters, obviously have a much greater need. In some jurisdictions security department representatives may represent the victim employer, actually present the evidence, and do the prosecuting, rather than a district attorney. Nevertheless, there is a need to avoid conflict with the district attorney. This could be in terms of scheduling cases for trial, or pursuing one as a misdemeanor when the district attorney might have information which would justify a felony prosecution to be handled by that office. Since most security representatives who might present cases in court are neither lawyers nor necessarily familiar with all of the nuances that may influence the outcome of a trial, good liaison with the prosecuting attorney's office may be critical.

Therefore, it goes without saying that there are many perfectly proper and legitimate ways in which security and law enforcement can and should cooperate. While the initiative for establishing liaison will usually come from security directors and managers, it is entirely possible that in some cases the first contact will be by someone in law enforcement. Regardless of who takes the first step, the tone should be set by the respective parties. This does not mean that at the outset each has to tell the other that their relationship must at all times be lawful, ethical, and moral. However, if at any time either party, directly or indirectly, asks the other to do something that is at best questionable and at worst unlawful, the other must be prepared to refuse, but in a way that will not jeopardize future opportunities for cooperation. To either make or give in to any such request is needlessly to risk one's personal integrity and even one's professional future.

NEWS MEDIA RELATIONSHIPS

It is not uncommon for security directors or managers to receive calls from the news media. They may want information about an incident that occurred or allegedly occurred, or they may ask for an interview about some aspect of the employer's security program. These requests can be fraught with danger, especially for the novice, the unsuspecting, or the person who will permit ego to outweigh good judgment. This is no less true for security directors and managers than it is for security officers. Representatives of the news media have a job to do, but so do security personnel. To antagonize the news media is unwise and best avoided. To give them what they want can cause problems and create work for security directors that otherwise might have been unnecessary. Therefore, the wisest course of action is to handle inquiries in ways that will cause neither hard feelings on the part of the media, nor problems for security. To do this in both the employer's and their own best interests, security directors and managers must be skillful.

Three illustrations of what can happen when members of the news media make contact may be helpful. In the first a representative of a national news magazine called several Fortune 500 corporate security directors in connection with a story she was writing on the subject of industrial espionage. Her principal interest was in learning what their companies did to prevent the loss of valuable information to industrial spies. All but one outlined in general terms what their organizations did. That one, interviewed for half an hour, was thanked for giving his time and for information about security of which the caller had been unaware. However, he was also told that he really had told her nothing about his company's program for dealing with the industrial espionage problem, to which he replied that he was happy that he had been able to do his job. When the names of the other security directors, their company names, and their statements appeared in the publication, it dawned on them that they had said too much, thus making it necessary for them to review their programs for countering industrial espionage and to modify them. If they did not, there was an increased risk that readers of the article might get ideas about how to spy on their organizations.

In the second a reporter asked questions that a security director felt could be answered without risk to the employer, and a story appeared in a newspaper. When it did, the security director was disturbed not only because it contained misleading information, but also because that information was attributed to the security director and was in quotes. Had it not been for a member of the employer's public relations staff who was a party to the interview and informed the corporate officers of the true nature of what the security director had said, the latter's superiors might well have had serious doubts about both his professional ability and his common sense.

The last involved a newspaper reporter interested in how businesses handled visitors to their facilities. He called the public affairs office of a major employer in the area covered by the paper and explained his interest. With the security director's cooperation, he got both his story and photographs of the visitor clearance procedure, but in ways that would not affect the process.

To minimize the risk of antagonism on one hand, or compromising the security program on the other, certain principles need to be kept in mind. First, earlier in the chapter we pointed out that security directors or managers have to make certain that all departmental personnel clearly understand that the director or manager, as the case may be, is the only person authorized to speak for and on behalf of the department. In other words, if subordinates are contacted by representatives of the news media regarding anything connected with the employer's business, the caller is to be referred to the person in charge of security, whatever his or her title. This helps prevent security employees from giving incorrect, invalid, confidential, or embarrassing information to the news media.

The next thing to bear in mind is the fact that many, if not most, businesses and institutions of appreciable size have their own public relations or public affairs departments. They, not security, are responsible for news media liaison, and security directors or managers should not be the ones to court the press, whether for business or personal publicity. Therefore, in a majority of cases a first call from the media for information about security matters or anything else will usually be to public relations. If a security matter is what prompts the call, and it is to the security director, the latter should first refer the caller to public relations. Wise security directors will then contact public relations and ask if they believe that an interview should be granted. They will then act on the basis of that advice. However, if the news media are calling because of a security-related emergency, only public affairs should be involved, since the security director's job is to deal with the emergency, not the press.

If there is no emergency, and public relations feels it is advisable for the security director to agree to an interview, the public relations employee through whom the request was made should be present for the interview if it is conducted face to face. If done by telephone, it should be as a conference call. This is a safeguard for both the person being interviewed and the employer, since the public relations representative is often better positioned than the person being interviewed to control the interview if questions asked border on the improper.

Even so, news media interviews should be treated by security directors much as if they were testifying in court. Beware of possibly misleading questions or those that tend to play on one's ego. Be certain that all questions asked are clearly understood. If not, ask for clarification. Answer questions carefully and to the point; do not volunteer information for which the reporter has not asked. If the answer to any question asked might compromise the security program, it should not be answered. However, while in this instance the interviewer deserves to be told why a question will not be answered, care must be exercised to avoid giving even a partial answer during the course of the explanation.

The pitfalls can best be avoided by security directors who have good relations with their own public affairs departments. They know which representatives of the news media should not be granted interviews and which ones should. They can also help handle difficult interviews by their very presence, just as that factor in and of itself can provide support for a misquoted security director whose superiors may be disturbed by what they read in a newspaper or magazine, hear on radio, or see on television.

EMERGENCIES AND DISASTERS

Of all the challenges that security personnel must face, perhaps none is greater than that posed when called upon to deal with emergencies or disasters. Furthermore, when an emergency or a disaster does happen, it may challenge everyone in the department, not merely its management staff.

Webster's New World Dictionary defines *emergency* as a sudden, generally unexpected occurrence or set of circumstances demanding immediate action; and a *disaster* as any happening that causes great harm or damage, a serious or sudden misfortune. Although these definitions indicate that disasters are emergencies, not all emergencies necessarily are the result of disasters. For example, if an explosion destroys a building, the disaster also creates an emergency condition. If, however, there is a bomb threat, security is faced with an emergency, but the threat alone is not a disaster.

The very fact that for the most part emergencies and disasters generally are unexpected, and happen suddenly, means that their occurrence is not limited to sometime between 9:00 A.M. and 5:00 P.M., Monday through Friday, when security directors and mangers are at work. They can happen at any hour of any day. It is also worth remembering that the causes of both emergencies and disasters can be either acts of nature or acts of people.

With scientific advances and the help of technology, acts of nature, with the possible exception of earthquakes, can be forecast and tracked. Even though the forecasting and tracking may not always be accurate, they at least provide some warning. This makes it easier for security departments to prepare for their arrival. This, in turn, may help minimize the scope of the damage. By the same token, rarely is there any warning, and certainly there is no tracking, where human-made events are involved.

Natural disasters include earthquakes, fires, floods, blizzards, snow or ice storms, hurricanes, tornadoes, and some types of explosions. However, it is also possible for some fires, floods, and explosions to be human-made. Riots and civil disturbances certainly are human-made events, as are all acts of terrorism, whether in the form of bomb threats or actual bombings, kidnappings, extortion, or hostage taking. Regardless of whether an emergency or disaster is caused by a natural or a human act, and no matter who may make the final decision as to how best to respond, security will probably be the first department involved, and its personnel will be expected to take some action to deal with the problem and to minimize any risk of loss.

It is precisely because of the unknown factors and uncertainties involved with events of this sort, and the fact that security directors neither have, nor should they expect to have, unlimited resources available for either emergencies or disasters or contingency planning that the challenge is so great. They know that they must develop plans for handling such events, but at the same time they must avoid certain pitfalls.

Among the issues raised in Chapter 2 was the need for security directors and managers to be flexible and capable of adjusting easily to new and developing situations. Nowhere is the need for flexibility more evident than when security is faced with an emergency, whether in connection with a disaster or otherwise. Highly regimented security departments with rigid operational plans or programs tend to suffer most when something unexpected and out of the ordinary develops and must be dealt with without delay. However, this is not the only danger. Other dangers lie in being either too casual and assuming that nothing will happen, or being inattentive to forecasts or other warnings and failing to take timely action in response.

Examples may be helpful. A luxury hotel security manager in a city rarely subject to snow or ice storms assumed that since none had occurred since he had been in this job, none ever would. Therefore, he saw no need even to discuss what the security and housekeeping departments working together should do if such a storm developed. Despite the fact that one day, local weather forecasters reported that an ice storm was on its way, the forecasts were not monitored and no preparations were made. When the storm struck, the need for a salt/sand combination for the sidewalks became obvious, but none could be bought because every vendor of such materials was sold out. The result? A guest slipped on ice at the main entrance, was hospitalized and in a coma, and the hotel was sued for over $1 million.

In another case, the security director of a multinational corporation read that the French government, long a haven of refuge for Basque separatists suspected of terrorist activities in Spain, had changed its policy. France would now agree to return them to Spain, where they might be apprehended and prosecuted by the Spanish authorities. Knowing of the ways in which the Basque separatist movement conducted its terrorist activities, this security director rationalized that it would probably show its displeasure with the French government by targeting a readily identifiable French target. Knowing, too, that employees who traveled to Madrid on business stayed at the Meridien Hotel, a subsidiary of Air France, France's national airline, the security director immediately instructed the travel offices for both corporate headquarters and the company's European headquarters to avoid making reservations at that hotel. Less than a month later the hotel was bombed by separatists.

These illustrations show how important it is to take nothing for granted, to be alert for any information that might help cope with an emergency or disaster, to be flexible, and to react promptly at the first sign of an emergency or disaster. In the first instance, involving an act of nature, complacency, inattention to readily available information, and a delay in taking action proved costly to the employer. In the second, a human-made situation, keeping abreast of activities worldwide, anticipating what conceivably could happen under the circumstances, and taking prompt action to protect employees helped save them from possible injury or death.

SUMMARY

For those whose primary interest in a career in security lies in becoming a security director or manager or possibly an inspector general rather than a teacher, salesperson, or consultant, certain considerations must always be borne in mind. To protect and conserve an employer's assets effectively requires a staff, the difficult part being to develop one that is neither too large nor too small. At the same time, an untrained or improperly trained security department not only will minimize its effectiveness but may result in a range of costly problems for the employer and embarrassment for the person in charge. To a large extent the same is true where supervision is concerned. Too many supervisors can be as bad as too few, and certainly, overstaffing at any level is a waste of the employer's money. Inadequately supervised personnel, even when properly trained, cannot perform their duties and discharge their responsibilities in ways that will most benefit the employer.

While the authority of security personnel has limits, the matter of their responsibility largely is a matter within the employer's discretion. True, some businesses and institutions define security responsibilities narrowly. However, as more and more fully realize the many ways in which security can benefit their operations, and as increasing numbers of business-oriented, educated professionals enter the field as directors and mangers, security responsibilities are being expanded. Security directors may also be responsible for safety, and whether directly or indirectly, they are becoming increasingly involved with environmental protection matters.

Records and communications are important, but not only for their historical value. Properly developed and used, they can be invaluable to security. A good records system can be used to forecast potential problems and help with risk management. It is also indicative of what the security department does, and in some cases, of the extent to which it helps pay its own way. Good communications are essential to every organization's success.

Law enforcement liaison and relationships with the news media are important; they are also delicate matters. Allowing one's ego to cloud one's thinking, which can be the case in both situations, can also be harmful. When this happens the employer generally, and its security program in particular, may suffer the consequences. Then, too, in dealing with either law enforcement agencies or the news media, security personnel dare not lose sight of the legal, moral, and ethical issues that may be involved if questionable or improper requests for information or other assistance are made.

No business or institution, regardless of its size or location or the nature of its activities, is immune to emergencies and disasters. Whether their origin is natural or human-made is immaterial; they must be dealt with. When one presents itself, many of the personal traits for which employers look when hiring security directors come into focus: flexibility, creativity, imagination, patience, decisiveness, and good communications skills in dealing with employees at all levels and outside agencies all assume heightened importance.

REVIEW QUESTIONS

1. In developing a security department, what key elements, other than size, should be taken into consideration?

2. Since wages and fringe benefits represent so great a part of a security department's budget, what can security directors do to provide a proper level of protection with a minimal staff?

3. Why is training so important, and to whom should it be given?

4. Why is the supervision of security personnel necessary?

5. Is there a prescribed standard for the ratio of supervisors to subordinates, and if not, who makes that determination?

6. Are the responsibilities for all security departments the same? If not, who actually decides on what they should be?

7. Why should good records be maintained by security departments?

8. What is possibly the greatest danger that can befall a security director or manager in his or her dealings with both law enforcement agencies and the news media?

9. What role should ethics play in connection with security department operations?

10. In planning for emergencies and disasters, which approach is best, one that is both detailed and very rigid, or one that is fluid and flexible?

NOTES

[1] CHARLES A. SENNEWALD, *Effective Security Management*, 2nd ed. (Stoneham, MA: Butterworth Publishers, 1985), p. 59.

[2] Napoleon I, *Maxims* (1804–1815).

[3] GEORGE BERNARD SHAW, "Preface on Doctors: The Technical Problem," *The Doctor's Dilemma (1913)*.

[4] *The Boston Globe*, August 16, 1991, p. 55

[5] *The Boston Globe*, October 19, 1990, pp. 1, 16.

[6] *The New York Times*, August 29, 1991, sec. B, p. 13.

[7] *The New York Times*, September 18, 1991, sec. B, pp. 1, 13.

[8] *The New York Times*, September 1, 1991, p. 18.

[9] *The New York Times*, August 10, 1990, sec. B, p. 4.

Chapter 4

PROTECTING AND CONSERVING ASSETS

Assets are an organization's lifeblood. An organization's real and personal property, personnel, and reputation have a bearing on its ability to obtain financing, grow, attract customers and employees, sell, and succeed. Few will quarrel with the idea that security departments should protect and conserve an employer's assets; all might not agree on what goes into developing and implementing a program designed to do just that. The use of security personnel for that purpose is almost universally accepted, but experienced security directors are quick to point out that security officers alone cannot possibly do all that has to be done if assets really are to be protected and conserved in the employer's best interest. Neither is there disagreement about the need to use at least some physical security to supplement the efforts of security officers.

Nevertheless, as much as a combination of security officers and physical security contribute to the protection and conservation of assets, they cannot possibly satisfy all the requirements for a sound loss prevention program. Business-oriented security directors know only too well that other factors must be taken into account. An employer's operating systems and procedures, effective controls and accountability, and the involvement of its line management can be equally important to the process. Furthermore, without executive management's support, no security program can succeed. As a result, each component, and the role it plays in the security effort, has to be understood.

PHYSICAL SECURITY

The role of security departments was discussed at length in Chapter 3. Now it is necessary to consider physical security, one of the most established ways of supplementing the work of security personnel. Locks, alarms, fences, shrubs, and safes often come to mind when thinking about physical security. However, with the passage of time and the advent of high technology, the application of physical security to the protection and conservation of assets has undergone considerable change. Security directors have a role to play in the area of physical security, but now they have many more tools at their disposal with which to provide that type of protection.

Because of the changing roles of security directors, and the changes that have taken place in the instruments of physical security, three questions need to be answered.

1. At what point in time and in what ways should security directors become involved with physical security?
2. Where does the use of physical security begin?
3. What equipment is available for the physical protection of assets?

The Security Director's Role

Security directors always need to be involved with the physical security of existing facilities. They have a special role to play when employers consider new construction or major alterations at existing facilities. Although physical security needs are pretty much the same in both cases, there may be deficiencies in existing buildings which, as a practical matter, either cannot be corrected or whose proper correction would be cost-prohibitive. However, for both ease and clarity in considering the subject, physical protection for each category will be examined.

One of the first things that security directors must do in all physical security matters, whether related to existing or to new facilities, is to determine what risks exist and what is needed to reduce those risks to the greatest possible extent. Although the identification and reduction of risks is discussed at length in Chapter 5, it is enough for now to say that security directors have to weigh the cost of correcting deficiencies against the dollar value of potential loss if no action is taken. If the expense involved to take corrective action is reasonable in relation to the possible loss, it is likely that approval to proceed with the project will be granted. On the other hand, if it far exceeds the amount that might be involved for a projected loss, the security director is left with two choices: either find a more reasonable way to solve the problem, or do nothing.

Even though the same two choices can exist in the case of either a standing facility or one about to be built or to undergo major alterations, with proper planning the expense factor may not be as great where major construction is involved. Of course, this will be true insofar as new construction or major alterations are concerned only in those cases where security directors are involved with the project from the time the plans appear on the drawing board until the work itself is completed. For example, the cost of retrofitting an existing structure to accept a new access control system may be more expensive than the cost of incorporating an identical system in the plans for a new building. This can be illustrated by a situation where a hotel chain's security director had a computerized access control system installed in a new property for less than $100,000; to install it in an existing hotel would have cost about $300,000.

Another advantage of becoming involved during the design stage lies in the fact that the very design and layout of a building can have a significant impact on a loss prevention program. Such diverse factors as a building's aesthetics, operating efficiency, and protection are not incompatible, despite the fact that there are some who would argue that the idea of physical security is inconsistent with the concept of a structure's eye appeal and its business operations. If security directors are allowed to work closely with architects and engineers during the design and layout stages, there certainly need not be a conflict between security and aesthetics. As for operating efficiency, since so much of a well-thought-out security program depends on controls and accountability, security can actually help rather than hinder it.

Whether old or new construction is involved, once security directors have determined the risks and estimated the cost of offsetting them, they must establish priorities for corrective action. This is discussed more fully in Chapter 5. In any event, funding for any significant hardware expenditures, and certainly all new construction costs, commonly are taken care of in what are called capital expense budgets. Although these budgets may be based on little more than estimates, contracts or purchase orders for work to proceed are based on more accurate figures.

Since potential suppliers of goods or services are reluctant to submit hard figures without having the buyer's needs clearly defined, a security director's next level of involvement consists of developing specifications for those products that appear to be able to satisfy the particular need, followed by cooperation with the purchasing department in preparing a request for proposal (RFP). Purchasing then sends copies of the RFP to those companies that sell the type of product or service being sought. For help in this respect it will look to the security director, who is familiar not only with products available, but also with the businesses that make or sell them. The latter then submit their detailed proposals together with prices.

Although proposals are sent to purchasing, the fact remains that purchasing cannot make a buying decision on security-related products or services without the security director's input, as only he or she is professionally qualified to evaluate what is being offered for sale. Again, purchasing turns to the security director for help before making a decision and awarding a contract.

Thus it becomes the security director's job to provide the evaluation. Of course, conscientious security directors will not be satisfied with evaluating only the product. They know that once an employer has been convinced to spend what could be a considerable amount of money for physical security, and since two critical elements of any security program are reliability and dependability, they would also be wise to evaluate the product's manufacturer, its vendor, and the latter's service department. For instance, recognizing that even the best product may on occasion be plagued with a problem, it is important to know if the manufacturer stands behind the product. Also, what is the vendor's reputation for reliability, dependability, and financial soundness? Does its service department have a spare parts and "loaner" inventory that will allow it either to make repairs with little or no lost time, or to provide the customer with a temporary replacement until its own unit can be repaired?

As one security manager discovered, not doing this can prove embarrassing, and possibly even costly. He recommended what normally was an excellent closed-circuit television camera, made by a manufacturer of good reputation, to help monitor the employer's parking lots. However, the product was sold by a local vendor, not the manufacturer, and instead of evaluating the vendor objectively, he relied on its sales presentation. After a relatively short time the camera developed a problem and the vendor was called. The camera needed to be taken to the shop for repair, but since the vendor had no "loaner" units in its inventory, temporary replacement was not possible.

Some time later the security manager resigned. His replacement began work before the camera was returned, but not before more than eight weeks had passed without it. It would be another eight weeks before the camera was back on the site. This incident resulted in the following questions being asked:

- ❏ How were the parking lots monitored during the 16 weeks that the camera was out for repair?
- ❏ If they were not monitored and no problems were encountered, why was money spent for the camera in the first place?
- ❏ If they were monitored through the use of a security officer because concern for the security of vehicles and employees was genuine, who paid the overtime for a regular security officer or the wages of one used on a temporary basis?

Consequently, security directors have a great deal to do where physical security is concerned. They are involved with determining what risks exist, setting priorities for corrective action, developing capital expense budgets when necessary, staying current on the subject of product availability, preparing specifications for proposals for security-related hardware, helping identify suppliers and evaluate manufacturers, vendors, and products for purchasing, and working with architects and engineers on design, layout, and all other aspects of physical security when new construction or major alterations are being planned by the employer. This is but another example of the breadth of activity in a security director's position. It helps to further illustrate opportunities to be both creative and imaginative in performing one's job.

Using Physical Security

Understanding the security director's role and its importance in relation to physical security is one thing; understanding where the use of physical security begins is another. Since security's mission is to protect and conserve all of the employer's assets, and physical security involves using products manufactured to help prevent losses, it is logical that physical security should begin at the employer's property line. Of course, that property line's location, as well as a definition of the various kinds of assets to be protected inside the building itself, will influence a security director's choice of a type of product.

For instance, security directors whose organizations have their facilities located on several acres of land have different concerns from those where the property line consists of a building's four outside walls. Furthermore, if in the first case the grounds are wooded, or partially wooded and partially landscaped, its needs will be different than if they are totally landscaped. Consequently, security directors who need to protect grounds obviously cannot limit their thinking about physical security to protecting only the structures on that land; they must take the entire picture into account.

The mere fact that a security director need not worry about protecting grounds does not relieve him or her of the responsibility for taking into account the neighborhood in which the employer's building is located. For instance, there is a greater risk that a warehouse located in an industrial area bordered by abandoned or vandalized buildings will be burglarized or burned than would be the case of a retail store located in a well-lighted, upscale neighborhood where there is a reasonable amount of both pedestrian and automobile traffic even when it is dark.

Each of the foregoing illustrations shares in common with the others a need for some form of access control. Of course, the physical security employed for that purpose will differ both in terms of whether controlled access is to land or merely to buildings, and also with regard to the nature of the business involved. The type of protection used to control access to the landscaped grounds of a resort hotel will be different from what might be used to protect land on which a manufacturing plant is located. Where land is not a factor, the fact remains that the need to control access to an office building is different from what reasonably can be used for the same purpose in a retail store.

Of course, security directors cannot be satisfied with merely controlling access to land, buildings, or both. They have to control access internally regardless of the environment in which they are working. Even businesses that literally invite the public to enter their premises, such as retail stores and hotels, cannot protect their assets unless they take steps to prevent members of the public from entering certain areas of the store or hotel. The public obviously is welcome to the sales floors in retailing, or to the restaurants and lounges in hotels, for without customers or guests neither can survive. On the other hand, retailers cannot allow customers into those parts of the store where stockrooms are located, and hotels cannot permit guests to enter the so-called "back of the house," where there are storerooms and food preparation areas.

Although mechanical means can be used for access control, it is also possible in some cases to help control access if security is taken into account when the building is designed and the space is laid out. For instance, that a building or fire code may require a minimum number of emergency exits does not mean that all of those doors must also be available for people to enter a facility. Locating a personnel office in the heart of a building instead of near the employee entrance can lead to security problems. Since architects and engineers may not always take such matters into account when new construction or major alterations are planned, it is important that security directors be actively involve with all such projects. At the same time, working with architects and engineers is but one of the many challenges that security directors must face. They cannot allow their interests in protecting the employer's assets to blind them to the fact that the employer also wants the facility to be both attractive in appearance and efficient from the standpoint of operations. To achieve this may require some compromise on everyone's part.

It is important to understand that while controlling access to grounds, buildings, and building interiors is an important aspect of physical security, by no means is this all there is to the subject. There also is a need to protect a building's contents. That includes such things as office and communications equipment, cash and negotiable instruments, and a wide range of information regardless of its form: hard copy documents, computer disks, or microfiche. Just as there are alarm systems to deter unauthorized access to buildings, there are alarms that can be used to protect both interior space and some types of tangible assets. In addition, various locking devices can be used to reduce the risk of theft of office equipment and information, and fire-retardant storage facilities are available to protect cash, negotiable instruments, and information. There are also storage cabinets in which computer disks and microfiche can be kept safely.

Courtesy of ADT Security Systems, Inc.

As a result, physical security measures are available and need to be used to protect not only grounds and buildings, but also building contents. Obviously, things that can be moved with relative ease, especially items that can be concealed, need to be protected against theft. However, this is not the only kind of loss with which security directors are concerned. They know that it is equally important to minimize the risk of having assets destroyed by fire, another factor that has to be kept in mind when planning physical security.

Physical Security Equipment

There are relatively few physical security needs that cannot now be satisfied with a choice of products. Often a security director's greatest problem may lie in the fact that so much is now available that deciding on any one item may be difficult, and even the need to look for the most cost-effective solution to a physical security problem may not make it any easier to choose. As a result, security directors faced with this situation may find it helpful to draw on their creativity in finding the most suitable approach to solving the problem.

Security directors concerned with protecting land, as well as the buildings on that land, will find that they can erect wooden or metal fences, with or without barbed or razor wire, use heavy shrubbery or architectural masonry, and even install alarms by themselves or in connection with the named enclosures. The alarms can be installed so as to let the security department know not only if there is an unauthorized penetration, but also at about what point in the enclosure it took place. However, as a practical matter, in some cases because the risk is so very slight, or the cost of erecting and alarming an enclosure is so great in proportion to the risk, nothing will be done. Then, too, if physical security measures are to be adopted, the choice may well be influenced by the nature of the employer's business. For example, while a chain link fence with either barbed or razor wire strands on top might be suitable as an enclosure to land on which there is a manufacturing plant or warehouse, it would be an unacceptable enclosure for a resort hotel.

The possibilities for access control have changed radically over the years. Locks and keys have always been used for this purpose, and still are. But while at one time security directors were limited in their choice to installing either dead or spring locks, today they can make their selection from a wide variety of products. They can use a combination of closed-circuit television and remotely controlled electric locks, or computerized systems that use coded identification cards in connection with either insert or proximity card readers, combination locks with or without a key override, or biometric systems that rely on matching either the retina of an eye with one stored in a computer's memory, or fingerprints.

Of course, the existence of so many possibilities for controlling access both to and within buildings requires security directors to consider factors other than cost-effectiveness

Courtesy of First Security Services Corp.

and control, and often may prompt the use of more than one type of product. In making their selection they also have to consider the volume of traffic that reasonably can be expected to enter a facility through a given door. For instance, if employees using a biometric system need more time to gain access than those using a proximity card reader, use of the biometric system at an employee entrance may be impractical if it would cause significant delays for employees arriving for work. On the other hand, biometrics at a computer room entrance, where the number of employees involved would be far less than at an employees' entrance, is worth considering.

In Chapter 1 reference was made to the fact that in 1858, Edwin Holmes established the first central station burglar alarm company, and that it was followed by the American District Telegraph Company in 1874. Today, one can still use such a system, but with the choice of it being an agency's or proprietary. Of course, there are also local burglar alarms that may be quite satisfactory under certain circumstances. However, not only have there been changes in types of burglar alarms, or intrusion alarms as they are now called, but there have also been changes in the methods used. Tape and magnetic contact installations are still in use, but now there also are systems that use infrared, others that use motion, and still others that are activated by a combination of body heat and motion.

Today's security directors must also appreciate the fact that intrusion alarms are not the only types of alarms which they must consider from the point of view of protecting and conserving assets. They must realize the importance of fire, smoke, and heat detection alarms, and understand how sprinkler alarms work. To protect employees in relatively isolated physical locations who may be vulnerable means that they have to think about panic or "help" alarms.

The use of alarms and other physical security equipment will also depend on either the nature of an employer's business or some aspect of its operations. For example, it may be wise to consider alarms to indicate an accumulation of water under a raised floor in a computer room since this could pose a serious problem in case of an electrical fire. Thermometers and humidity indicators can also be important to computer operations.

Security directors for banks and other cash handling operations cannot overlook the possible need for holdup alarms. However, bank security directors also have to be concerned with vaults, safe deposit boxes, closed-circuit television or time-lapse cameras, and securing automated teller machines. A good deal of bank physical security is covered by the standards prescribed by the U.S. Congress when in 1968 it passed the Bank Protection Act.[1]

Of course, like so many other instruments of physical security, closed-circuit television is by no means limited to use by banks. It can be and is used for surveillance purposes by security directors for other businesses and institutions, such as retailers, hotels, manufacturers, medical centers, shopping malls and plazas, and transportation.

However, it would be a mistake to assume that devices for access control, alarms, and closed-circuit television are the only aspects of physical security that have a rather universal application. That facilities have fire and smoke alarms is no excuse for not having fire suppression equipment. This could be in the form of sprinklers, extinguishers, or perhaps Halon for computer rooms. Neither would a combination of fire and smoke alarms and fire suppression equipment be an acceptable substitute for fire-resistant safes, file cabinets, or other suitable storage facilities in which vital records and other documents, or computer tapes and disks, can safely be kept. Two-way radios frequently are used for direct communications between security offices or control rooms and security officers on post.

Security directors also need to be mindful of other physical security equipment that might be useful for particular types of industries or situations. For example, those employed by airlines have use for x-ray machines, metal detectors, and possibly "sniffers" or other explosive-sensing devices. Devices for tagging items to prevent their theft are used not only in retail stores, but also by libraries. Tracking equipment can be used to monitor vehicles, and seals are used to help ensure full truckload deliveries of merchandise. Bar codes are used to both identify and help locate movable assets. Bulletproof glass or similar materials can be used to help protect employees who might handle substantial sums of money and who thus may be confronted by armed robbers. Certain types of pads and cables can be used to reduce the risk of office machine thefts. Time recording locks are used to help prevent thefts from storerooms. Time-lapse cameras can be used to monitor their use further, and these cameras also work well for surveillance purposes in an environment such as a manufacturing plant, where immediate identification of persons is not necessarily critical. Emergency power cutoffs near exits from computer rooms or other areas in which there are high-voltage electrical systems help reduce the risk of irreparable damage to equipment and of a more general electrical fire. Anti-eavesdropping equipment can be used to help reduce the risk of industrial espionage.

Thus where physical security equipment is concerned, it is important to recognize not only that changes have occurred and new products have been developed, but also that much of this has happened with such rapidity that what may appear to be "state of the art" today can be obsolete tomorrow. This makes it necessary for security directors to do two things: keep abreast of what goes on in the field and pay particular attention to those products that might have application to their organizations, and not buy a product just because it is new but be willing to buy it if satisfied that it will be a sound investment and make a significant contribution to the overall security effort.

SYSTEMS AND PROCEDURES

Important as physical security is, the quality of the employer's operating systems and procedures will have an impact, be it good or bad, on the organization's loss prevention program. If the impact is good, success is much more easily attainable; if it is bad, even the best of security programs will find it difficult to succeed. Of course, there are also times when even what may seem to be the best operating systems and procedures can be refined and improved. Frequently, those not directly involved with a particular aspect of operations can make suggestions that are quite helpful, and there is no valid reason why security directors cannot play that role. However, to do so they will be faced with yet another challenge.

Operating systems and procedures deal with the ways in which businesses and institutions function. For instance, all aspects of personnel management, not merely the hiring and firing processes, are important from both a business and a security perspective. Since no organization is completely self-sufficient, it necessarily has to buy things. This means that security directors need to understand how the purchasing department operates. It is doubtful that there is any kind of business or institution that does not ship and receive things. Therefore, shipping and receiving procedures have to be understood.

These activities are common to virtually all types of organizations, but there obviously are others that are more or less unique to a particular industry or set of circumstances. Operating systems and procedures are different in manufacturing than they are in retailing, and even within manufacturing they will vary depending on the type of product made. In retailing there are such issues as pricing, markups and markdowns, special promotions, employee discounts, and seasonal operations. Hotels must take into account such diverse operations as housekeeping, engineering, front office, sales, banquets, food and beverages, cashiering, and guest relations. Transportation must have systems and procedures for maintenance and repairs, whether of motor vehicles or aircraft. Medical centers share many of the systems and procedures found in hotels, yet they also have to regulate the distribution of medications to patients and the disposal of hazardous waste. Banking and other financial institutions have procedures for the handling of cash and other negotiables. Academic institutions deal with admissions, and so does the entertainment industry, even though their admissions are of a different kind. Research and development organizations, public utilities, the construction industry, and real estate management all have their own operating systems and procedures. Even government must have operating systems and procedures in order to function. In other words, no organization of any appreciable size can hope to function at even a reasonable level of efficiency without first developing and implementing systems and procedures.

Thus the initial challenge facing security directors is to be able to understand fully their employer's operating systems and procedures. If they do not, they cannot and should not even try to recommend changes affecting other departments' functions. Second, if loopholes that could adversely affect the protection and conservation of assets appear in operating systems and procedures, security directors need to be able to offer ideas that will help to correct those deficiencies. Last, but by no means least, they have to be able to make their suggestions in ways that will neither offend nor alienate other department heads. Perhaps a few examples of how this can be done will clarify the security director's role in this respect.

The main plant of a company licensed to process raw opium into morphine for sale to pharmaceutical manufacturers was located in a number of buildings, each occupying a city block. This resulted in the plant being bisected in several places by city streets. The distance between the building in which the processing was done and the one where the packaging and shipping took place was approximately two city blocks. Consequently, when the raw opium-to-morphine conversion was completed, arrangements had to be made to move the 55-gallon drums from the first to the second building. This routinely was done 24 hours before the scheduled transfer, despite the fact that the equipment and a driver could be made available with only an hour's notice. While enroute, the driver reported his progress to the transportation department by two-way radio using clear language. The combination of a 24-hour lead time and clear communications made each such transfer vulnerable to possible hijacking or robbery. The solution: Give the transportation department only the one hour's notice that is actually needed, and devise a simple but easily changed code for the driver's use while enroute.

To minimize the risk of either assets or the personal property of employees being removed from its premises without authorization, another company's procedure required all employees taking anything other than a briefcase or a purse from the building to use a parcel pass. In addition to listing what was being removed, each parcel pass had to have an authorizing signature, invariably that of a supervisor or the department head. However, the loophole lay in the fact that it was not unusual for supervisorss or department heads to sign their own parcel passes. The simple solution was to change the procedure by prohibiting anyone from signing their own parcel pass and requiring those who otherwise could sign to get an authorizing signature from a superior.

Notwithstanding the sensitivity of information generated by a major corporation's research and development facility, several copying machines were located throughout the building. It was not uncommon to see lines of employees waiting to use the machines, not always for business purposes. The availability of the machines was wasteful not only in terms of time spent while employees waited to make copies, but also to the extent that they often were used for personal reasons. Of course, this also increased the risk that there could be unauthorized copying of proprietary information. The change adopted resulted in creating one copy room with three machines, and assigning one full-time employee to copy documents brought to him for that purpose by other employees. The savings in time and copy paper more than made up for the salary of the person assigned, and the risk of having unauthorized copies made was for all practical purposes eliminated.

Employees who incur business-related expenses are entitled to be reimbursed by their employers. Normally, this is done by having employees submit expense reports that have been approved by their managers. However, it is not unusual for companies not to set deadlines for filing expense reports since they assume that persons spending their own money for business purposes will want to be repaid as soon as possible. This was the procedure at one company until quite by accident it discovered that an employee had submitted several fraudulent expense reports at one time, all covering expenses that allegedly had been incurred months before, thus making verification difficult. The procedure was changed; thereafter all expense reports had to be submitted within 30 days or reimbursement would be denied.

A supermarket chain's regional warehouse received shipments by rail. The normal procedure was for freight cars to be shunted in early each morning on tracks paralleling the dock. Unloading began when the forklift operators came to work. Merchandise was then moved into the warehouse, but as a rule not all of it could be transferred from the dock to the warehouse by the time their workday ended. The freight cares moved in that morning would be moved out during the night so that new ones could again be dropped off early the next morning. Therefore, all freight cars had to be emptied. Goods not placed in the warehouse would stay on the dock overnight. The risk of loss was evident. However, by the simple process of having two forklift operators report for work an hour later than the others, and work an hour later, it was possible to clear the receiving dock completely and to do it without the employer having to pay overtime. As a result, the risk of loss was markedly reduced with no extra cost to the employer.

These few examples are indicative of ways in which creative security managers, who really understand their organization's operating system and procedures, can make significant contributions that can help both operations and security. By the same token, it is improbable that any of the recommended changes could have been made and accepted by the department heads primarily affected if the security directors involved had not taken the time not only to learn the business, but also to get to know and understand the operating needs and concerns of the other department heads.

CONTROLS AND ACCOUNTABILITY

In many respects it is rather difficult to separate systems and procedures from controls and accountability. The one logically leads to the other, for no matter how good an organization's systems and procedures, there must be acceptable controls and a high level of accountability if assets are to be protected. From a security viewpoint the critical phrase here is "acceptable controls," not just controls.

It is only natural to rationalize that the better the controls, the better protected are the employer's assets. Although this is true in theory, it may not always be true in practice. In fact, it is possible that under certain conditions there may be too many controls. In those cases the controls that security directors might like to see in place may be unacceptable. Therefore, security directors need to remember that businesses must be profitable to survive, and even nonprofit institutions must make every effort to at least break even in terms of trying to balance their income and expenses.

The U.S. Department of Defense Industrial Security Manual understandably imposes strict controls over classified information to maintain lead time in the development of new weapons systems considered crucial to national defense. There are also some security directors whose controls over all assets, including proprietary information, parallel in strictness the government's control over classified information. No one quarrels with the idea of controls for the protection of assets. However, those few security directors who do try to impose too much control are shortsighted by failing to appreciate the fact that non-defense industries must also be able to stay ahead of their competitors. Therefore, if the controls imposed by security managers to protect assets are so tight that they make it difficult, if not almost impossible, for employees to do their jobs in keeping the employer ahead of the competition, in the final analysis the security program has not succeeded; it has failed.

That controls cannot be too tight does not mean that accountability cannot be strict. Despite these differences in approach, the fact remains that acceptable controls and strict accountability go hand in hand. While accountability will not interfere with job performance and the benefits to the employer can be substantial, employees who know that they can be held accountable are less inclined to do anything wrong. Furthermore, the few who are willing to risk their jobs by doing something improper, criminal or otherwise, can be more easily identified so that appropriate action can be taken.

Perhaps a few examples of how controls and accountability can benefit an employer are worth examining. The kitchen of a major hospital sent food to the floors for each of the three daily meals. Some of the food was fully prepared; the balance was not. For instance, it was not uncommon for eggs to be uncooked, and at least once a day loaves of bread, butter, margarine, packaged sugar, and condiments would be on the food carts for each floor. However, neither was it uncommon for the carts to be delivered to the floors with some of the foodstuffs that had been entered on the floor's diet slips missing. Despite the fact that designated kitchen employees were supposed to get the carts personally to the floors, some would give them to elevator operators instead and ask them to drop off the carts. The solution was to make extra copies of the diet slips, which now included the names of the kitchen employees and which also served as receipts to be signed by head nurses when the carts were delivered to the floors. From then on, those assigned to make deliveries knew that if they asked elevator operators to do their jobs for them, and there were any shortages, they would be held accountable for those shortages that might appear.

A company that sold radio components for assembly by customers had problems when parts that should have been included in each kit were not. This necessitated replacing missing parts at no charge; it also affected the company's reputation. Since kits were put together, based on order tickets, by employees working in assembly line fashion it was evident that only employees could be responsible for missing parts. The problem was solved when assembly employees were required to initial order tickets as they put their components in trays enroute to the packaging area and they were told that their initials meant that all components previously placed in the trays were there when they added the ones for which they were responsible.

Employees engaged in research and development for a major manufacture were issued prenumbered engineering notebooks in which all data were recorded. The very nature of their work meant that the notebooks' contents were sensitive and needed to be protected. If employees left either the research group, or the company's employ for any reason, the notebooks were to be turned in. However, as long as a person continued to do any research, there was no real accountability for the notebooks, and as a result, for their contents. Therefore, it was quite common for employees to retain custody of the notebooks that had been issued to them whether or not they had further use for them. As a result, as time passed the risk of old ones being improperly maintained and protected increased. Both accountability and security improved when a program of random inventories of engineering notebooks was instituted. Thereafter all notebooks issued were accounted for, and those no longer in use were recovered and stored in a safe place.

Still another manufacturer called for the use of a printed form for the movement of materials from one of its sites to another. That the forms were not numbered meant that since they could not be controlled and accounted for it was likely that materials moved really were not accounted for. In addition, not requiring unit counts to be listed on the forms meant that a receiving facility had no way of knowing if the quantities shipped and those received were the same. In other words, if the form only listed 10 boxes of parts without specifying the number of parts per box, as long as the 10 boxes were received there was no way of knowing whether each should have contained 10 or 5 units, or what might have happened enroute. Modifying the forms by having preprinted numbers added to each, and having both the number of units per box as well as the number of boxes listed for each transfer, solved the problem.

An organization that operated a large enough truck fleet to justify having its own regional repair shops and service centers found the cost so high that it was about to make a change and have maintenance done by others under contract. The expense involved primarily the frequency with which a number of parts were used and the inventory that had to be kept as a result. Although controls existed in the form of written repair orders, and the issue of parts to mechanics by a parts clerk, there was no real accountability. All any mechanic had to do was ask for whatever was needed to repair or service a vehicle. However, it seemed only logical that what parts had to be replaced, whether they might be fan belts, spark plugs, or anything else, would first have to be removed from the vehicle. Therefore, it would not be illogical to have all parts to be replaced turned into the parts clerk before new parts would be issued. With accountability the cost of parts for repairs was so reduced that the employer found it less expensive to maintain its shops than it would have been to have the work done by contractors.

Thus there is a definite relationship between systems and procedures on one hand, and controls and accountability on the other. The best of systems and procedures are meaningless unless supported by controls and accountability, and security has a role to play in the development of both. This is where security directors often have to rely on a combination of their personalities, creativity, and an understanding of the employer's business if they are to contribute to a well-run, profitable operation. No one seriously can doubt that this can be both very challenging and stimulating. Seeing the results of one's efforts can be most rewarding.

LINE MANAGEMENT'S ROLE

In Chapter 2 the importance of security directors and managers developing and maintaining good relationships with their co-workers was discussed. If employers and their security directors or managers see security as little more than a form of private policing, compatibility with co-workers may be enough. However, much more than compatibility has to be involved if security programs based on the concept of protecting and conserving assets are to succeed. For this the active involvement of all line managers and supervisors is a must. While good relationships alone are not enough, they can make it much easier for security directors to sell the idea that although good security is every employee's business, in particular it is the business of line management.

Simple logic validates this statement. For instance, no security director or manager, and no security department, regardless of ability or efficiency, possesses all of the resources and skills that are necessary to protect and conserve all forms of assets. Therefore, skilled security directors will identify those line managers who can help provide the resources and skills which neither they nor their departmental personnel have, and they will also enlist their help in implementing their security programs.

Examples of how other managers can provide skills or other resources can best illustrate the need for cooperation if employers are to benefit. The management information systems director of a multinational corporation informed the security director of an unusually high volume of electronic mail traffic between certain hosts in the United States and a remote site. The contact itself was not the cause for concern; the amount of contact was. It suggested that perhaps proprietary information was being transmitted to an unauthorized recipient. With the help of a member of the telecommunications staff and a management information system manager, the security director succeeded in isolating the problem and identifying the responsible persons.

In another instance the director of internal audit brought to the security director's attention the fact that one of the company's overseas audit managers had reason to believe that three managers in that area, and one at corporate headquarters, might be engaged in a conflict of interest and possibly an attempt to defraud the employer. Because of the distances involved and the need for prompt action to obtain and protect any physical evidence that might be developed, the security director solicited the help of both the manager who suspected that there was a problem and a member of the international legal staff, and under his guidance and coordination they handled the overseas aspects of the investigation while he took care of the corporate headquarters phase.

While these are illustrative of managerial involvement when called upon by the corporate security director, the fact remains that managers and supervisors down the line have to become active participants in any successful loss prevention program. However, when removed from a corporate headquarters environment this can be harder to accomplish. Not infrequently when the subject of security is raised, line managers and supervisors will react by saying that there is nothing in their job descriptions about security. Although this is true, they need to be reminded that being a manger or supervisor means being willing to assume all of the obligations that go with the job, which includes protecting and conserving the employer's assets.

In one case the manager of a manufacturing plant, upon the completion of a corporate security audit and noting the deficiencies cited in the audit report, asked the security director what he might to do get his line managers more involved in improving the plant's loss prevention efforts. The security director suggested that the plant manager inform his direct reports that effective immediately he would take into consideration the security records of their respective departments whenever he had to write their performance evaluations. Since bad reviews would affect salary increases, this obviously was something that no one wanted. To reduce the risk of this happening, the plant manager's direct reports passed this same message to their section managers, and so on down the line. When the plant had its next corporate security audit the number of deficiencies decreased from 17 to two.

Security directors cannot lose sight of the fact that the objective is asset protection. Reaching that goal is far more important than the matter of who gets credit for a successful program. If the effort does succeed, their accomplishments will be acknowledged. Consequently, recognizing that the most practical approach to security emphasizes prevention, and that so many of the risks that could result in losses to the employer are not always easily or readily seen by security personnel, line managers definitely must play a role in the process.

The security staff can help prevent the theft of tangible assets, but the theft of time by employees, or the production of poorly made products that can mean rework or scrapping and are costly to an employer, are not matters with which security personnel can or should be expected to deal. Security officers making rounds can secure an unlocked file cabinet and report the infraction, but neither they nor security directors can prevent the unauthorized disclosure of proprietary information in a paper to be read by an employee at a professional meeting. Security directors can suggest ways to reduce the risk of kickbacks to purchasing department personnel, but they cannot oversee their implementation. They can recommend ways to reduce losses in hotel kitchens, but they are not in a position to monitor food and beverage operations. In each of these instances security can make a meaningful contribution to loss prevention, but the ultimate responsibility for effective oversight necessarily must rest with those most familiar with their own departmental activities. Security directors have to understand that they can author security policies and procedures designed to provide optimum protection without adversely affecting business operations, but the results will be less than satisfactory without the complete cooperation and participation of the entire line management staff.

EXECUTIVE MANAGEMENT SUPPORT

Perhaps the most critical issue facing security directors in any business or institution is the ability to gain and retain the full support of the organization's executive management team.

Without it even the most enlightened, creative, experienced, and professional of security directors or managers cannot hope to succeed. With it so much can be accomplished.

Part of the problem lies in the fact that even today some executives still consider security as nothing more than a necessary evil. Others do not really understand how much benefit can be derived from an effective program, instead continuing to think of security as but an extension of policing into the business world. There are still others who are quite supportive of the idea of security programs but who have been disappointed by some security directors with whom they have had contact. Thus they now are prepared to offer only passive support. Consequently, regardless of which category an organization's executives fit into, security directors have to be ready to add the roles of educator and salesperson to their repertoire. Of course, while those who have executive management's unqualified support are fortunate indeed, they cannot afford to become so complacent that they risk losing it.

Support has to be shown in more than one way. To endorse the security program by a willingness to provide an adequate staff, pay good salaries, spend money for hardware and other devices, encourage professionalism, and approve security policies and procedures is one way of evidencing support. However, equally important is the need for an organization's executives to accept and comply with those policies and procedures. In other words, they must lead by example, not merely by telling others what to do. What follows are some of the ways in which executives can openly show their support for the security program.

A multinational company's security director proposed having two three-day seminars a year at the organization's corporate headquarters. The security managers of all the organization's major facilities would be required to attend. Despite the expense involved in bringing together employees not only from the United States, but also from Europe, Australia, Singapore, the Philippines, Thailand, Hong Kong, and Japan, executive support was unanimous. In addition, a vice president either opened or actively participated in every seminar.

Upon getting his first copy of a security audit report, the new senior vice president for manufacturing of a major company addressed a note on the front page to the corporate security director asking the latter to keep him informed of the progress made in implementing the security director's recommendations. At the same time, a copy of that note was sent to the manager of the plant that had been audited. This clearly indicated to all of the plant managers that the manufacturing vice president supported the program.

A Fortune 500 company did not require its employees to wear their photo identification badges; it did require them to have them on their persons at all times while at work. Nevertheless, the corporate officers always wore theirs. The president of another company, with a visitors' parking lot directly in front of the entrance to the corporate headquarters building, not only never parked there but on one occasion asked security to tow the executive vice president's automobile because it was in the visitors' lot. At still another organization employees leaving the premises with anything other than briefcases or attaché cases or women's purses were required first to get a parcel pass that authorized the removal of the item. The corporate officers never objected to getting passes for things they wanted to take. Neither did they ever refuse to open a parcel so that its contents could be examined to make certain that what they were taking was what was listed on the pass.

These are but some of the ways in which any organization's executives can show their support for security. By complying with security policies and procedures, they set a good example for everyone. However, when support is lacking, and when executives flaunt policies and procedures by ignoring them, subordinates are resentful and will look for ways in which to show their displeasure. Consequently, much more is involved for security directors than dealing with executives. Executive avoidance of security programs will only serve to encourage employees to circumvent security. It may also lead to significant problems, including possible losses, for the employer.

SUMMARY

As a practical matter the security directors or managers of any organization are responsible for developing and overseeing the implementation of their employers' loss prevention programs. Assuredly, it is they who will be held accountable for program failures. Nevertheless, if asked where effective security programs begin, the answer would have to be in the executive offices and at the employer's property line. Certainly, a security director's efforts will not be taken seriously by others in the organization if there is the slightest hint that loss prevention is not fully supported by the organization's executive management team. Therefore, successful programs that provide optimum benefits are those which are fully supported by the executives by word, by deed, and by example.

Physical security is essential. Applied realistically, it can help protect and conserve assets in reliable, cost-effective, innovative, and inoffensive ways. But physical security unsupported by realistic operating systems and procedures, which logically should lead to good controls and accountability, can provide only partial protection for assets. At the same time, even the best operating systems and procedures, and the levels of control and accountability for which they call, are of little or no value without the total involvement of line managers and supervisors. In the last analysis they are the ones who must maintain the integrity of the operating systems, procedures, controls, and accountability, all of which are in fact as much a part of an effective security program as is the physical protection provided and the security staff. Coming full circle, no one can doubt that if executive management's support is forthcoming, line management's involvement will be assured.

REVIEW QUESTIONS

1. If physical security begins at an organization's property line, what does *property line* mean?
2. Does the need for physical security apply only to the protection of grounds and buildings? If not, to what else does it apply?
3. Can physical security be used as a substitute for security officers? If so, under what circumstances?
4. Is it possible to eliminate security officers entirely by using physical security measures?
5. What purpose do operating systems and procedures serve?

6. Why is it important for security directors and managers to understand the operating systems and procedures used by their employers?
7. Is it proper for a security director to suggest ways in which to improve systems and procedures?
8. Why are controls and accountability important?
9. Can security programs be successful without the involvement of line management? If not, why not?
10. Why is executive management's support for security programs so critical?

NOTES

[1]Bank Protection Act of 1968, Pub. L. No. 90-389, 82 Stat. 295.

Chapter 5

RISK MANAGEMENT

Virtually every organization assumes some risks from its very inception. As used by insurance companies, the word *risk* refers to the things for which they are providing insurance. In other words, the risk insured could be almost anything of value, such as persons, buildings, motor vehicles, inventory, accounts receivable or payable, and so on. Most organizations of any appreciable size have risk management departments supervised by employees at either director or manager level whose job it is to evaluate the perils to which their employer is exposed, and to obtain the best value in the way of insurance coverage which they feel the employer needs. The perils might include fire, burglary, larceny, hurricane, errors and omissions, injuries to both employees and third parties, and so on.

Aside from those very few companies which, for one reason or another, are self-insuring, virtually every business or institution, regardless of size, has insurance. However, when insurance companies write policies for their customers the latter are given an opportunity to save money on their premiums by having a so-called deductible clause. Although the amount of the deductible may vary, it means that unless the insured policyholder suffers a loss that is greater than the amount of the deductible, the insured absorbs the loss by itself. In other words, the policyholder insures itself up to the amount of the deductible. Consequently, successful security programs that help prevent losses actually save money for their employers.

Nevertheless, it is somewhat ironic that while risk management departments are so widely accepted by the business community, some executives still fail to see the importance of security departments. Objectively speaking, who really is more directly involved in managing risks for an organization than its security director? True, risk managers try to minimize an organization's losses through the medium of insurance coverage, but it is security directors or managers who are charged with developing and implementing programs designed to prevent them from occurring in the first place. Then, too, security directors also have to be concerned with protecting and conserving those assets that may not always lend themselves to being insured, and where an employer may have to resort to costly legal action to try to recover if a loss is suffered.

Consequently, one might well argue that in fact security directors are the real risk managers in any organization. This, in turn, means that they have to be able to identify those things that pose risks to their employers, they need to be able to analyze those risks in terms of setting priorities, they must be ever alert for ways to reduce those risks which simply cannot be eliminated, and they also need to be able to determine the extent to which there is compliance with security policies and procedures designed to reduce those risks.

IDENTIFYING RISKS

Although insurance companies and risk managers use the word *risk* to define that which is covered by insurance, the word has a different meaning when used in connection with security. Here it means to expose something or someone to the chance of injury, damage, or loss; it is a hazard. Therefore, from a security point of view, one must first ask: What are the assets (which can include people) that are exposed to the possibility of injury (and death in the case of persons), damage, or loss? A realistic answer is: almost everything of value to an organization. This would include tangibles, intangibles, and employees. In some cases it might even be extended to include third parties such as retail store customers, hotel or motel guests, and passengers who use any form of public transportation. Consequently, since all assets have value to an organization, identifying them is not a particularly difficult task.

Despite this, however, not all assets are of equal value to an employer. For example, computer manufacturers use precious metals in making printed circuit boards, and the boards themselves are what enable the computers to operate—but not without cable for electrical connections. Therefore, while all three have value to the manufacturer, the precious metals and printed circuit boards have a greater value to the manufacturer than do cables. Retailers may offer diamond as well as inexpensive costume jewelry for sale, but obviously the diamonds are more valuable. The bread and roast beef served by hotel dining services both have value, but their value is unequal. A drugstore values its inventory, but prescription drugs are more valuable than candy bars. Stockbrokers may receive proxy votes from stockholders in behalf of customers preparing for their annual meetings; they also have bonds on hand. Both have value, but needless to say, bonds, which may be worth millions of dollars, are by far the more valuable. As a result, trying to decide how best to relate these values to the need for a particular level of protection is more difficult than is the task of identifying the assets involved.

RISK ANALYSIS

If not all assets are of equal value, it must follow that not all assets require the same type of protection. Thus allowing for differences in values is not the only factor that has to be considered in developing effective security programs. The risks that could affect individual categories of assets need to be analyzed. This is true not only in helping to determine the various levels of protection required by those categories but also in helping to set priorities for putting that protection in place.

In analyzing risks security directors and managers have to deal with reality, and one of the realities is the fact that in their work they will find few, if any, absolutes. That definitely is true where the subject of risk analysis is concerned. The least expected incident may occur, yet based on historical data it is so unexpected that there has been little or no thought given to preparing for just such an occasion. On the other hand, making preparations on the basis of forecasts which, in turn, are based on historical data may prove to have been meaningless since the anticipated events never occurred.

Of course, historical data should be taken into consideration, but that should not be the only criterion relied upon. By the same token, the very nature of risk analysis is such that the best one can do is attempt to be reasonable and prudent in analyzing risks so that priorities for levels of protection can be set and suitably implemented. For this to happen, two questions must be asked repeatedly for each category of assets.

The first deals with possibility, the second with probability: in other words, what might happen as against what is likely to happen. From the security director's perspective it is the probability factor that needs to be rated higher on the scale than the possibility factor and which deserves more consideration. For instance, although an earthquake might possibly occur anywhere in the United States, there is a far greater probability that one will occur on the west coast. Similarly, snow might fall anywhere on the east coast of the United States, but there is far more probability of a blizzard striking the New England states than there is of one hitting Florida.

This same line of reasoning has to be applied in terms of analyzing the risk of injury to or loss of assets. All buildings may catch on fire, whether the fire itself is caused by an act of arson, an accident, an electrical problem, or an act of God. That is a distinct possibility. However, the probability of a building that is sprinklered and both constructed of, and furnished with, fire-retardant materials being completed destroyed and the occupant being put out of business, even if only temporarily, is relatively slight. This would not be the case if the building were not sprinklered and its furnishings were not fire retardant.

The risk of an explosion is more likely for a company that uses chemicals or gases in its business than it is for a manufacturer of women's dresses or men's suits. Banks are more likely to become the victims of an armed robbery than is the corporate headquarters of a manufacturer of sporting goods. A multinational corporation with operations in one or more countries that suffer from political, social, or economic unrest is more likely to become the target of anti-American terrorist organizations than would be true for a chain of retail specialty stores all of which are located in suburban shopping malls or plazas in the United States. Certainly, the clothing manufacturer might have an explosion, and the sporting goods manufacturer's headquarters might be robbed. It is equally possible that the retail specialty chain might be targeted by a terrorist organization.

Nevertheless, it is on the probabilities that security directors must focus their attention, and even then the parent organization's size may require them to consider further refinement. If the employer's business consists of but a single location, viewing the probabilities in relation to asset categories is one thing. If multiple sites are involved but all are within the boundaries of the 48 contiguous U.S. states, it is another. However, it is yet another thing if some of the company's facilities are located internationally. Furthermore, in the latter instance consideration has to be given to the likelihood of an incident occurring to employees whose work makes it necessary for them to travel from one location, which for all practical purposes is risk free, to another where the risk of something happening is relatively high. Such a situation was described in Chapter 3 with regard to terrorist activities engaged in by the Basque separatist movement.

Consequently, risk analysis needs to take three factors into account. The first is the probability that something might happen that will have an adverse impact on the business or institution. Second, since not all assets are of equal value, it is important to ascertain which assets are most vulnerable. Third is the matter of how many locations are involved and where they are, inasmuch as geography may also have a bearing on probability.

SETTING PRIORITIES

Like all business or institutional departments, security has a budget and is expected to operate within that budget. Although it is true that if a security director recommends a capital expenditure that will greatly improve protection, is cost-effective, and will have a short-term payback, extra funds may be provided, the fact remains that normal security operations should be based on minimizing risks and losses. Therefore, additional monies will not be forthcoming to cover those operations, and security directors have to bear this in mind in the preparation and submission of their budgets. Consequently, despite their concern with protecting all assets, what money is available must be spent wisely. This poses a challenge since it requires them to set priorities.

It might seem that setting priorities should not be a very difficult task since it is something everyone does every day. Students will give a higher priority to studying for an examination than they will to studying for a regular class session. Hospital emergency room personnel will give a higher priority to treating a patient losing a lot of blood from being stabbed than they will to someone with a simple fracture. It is not uncommon for airlines to give priority handling to the checked-through baggage of first- and business-class passengers, something they do not do for other passengers.

In these and similar cases, priorities are set on the basis of things that are known. The student knows that passing an examination is more critical than being able to recite in a single class. Emergency room personnel know that profuse bleeding can cause complications and conceivably death, and airlines know that catering to certain classes of passengers is good for business. By way of contrast, in trying to set priorities, security directors have only probabilities on which to rely since there is no assurance that any given incident will occur at any particular time or place as was illustrated under the heading "Emergencies and Disasters" in Chapter 3. Thus in setting priorities, they find themselves relying largely on their professional education and experience.

What, then, needs to be considered beyond the issue of probability in setting priorities? The answer obviously is the impact on the organization should any given probability become a reality. Perhaps this can best be illustrated. The research and development department of a pharmaceuticals manufacturer is working on a new cancer-curing drug which, when fully developed, tested, and approved for use, can mean untold millions of dollars in business for the company. In the warehouse of its main plant it has an inventory of a proprietary but not necessarily unique cold medicine valued at $4 million. At this time, protecting the research and development data against compromise, theft, or any other form of loss would rate a higher priority than would protecting the inventory of a product that while already on the market is competing with other cold medicines.

A fire breaks out at a hotel. Despite the fact that the building and room furnishings are of fire-retardant materials and the facility is sprinklered, the presence of some flammables is unavoidable. Guests, some of whom are disabled, and employees have to be evacuated. Help for disabled guests in evacuating the property would deserve a higher priority than help for guests and employees who are able to leave the hotel without assistance.

The chairman of the board and chief executive officer of an international organization that does $100 billion a year in business is planning a visit to one of the company's offices in a country where there is considerable anti-American terrorist activity; both he and the company have a high profile. At least some of the terrorists have in the past resorted to kidnappings for the dual purpose of getting money with which to continue their activities, and for the publicity that the kidnappings attract. At the same time the organization's vice president for manufacturing, who has a low profile outside the company, is going to visit a plant where there is no known terrorism. The chairman's protection deserves a higher priority than the vice president's under the circumstances.

To expand on these examples, like any business, the pharmaceutical company would not like to suffer the loss of any inventory. However, the impact from the loss of data which could result in untold future profits and favorable publicity while benefiting humankind would be far more costly than the loss of the inventory, which despite a $50,000 deductible clause, is insured. The hotel's liability, adverse publicity, and loss of future business if the needs of disabled guests were ignored in case of a fire requiring evacuation conceivably could put it out of business. Any injury to the board chairman, who is the one person largely responsible for the company's success, or possibly his death if he is kidnapped and the kidnappers' demands are not met, would be far more harmful to the organization than would be an incident involving the manufacturing vice president.

Consequently, for each class of assets, security directors must weigh the probability that something could happen which would result in a loss to the organization. Next, they have to consider the degrees of probability involved relative to each of the categories since some incidents may be more likely to happen than others even though it is probable that both could occur. As an example, a bank might be robbed during banking hours; it also might be burglarized at night and safe deposit boxes emptied. However, a robbery is more likely to occur than is a burglary. Finally, they must take into account the impact on the business or institution if there is an incident that results in a loss of any sort. Only after completing such an analysis can priorities be set. Logically, the highest priorities must be given to protecting those assets which if lost or damaged would have the greatest adverse impact on the organization's ability to continue to function, perhaps even to survive.

REDUCING RISKS

Risks rarely can be eliminated completely. In addition, since organizations are composed of people, and people are fallible, some losses are bound to occur. Therefore, security programs must be designed to reduce risks to the lowest possible level and to keep the dollar amount of those losses that might be classified as unavoidable to an absolute minimum. To do this, security directors will employ different methods depending on any given situation. To reduce the risk of travel-related incidents and increase the level of executive protection, they may report to issuing timely memoranda based on access to available intelligence information. In cases of emergencies or disasters, they will act to minimize the risk of loss mainly by relying on on-site evaluations of a situation. For the most part, however, the primary mechanism for minimizing both risks and losses will be through the use of security-related policies and procedures.

Chapter 2 emphasized the importance of security directors developing and maintaining good relationships with their co-workers. The need for line management involvement was cited in Chapter 4. Nevertheless, the fact remains that no matter how good the relationships may be, or how willing line managers are to become involved, employees generally, and line managers and supervisors particularly, need guidance. That guidance should come in the form of policies and procedures that have organization-wide distribution and application.

Using the term *security related* should be understood to mean that there can be policies and procedures that are the result of collaboration between security and another department, and which may in fact be issued under another department's auspices. The subject matter of such policies and procedures will depend largely on the extent to which the security program has executive support, the scope of the security department's charter, and the security director's ability to work with other department heads.

As an illustration of a collaborative effort there might well be a human resources policy and procedure dealing with employee terminations for cause which, under certain circumstances, would require notification to or clearance by the security director. There might be a security policy and procedure on the protection of electronically generated, transmitted, and stored information written with the help of the director of the organization's management information systems. If the security department is also responsible for safety, safety policies and procedures dealing with such matters as safety glasses and shoes and hearing protection might be developed with aid from both an organization's medical department or occupational nursing staff and its risk management department, while other aspects might require the law department's assistance.

However, in addition to such collaborative efforts as those mentioned, most security policies and procedures will deal with matters more likely to be associated with the protection function, and they will be written by security directors and managers. A sample of security policies and procedures might well cover such diverse subjects as investigations, bomb threats, the protection of proprietary information, the protection of assets in transit, parcel inspections, employee identification, access control to the organization's facilities, fires and other emergencies, security audits, security conferences, proposals for and the use of contract security services, the use of cameras of any kind by either employees or third parties at any of the organization's locations, and searches and seizures by security officers.

To the greatest extent possible the procedural part of security policies should be in the form of guidelines rather than as hard and fast steps to be followed. This actually can help with implementation since it recognizes that line managers are intelligent and capable of exercising good judgment. It can also reduce the number of times that the policies and procedures have to be revised because of changes, often relatively minor. Of course, there will be some that will best serve the purposes of the security program by combining some rigidity with flexibility, and others where there is no room for flexibility. As an example of the former, the order in which corporate headquarters personnel are to be informed of certain types of incidents should be precise, although local management would have discretion in terms of how to deal with the problem. On the other hand, in a matter as delicate and potentially damaging to both employees and public relations as searching parcels, purses, or briefcases being carried from a facility, it is often best to prescribe in detail under what circumstances and how the searches are to be conducted.

No matter how well written and intended security policies and procedures may be, unless they are properly implemented, they are useless. Furthermore, even with line management cooperation there can be personnel changes that can affect policy implementation. This, in turn, means that security directors or managers need a mechanism that will enable them periodically to determine the stages of implementation, and once policies have been implemented, the status of compliance.

SECURITY AUDITS

Security audits, both those conducted by the persons in overall charge of security and where applicable by local security managers can serve a fourfold purpose. First, they give the auditor an opportunity to review the physical security status of the facility being audited. Second, they allow the auditor to review security department operations for any shortcomings that may be noted. Third, they are a good way to follow up not only on security program implementation and maintenance, but also on the extent to which the audited site is in compliance with all security-related policies and procedures. Last, but by no means least, they give the auditor a chance to get the cooperation of the person responsible for the audited site in terms of recommendations that may result from the audit.

For the security program generally and the audited facility particularly, to get the most out of any security audit, it is best for those conducting the audit to have a format they can follow. If they do not, even the most experienced and knowledgeable security director or manager risks overlooking an item simply because the audit itself is designed to examine so many security-related issues. It is also possible that occasionally a single organization may find it advantageous to develop two formats for its security audits, due to slight differences in the types of sites to be audited.

As an illustration, a manufacturing organization that also has its own sales and service offices may find it useful to use one type of format for all its plants and another for its various offices, even though both are basically the same. Although the same general headings can be used in both cases, as a practical matter, certain differences between the types of operations involved may be unavoidable. For instance, physical security would be a subject for auditors to consider whether they were working at a manufacturing plant or at sales and service offices. However, although the protection afforded a manufacturing plant's outside fuel storage facilities would be a legitimate subject for examination, it normally would not be a factor where the company rents space from a third party in which to house its sales and services offices. The same might be true of access control to a building. Similarly, reviewing security department operations would be a proper audit function at a plant, yet in all likelihood such a department would not even exist in a building owned by someone else who is the landlord for the company's sales and service offices.

On the other hand, auditing administrative and operational matters in both manufacturing and sales and service office environments would cover virtually identical issues. Certainly, such things as the protection of proprietary information, including its destruction, the proper issue and use of standard employee photo identification badges, visitors' escort requirements, and the protection of blank check stock would apply equally. Thus the possible use of separate but definitely similar audit formats is likely.

Turning to the first of the fourfold purposes of security audits, it is unwise to assume that there can be no physical changes that might affect security, and therefore there is no need to look periodically at the situation at each site, or at least at each principal site. New construction or major alternations certainly can have an impact on security and may require new or different physical security measures. Even when this is not the case, is the integrity of the site's physical security respected and maintained? For instance, are all doors with locks secured after hours unless an authorized employee actually is working in the area, and are keys to file cabinets locked up or are they left under desk calendar pads, as so often happens? If doors are not closed and locked, or keys are left where they can be used by anyone, there are deficiencies.

Security departments can be just as guilty as other departments in terms of operating deficiencies. This is a chance to look at such things as whether the department is under- or overstaffed and if the training of security personnel is both appropriate and given with sufficient frequency. Since maintaining good records is so important to efficient and effective security operations, are the records audited adequate, clear, and can they be used for more than historical purposes? This is also an opportunity to see if requests for the issuance of photo identification badges and keys to employees, and approvals for the removal of assets from the site, have been properly authorized and to review all aspects of departmental operations for the purpose of finding ways to improve them.

Of course, one of the most valuable contributions made by security audits is the opportunity they provide in terms of determining the extent to which all aspects of the organization's security program, including security-related policies and procedures, have been implemented, and the extent to which the site being audited is in compliance. Although it would seem that if implementation has occurred, compliance will follow automatically, this is not always true. As an example, a hotel chain might send all its general managers a policy and procedure that calls for monthly food, beverage, and housekeeping inventories to be reported to him or her, but which also says that in between the monthly inventories, each food and beverage manager, executive or sous chef, and executive housekeeper will on a weekly basis randomly inventory at least one asset for which their respective departments are accountable. The general managers inform their department heads of the policy, and since monthly reports are to be submitted to them, they obviously will know if there is implementation and compliance with that part of the policy. However, unless they or someone else asks periodically for data on the random inventories, those who are supposed to take those inventories may not be complying with policy.

The way in which security directors do audits and can relate to those in charge of the sites being audited ultimately can have a major impact on the success or failure of the overall security program. Consequently, in many respects this last of the fourfold purposes may well be the most important. It involves the question of whether security audits should be announced in advance, by whom, under what circumstances, and with what frequency should they be conducted, and how, under what circumstances, and to whom the results should be reported.

There are two schools of thought on the subject of whether to give advance notice of security audits. One advocates unannounced audits on the theory that the element of surprise prevents people from correcting deficiencies in anticipation of an audit; therefore, it helps to detect deficiencies. The other theorizes that even if deficiencies are corrected in anticipation of an announced audit, a purpose is served since everyone at the site to be audited has to think about security from the time when preparation for the audit begins through its completion.

Although both approaches are used, security directors who give advance notice almost invariably find that their visits are a source neither of resentment nor of embarrassment to those in charge of the sites audited. Causing persons to resent having security audits made of their facilities, or embarrassment because the number of deficiencies found imply that they are incompetent managers, can do the overall loss prevention program far more harm than good. It makes them considerably less receptive to any recommendations made. Understanding this, prudent security directors have few qualms about letting facility or site managers have advance notice of audit schedules.

An organization's size in terms of the number of sites involved usually will be a major factor in determining both who will conduct security audits and the frequency with which they will be made. If there is only one facility, the head of the security department, no matter his or her title, should do the audits, preferably at least one complete audit of the site a year. On the other hand, when multiple facilities are involved, unless all are located in close physical proximity to each other it is unrealistic to expect the security department head to audit each location annually. Nevertheless, he or she must be involved with the audit process, and if geographic locations are a factor, an audit schedule can be developed in a way that will allow a security director to at least audit all of the organization's principal facilities on a regular basis even if not annually. For instance, one multinational company's corporate security director would schedule annual audits of all major U.S. and Mexican facilities, audits of all major European sites every 18 to 24 months, and audits of all major Far East and Pacific area installations every 24 to 36 months.

Regularly scheduled audits conducted by the security department head also provide an opportunity to involve other security personnel in the process and to use the audits as a learning vehicle for those who are less experienced. A single-site security manager might find it beneficial to involve security supervisors in the audits, using a different supervisor each time. The corporate security director cited in the preceding paragraph used an audit team concept, the other team member being a security manager from a site other than the one being audited. This brought a fresh approach to each audit. It also gave the security manager on the team and the one whose site was audited an opportunity to get to know each other better and to exchange ideas that each might find useful.

A question often asked is whether an annual security audit really is sufficient in terms of trying to maintain a high-quality program, and the answer is "no, it is not." Of course, if only one facility is involved, there is no reason why the security department head cannot do two a year. To attempt to do more can be counterproductive in terms of maintaining good working relationships with other managers. It is also unnecessary since an experienced security manager invariably will notice any existing deficiencies simply by walking through the facility.

Where multiple sites are concerned, self-audits can be conducted by the site security managers. They can be scheduled for regular intervals following a so-called corporate security audit so that in practice the sites are audited twice yearly. If among the multiple sites there are international facilities, the same principle can be followed with regard to frequency. To make certain that these audits are thorough, the checklist developed for corporate audits can be used.

Still another method can be employed for an occasional audit of any single facility even when part of a multisite organization. The security manager can distribute copies of the checklist used for regular audits to individual department heads and ask each to audit a department other than his or her own. When done under the security manager's guidance, this approach can be substituted for one of the regular audits conducted by him or her. Using this method occasionally serves a secondary purpose. It tends to make the participating managers more conscious of just what is involved in the maintenance of an effective loss prevention program, and it can also lead to an even greater degree of cooperation with and understanding of the security department's role in the organization.

Although it is expected that an audit will be followed by a written report, knowledgeable security directors or managers will make it a point to discuss their findings with the person in charge of the particular facility or site audited before they put anything in writing. This precludes the facility or site manager feeling that the audit's primary purpose is to criticize their operation. It also helps to make certain that any recommendations for corrective action can in fact be implemented with relative ease, and to ensure that the manager who will have to initiate that action is committed to doing so in the best interests of the overall security program.

As for the audit reports, copies should be given to the person in charge of the audited facility, to that person's superior, and to the auditor's superior. To illustrate, in one large manufacturing organization, which also had its own sales and service offices, when the corporate security director audited any site, one copy went to the plant's or office's manager, another to the appropriate divisional vice president, and a third to the security director's superior. Certainly, the manager affected needed a copy in order to understand the nature of the problems encountered and to be able to take corrective action. Since it was important for the appropriate divisional vice president to know to what extent a facility for which he or she was responsible might be deficient, and whether the recommended corrective action might require additional funding, it was only logical for a copy to be made available. If, on the other hand, there might be some resistance to making needed changes in any facility's security program, the security director's supervisor had to be informed to be sure of executive support, and that could best be done by giving a copy of the report to that person. This also minimized the risk of the security director being blamed if something occurred at an audited facility after it failed to act on an audit report's recommendations.

SUMMARY

In reality, security directors or managers are also risk managers. Their main task is to try to prevent the loss of assets. Making certain that there is adequate insurance to cover a loss which might occur is someone else's responsibility. To do this they must be able to identify those risks that might have the greatest effect on their organizations and to distinguish between those events that are possible and those that are probable. They must be able to analyze the probabilities and determine which ones, based on their experience and in their judgment, pose the greatest threat to the organization and would have the most severe impact on it. Unless all of these factors are considered together, setting priorities for the institution and implementation of steps necessary for the protection and conservation of the employer's assets, and the prevention of losses, can be extremely difficult, if not almost impossible.

Having identified the risks, analyzed them, and set priorities for their reduction is one thing; reducing them is another. Risks can be reduced, and losses minimized, by bringing together physical security, systems and procedures, controls and accountability, the involvement of line management, and the support of the executive management team, all of which were considered in depth in Chapter 4. However, since no organization genuinely interested in its own protection can afford to become complacent, a mechanism needs to be put in place to make certain that the risk reduction measures are maintained. For this, security audits can be a most useful and important tool. Conducted properly at regular intervals, they enable all levels of management to learn if the security program is being followed, to detect any deficiencies and take corrective action, and to keep abreast of changes that may have taken place and for which some program adjustments may be required. They can also be used as a learning tool for the development of less experienced security personnel and, on occasion, to help heighten the awareness of line managers with regard to the breadth of security's concerns.

REVIEW QUESTIONS

1. What is meant by the word *risk*?
2. Why are security managers risk managers in many respects?
3. Why is risk identification a relatively easy task for security directors and managers?
4. Explain the difference between possible and probable risks.
5. What is meant by the term *risk analysis*?
6. Why is risk analysis important from a security point of view?
7. What elements must be considered in setting priorities?
8. Name five factors that together help reduce risk.
9. What purposes do security audits serve?
10. By whom and with what frequency should security audits be conducted?

Chapter 6

LEGAL AND INSURANCE CONSIDERATIONS

No security department can hope to function either efficiently or effectively unless the department head is prepared to take both legal and insurance considerations into account in terms of the training of departmental personnel and departmental operations. While the activities and operations of both law enforcement and security departments are affected by legal principles in varying degrees, they are also affected by them in different ways. Although this does not mean that all police or security executives should be lawyers, neither can they afford the luxury of total ignorance of those laws that have a bearing on how they, and their subordinates, perform their duties.

Criminal law, and some aspects of constitutional and tort law and the rules of evidence, have an impact on how police and security departments function. However, depending on the nature of an employer's business, security departments, unlike law enforcement agencies, may also be affected by other facets of the law. In addition, as noted in Chapter 5, security department operations and those of an employer's risk management department must complement each other since both are interested in helping to reduce risks and losses. This complementary relationship is a somewhat different one from that which tends to exist among or between government departments, yet without it businesses and institutions might find it difficult to function effectively.

ETHICAL BEHAVIOR

Before focusing on the law–security relationship, however, it is important to point out the importance of ethical as well as lawful behavior on the part of security personnel. In Chapters 2 and 3 it was pointed out that one of the features distinguishing security from policing, and security directors from police chiefs, is the ability of security directors to move forward with relative ease and speed in implementing new programs as long as they are lawful. Nevertheless, this truism standing alone is not enough. Security personnel may indeed operate within a perfectly lawful frame of reference, yet if their conduct is unethical or immoral, they may well do harm to one of their employer's principal assets: its reputation.

Security directors need to face the fact that this can happen most often when overzealous security officers, who also may be poorly trained and inadequately supervised, exercise their authority incorrectly if not improperly. They also need to admit that security directors themselves, despite or perhaps because of their training, may be no less guilty of lawful but questionable behavior. The greatest danger of this happening, whether at the level of security officers or of supervisory and management personnel, usually relates to their work in conducting searches or interviewing persons suspected of wrongdoing.

There may be occasions when good reason exists for acting in accordance with an existing policy and procedure that permits searching parcels and bags being taken from the premises by employees. Perhaps there have been thefts of either assets or the personal property of some employees, and there is a sense of uneasiness on the part of everyone. The Fourth Amendment to the U.S. Constitution reads:

> The right of the people to be secure in their persons, houses, papers, and effects, against unreasonable searches and seizures, shall not be violated, and no warrants shall issue, but upon probable cause, supported by oath or affirmation, and particularly describing the place to be searched, and the persons or things to be seized.

In *Burdeau v. McDowell* the U.S. Supreme Court held that the provisions of the Fourth Amendment did not apply to the acts of private persons; they apply only to the acts of government agencies.[1]

Based on this, security officers are instructed to search all briefcases and attaché cases, women's purses, and shopping bags or boxes being removed from the site by employees, and searches are conducted accordingly. However, there is a noticeable difference in how security officers search. All employees carrying things are stopped, but those who are minorities are subjected to a much more thorough search than are others. They are asked to empty their bags completely; others merely are asked to open them for inspection. Here the searches are perfectly lawful, but the blatant discrimination shown toward one classification of employees is neither ethically nor morally correct.

A security director announces to other security directors that he has access to good background information about people which he is willing to share with them. In fact, the information to which he refers is based on items clipped from newspapers about anyone whose name appears in connection with a story about an arrest, trial, or conviction. One must question the ethics of a security director who, despite the fact that there is nothing unlawful about his conduct, willingly provides information about someone who has been arrested, without any disposition data, knowing that conceivably it could prevent that person from getting a job.

Even before the U.S. Congress enacted a law in 1988 prohibiting private-sector employers from using the polygraph, or lie detector, to screen applicants for employment,[2] a number of states had passed similar legislation. Nevertheless, a security director for a company that did business in several adjoining states sent applicants from a state that prohibited the polygraph's use to a neighboring state that did not, in order to circumvent the law of the state in which the applicants ultimately would work. As the local statute then was written this was not unlawful; ethically, this security director's behavior was questionable.

On those occasions when security personnel may be acting lawfully but unethically, their unethical behavior may well prove to be far more noticeable than anything else which they have accomplished. Therefore, such conduct should not be tolerated in any security organization. Security directors have every right to insist on high ethical and moral standards on the part of all security personnel. To accept anything less can be construed as a lack of professionalism on the part of the entire organization.

GENERAL LEGAL PRINCIPLES

Each day that a legislative body is in session, be it the U.S. Congress, a state legislature, or a city or town council, new laws or ordinances may be passed and old ones amended or repealed. This also is true of regulations or standards which may be issued, modified, or repealed by administrative bodies at federal, state, or local level. Whenever a United States or state court sits, or an administrative law court is in session, existing laws may be affirmed, invalidated, or newly interpreted, and have a bearing on people's lives and the ways in which businesses and institutions can function. Therefore, virtually every department in a business or institution can be affected by some legal principles.

For instance, personnel departments are affected by labor and equal employment opportunity laws, purchasing departments by principles of contract law, and research and development groups by certain aspects of patent or copyright law. While other departments are also affected by those areas of the law that bear on their particular operations, the fact remains that security departments can often be affected by a greater number of legal principles than can any of their counterparts in the business organization. Thus it is especially important to understand the law–security relationship in general terms.

There are certain legal principles that apply to every security department regardless of the employer's size or the nature of its business. While those related to crimes and torts are discussed in greater detail later in this chapter, and those based on safety and environmental issues are dealt with in Chapter 9, the fact remains that other aspects of the law need to be considered from a security viewpoint to avoid legal problems in the course of protecting an employer's assets. There may be matters of contract, agency, labor, insurance, civil rights, constitutional, copyright and patent, real and personal property, immigration, and in some instances even international law. In addition, of course, there may be regulatory matters based on states' laws.

Regulatory Matters

A good example of state regulation is the very existence of a security department. The mere fact that it exists implies the use of security officers. As pointed out in Chapter 3, security officers may be proprietary—that is, employed directly by the business or institution for which they work—or they may be contract personnel. In the latter case they work for an agency which, in turn, provides security personnel to businesses and institutions on the basis of a contract. In either case they may be unarmed or armed.

An initial legal issue that would have to be resolved would deal with the subject of state regulation. For the most part, none of the 50 states tends to regulate proprietary security personnel, unless they are to be armed. That aside, all have some regulation of such diverse but security-related activities as contract and armored car services, and private investigators. Even then, the extent to which there is regulation varies from state to state. According to the 1976 Report of the Task Force on Private Security, Arizona, Kansas, California, and New Mexico were rather heavily regulated, whereas Alabama, Kentucky, Washington, Virginia, and Wyoming were among the least regulated.[3]

If security personnel are to be armed, whether they are proprietary or contract, there must be compliance with any existing licensing and possibly training requirements. Some states regulate the types of uniforms and badges that can be worn by security personnel to avoid confusion between them and sworn police officers. There are also states that regulate the types of emergency lights that can be used on security vehicles to prevent confusion with police and fire apparatus.

To the extent that there may be any regulation at all of proprietary personnel, security directors must make certain that their organizations are in full compliance with the laws under which their security officers work. An illustration of this point would be a situation where they are to be armed. Although those who use contract services are not legally responsible for regulatory compliance by the agencies, prudent security directors nevertheless will take steps to verify compliance, to minimize the risk of embarrassment to their employers or themselves.

Constitutional and Civil Rights Laws

By no means are regulations alone the only legalities that have an impact on security operations. For example, the risk of loss to an employer might be reduced if all applicants for employment were carefully screened before being offered jobs. Therefore, security directors might like to see certain questions asked either on applications or during interviews conducted by their personnel or human resources departments. Although some might be unhappy because those questions are not asked, they must also accept the fact that there are federal and state laws against discrimination, and laws that protect individual privacy. These laws, passed by the U.S. Congress and individual states, can be traced to provisions found in and interpretations of the Constitution. Therefore, to provide equal employment opportunities for everyone, there are strict limits on the types of questions that may be asked of applicants.

Contract and Insurance Laws

To illustrate how laws relating to contracts and insurance can be factors, purchasing departments handle the mechanics involved in soliciting proposals, whether for contract guard services or buying security-related equipment, and for entering into agreements with vendors. Since one of the fundamental principles of contract law is that there must be a meeting of the minds between the parties to the contract, this means that requests for proposals should contain all of the specifications, including those relating to what insurance coverage prospective vendors must carry, so that the latter know precisely on what they are bidding.

Suppose that the request for proposals deals with the provision of contract guard services for a two-year period. Inasmuch as another contract law principle, known as the Statute of Frauds, states that all contracts that cannot be performed within one year should be in writing, it is obvious that entering into this contract orally would be imprudent. Furthermore, since once selected it is not uncommon for contract agencies to submit their own contract forms for execution, it is wise to remember that it is only natural for people to look out for their own best interests. As a result, their contracts will tend to protect their interests more thoroughly than they do the interests of their customers. Therefore, it is preferable for security directors to work closely with their employer's law department and reverse the procedure by having contractors sign contracts prepared in house.

It is also important to require all vendors, of whom certain types of insurance coverage may be required, to submit copies of certificates of insurance before they start work. The mere fact that all states require Workmen's Compensation Insurance, or that their insurance requirements for motor vehicles may be as high as those which the buyer wants vendors to have, will not automatically guarantee full compliance. Only by having copies of insurance certificates can there be reliance on the fact that the coverage called for in the request for proposals has been satisfied. In addition, for self-protection, vendors' insurance companies should be required to notify the vendors' customers of any cancellations of insurance. These steps are necessary to protect the employer should a vendor of services or equipment have problems that could have an impact on the buyer and for which the vendor's insurance should provide coverage.

Fidelity bonds are another type of insurance with which security directors need to be familiar. A fidelity bond is a contract that can provide protection against losses arising from a lack of honesty, integrity, or fidelity of an employee or another person holding a position of trust,[4] and not infrequently customers will ask contract agencies to have employees assigned to their sites bonded. However, if unaware of the fact that fidelity bonds may be written to cover only certain types of offenses (and different courts may interpret the terminology used by the insurance companies in different ways), security directors might assume that all bonds are the same and that their employers have more protection against the dishonest acts of a contract security officer than is actually true. For instance, although a bond covering losses caused by "fraud or dishonesty" ordinarily would be extended beyond criminal acts, with the words being given a broad interpretation, some courts would construe the words *larceny* and *embezzlement* strictly, thus limiting the bonding company's liability to losses caused only by acts that amount to the crime or crimes named in the bond.[5]

Agency

How can security operations be affected by the principles of agency law? Suppose that a security department consists of both contract and proprietary personnel, and on one occasion a proprietary security officer falsely arrests a customer. On another a contract security officer hits a visitor to the site. Both victims file law suits against the company based on offenses called torts. Should the security director's concern be limited to the first case because an employee is involved, or should he or she be equally concerned about the second, even if it is a contract agency employee who is involved? If at all acquainted with the principles of agency law, it would be clear to the security director that from a legal point of view there would be no difference as far as the employer's liability is concerned.[6]

To illustrate this principle's application, particularly as regards the use of contract personnel in the mistaken belief that this can help avoid liability, there is the *Safeway Stores, Inc. v. Kelly* case. Kelly sued because of certain acts on the part of a security guard working at a Safeway Store. In defending itself Safeway argued that it was not liable since the guard was not a Safeway employee but someone who worked for an independent service used by Safeway. Nevertheless, the court found Safeway liable based on the fact that although the guard may have worked for a guard company, while at the store the guard acted "within the scope of his employment" and under the direct control and supervision of Safeway's management, not that of the guard company.[7]

This example brings to mind two aspects of the law already mentioned. First, although no reference is made to the agreement between Safeway and the guard company, is it possible that with a carefully prepared contract there might not have been any serious question about Safeway's role? In other words, how clearly did the agreement spell out the matters of control and supervision? Also, what did the contract require of the guard agency in terms of insurance should an event like this ever occur?

Labor Law

One rightly assumes that an organization's personnel or human resources department is the one principally involved with labor matters. If so, in what way might labor law have an impact on security? As an example, suppose that although an organization is nonunion, there has been some talk among employees about forming a union. A security director who does not think that labor law can affect security department activities, but who knows that executive management would prefer to maintain the status quo and who wants to show that he or she has the company's best interests at heart, decides to find out whether there is any truth to the rumors that a union is being organized. Under the circumstances the security director considers using one or more means to that end: surveillance, undercover operatives, or suggesting to certain employees that they gather and report information about any organizational activities.

That security director's lack of awareness could result in problems for the employer which conceivably might prove to be far more serious than having a union shop. It could mean litigation with the National Labor Relations Board, an agency of the U.S. government, as the plaintiff. Although not all of the U.S. Circuit Courts of Appeal necessarily agree as to whether surveillance alone is an unfair labor practice, there is agreement that it is unlawful if it interferes in any way with employees who exercise their rights or with a labor organization.[8] At the same time, there does not appear to be any disagreement among them about the fact that using labor spies or undercover operatives is a violation of federal law.[9] So is suggesting to certain employees that they gather information about union organizing activities, regardless of whether or not their doing so is coercive.[10] This shows how a security director, oblivious to the relationship between the law and security, might cause an employer needless expense in having to defend a law suit, a rupture in employer–employee relations, and a good deal of embarrassment.

Immigration Law

Employers are required to take steps to ensure that whereas not all employees are required to be U.S. citizens, all employees are in the country legally. Normally, this is a personnel department responsibility. It is regrettable that in their desire to be competitive, some businesses will violate the law by hiring people who have entered the United States illegally. These businesses are not necessarily very small, but their operations are labor intensive. In other words, there is tremendous emphasis on productivity in what otherwise may be relatively boring work for which their workers are paid the minimum wages or less. Although employing illegal aliens is unlawful, these businesses rationalize that no matter how poor the working conditions or wages are, the fact that their employees are in the country illegally means that they dare not complain to anyone. The fact that such businesses may be violating the law does not necessarily mean that they would not have security departments. Thus aside from the obvious illegality, such a situation poses an ethical dilemma for security personnel unless they are wholly unfamiliar with the law's requirement that only citizens or aliens admitted legally may be employed. In any event, it would be most unusual for a security manager to claim ignorance of such a practice on an employer's part, and hard to explain in the event of prosecution by the government.

Real and Personal Property Law

Since a primary role for a well-organized, fully integrated security department is the protection and conservation of all of an employer's assets, at least some understanding of real and personal property law is needed. The term *real property* applies to real estate and includes those things that are considered permanently attached to a building or other structure. *Personal property* covers all other assets, both tangible and intangible.

For example, one concern of all security managers is trespass, that is, when one person illegally enters upon the land of another. The property upon which the entry is made could be the landscaped grounds of a facility, its parking lots, or a building itself. To help protect against an act of trespass, and to prosecute successfully those who do, the law requires the property to be "posted." There must be signs which state that the property is private, that trespassers are to keep out, and that if they do not, they will be prosecuted. However, actual posting requirements may vary from state to state. Therefore, security directors need to know more than what really constitutes a trespass on the employer's property. They also have to know what the states in which the company has real property require in the way of posting, and whether in an action of trespass the property owner has to prove that the trespasser actually saw the warning notice.

In addition, it helps to understand that under certain circumstances the mere fact that a person was a trespasser will not necessarily protect an employer from being sued if that trespasser was a child. In fact, in states that follow what is known as the attractive nuisance doctrine, an organization could even be under an affirmative duty to protect children who might be injured on their property, despite the fact that those children are trespassers on that property.[11]

Turning to an example of an employer's personal property, aside from things like money and other negotiable instruments, such as checks, stocks and bonds, tools, records, raw materials, finished goods, inventory, equipment, supplies, and so on, intellectual property may well be involved. This would be particularly true of organizations that either do any research and development or are engaged in activities that produce materials capable of being patented, copyrighted, or classified as trade secrets.

Security directors rarely have the technical backgrounds which would permit them to participate in the research and development processes, but that does not alter the fact that they may be called upon by their employers for advice with respect to protecting such intellectual property. For instance, an organization's staff might generate materials that are either patentable or capable of being copyrighted. Once letters patent have been issued for a new and patentable item, or an item has been copyrighted, the person or organization to whom the patent or copyright has been issued has a degree of protection according to federal laws. However, since both patents and copyrights do expire after prescribed periods of time, a business or institution might ask its security director whether he or she thinks the employer would enjoy a greater degree of protection by considering the items as trade secrets.

Security directors who have at least some understanding of patent, copyright, and trade secret law might well find the trade secret classification attractive since there is a legal basis for such protection which goes back to British cases in 1851[12] and 1889,[13] and a 1917 decision of the U.S. Supreme Court,[14] and unlike patents and copyrights, trade secrets are not affected by arbitrary time limits. However, if that is their preference, they should be aware of the fact that in 1948, New York state courts hearing trade secret cases started to take into consideration the efforts made by trade secret owners to guard those secrets, including what was done to educate their employees to the fact that the information was secret, and the success of their efforts in this regard,[15] a position adopted in 1953 by the U.S. Court of Appeals for the Seventh Circuit.[16]

Department of Defense Contracts

Although there are businesses and institutions that do work for a variety of U.S. government agencies, those who do so as contractors to the Department of Defense have special security requirements imposed on them by the government. As an example, both private businesses that supply anything to any branch of the armed forces, and academic institutions engaged in research projects for any of the armed forces, would fall into this category. They are given security guidance in the form of the U.S. Department of Defense Industrial Security Manual for Safeguarding Classified Information.

Security personnel need to understand that the manual itself is issued under the authority of a Department of Defense directive and that it relates to what the department refers to as the DD Form 441 and the DLA Form 1149. The former officially is known as the Department of Defense Security Agreement, the latter as the Transportation Security Agreement. In other words, these are the written agreements or contracts executed between the Department of Defense and the businesses or institutions that do work for it.

From a legal perspective it is also important for security managers to appreciate the fact that if their employers do work for the Department of Defense, by no means are the two cited agreements (DD Form 441 and DLA Form 1149) the only things with which they have to be concerned. There are a number of federal statutes, executive orders, and regulations that are equally binding on businesses and institutions that are Department of Defense contractors. To mention but a few, there are the Espionage Acts, Sabotage Acts,

Internal Security Act of 1950, National Security Act of 1947 as amended, National Aeronautics and Space Act of 1958 as amended, Federal Aviation Act of 1958 as amended, International Traffic in Arms Regulation, and Executive Orders 10104, 12065, 10865, and 10909.

International Law

Since there may be differences among the laws of the 50 U.S. states, it obviously is no surprise that different countries have different laws. Therefore, security directors who work for multinational organizations need to be aware of the fact that each country in which their employers have facilities or do business has its own laws, regulations, and standards, and that those laws, regulations, and standards probably are different from those in the United States.

As an illustration, despite the fact that so many U.S. laws and laws of the 50 states have their origins in the old English Common Law, there still are differences between laws in the United States and those of Great Britain. That being the case, imagine what differences may exist between laws of and in the United States and those of countries other than Great Britain. These differences exist in virtually all aspects of the law, not merely in the fields of criminal and tort law or in the rules of evidence. Practices that may be lawful in the United States may be unlawful in other countries, and some that may be lawful there may be unlawful here. For instance, it is quite common for security officers in the United States to be equipped with two-way radios, yet in some countries it is unlawful for private persons to own or even use them. In some foreign countries many private persons, security officers included, can own and carry pistols and revolvers without any licensing formalities; in others, private ownership of firearms is prohibited. In the United States the general rule regarding firearms is that private ownership is allowed, but there are certain licensing requirements. U.S. law prohibits bribing foreign officials in an attempt to get business from them or the agencies for which they work, yet in some countries it may be almost impossible to do business without paying off certain officials.

CRIMES AND TORTS

Crimes and torts are the legal subjects that generally come to mind first when thinking about security operations. There is no denying their importance both in terms of what security personnel can and should do, and what they cannot and should not do. A misunderstanding of what might develop from a failure to appreciate fully the impact of improper conduct on the part of security officers where crimes and torts are at issue may lead to legal action against their employers and risks liability. Consequently, an understanding of what might happen is crucial.

First, however, what is the difference between a crime and a tort? A crime is an offense against the state; a tort is an offense against a person. In a criminal case the state is the plaintiff and brings the action for trial in criminal court. In a tort case the injured person is the plaintiff in a lawsuit in a civil court. A defendant found guilty in a criminal case is usually punished by being either fined, or confined in a correctional facility, or possibly both. A defendant who loses in a civil case usually pays monetary damages to the plaintiff. It should also be noted that some actions may be both crimes and torts, with the defendant being tried separately in both criminal court and civil court. An assault and battery is a good example of an action that is both a crime and a tort.

It is also important to understand that not all crimes are classified or treated in the same way. Within the criminal law a distinction is made between felonies and misdemeanors. Felonies are considered more serious crimes, the most serious being a homicide or the killing of another person. Within the framework of homicides there are degrees of seriousness, with murder the most serious. However, there are different degrees of murder. Manslaughter, the other form of homicide, also has different degrees. Of course, homicides are not the only felonies in the criminal law. For example, armed robbery or the theft of an automobile are felonies. Misdemeanors are less serious offenses. As an illustration, a theft of goods worth less than $50 would be a misdemeanor in most states.

Regardless of whether an offense is to be tried as a felony or as a misdemeanor, the prosecution's objective is to establish criminal liability. For this it must show not only that a criminal act took place, but also that the person knew that what he or she was doing was wrong and intended to do it anyway. For a conviction the prosecution must also prove the defendant guilty beyond a reasonable doubt. By way of contrast, to establish liability in a civil action such as a tort, the plaintiff only needs to prove its case by a preponderance of the evidence. Thus while in a criminal trial for assault and battery the state must prove the defendant guilty beyond a reasonable doubt, the plaintiff suing the same defendant for the same offense but in civil court does not need as much proof to win.

Crimes and torts are matters of concern not because one expects security personnel to commit homicides or armed robberies but because of the ways in which they perform their duties and how that could result in charges being filed against them and the businesses or institutions for which they work. There is also a need to be aware of the fact that occasionally, lawsuits may be brought not only because of something that security personnel did, but also because of something which they should have done and did not do.

The problems with which security personnel most often are involved in the areas of criminal and tort law relate to such issues as false arrest, false imprisonment, searches and seizures, confessions, and libel and slander or defamation of character. As discussed in Chapters 2 and 3, the duties, responsibilities, and authority of security personnel usually are dictated by the employing organization's executive management. However, they cannot grant security personnel more authority than is allowed by law. This is particularly noticeable when the subject of arrests arises. Although the owners of a business or institution have a right to protect their assets and can delegate this authority to their protection staffs, neither they nor their security personnel have an unquestioned right to make arrests.

Since executive management would have a right to make a "citizen's arrest," they can authorize security personnel acting in their behalf to do the same. The common law right of private persons to make an arrest without a warrant for a felony has been affirmed by the U.S. Supreme Court,[17] and private persons also have been given the right to make arrests for misdemeanors if committed in their presence. Thus the obvious question is: Just what is an arrest?[18] Is the impression that one might get from watching motion pictures or made-for-television movies—namely, that the person being taken into custody has to be told that they are under arrest, or physically restrained, or both— the correct one?

The answer is "no, it is not." In fact, on the basis of court decisions, it is even possible that a situation could arise where no arrest is intended, yet in his or her own mind a person might believe that he or she were under arrest. Generally speaking, there is an arrest when a person is seized or detained by being physically restrained, by any act indicating an intention to take that person into custody and that subjects him or her to the actual control and will of the one making the arrest, or when the person consents to the arrest.[19] If a person understands that he or she is in the power of the one making the arrest and therefore submits, there is no need for force to be applied or for a manual touching of that person's body.[20] Furthermore, if a party making an arrest claims to have the authority to do so and tells a person by virtue of that pretended authority to accompany him or her, and the other person does, with both going where the one claiming the right to arrest says to go, there has been an arrest and imprisonment within the meaning of the law.[21]

Therefore, if security officers identify themselves, ask a person to go with them, and the person does feeling they have no choice, an arrest has been made even if it was not necessarily the security officer's intention to make an arrest. Should this happen, that person could sue both the security officer and the employer on the grounds that the arrest was made by someone who had no legal authority to do so. Generally speaking, a person suing for false imprisonment, which usually goes hand in hand with false arrest, would not have to prove malice or probable cause to prevail in court.[22]

It should be understood that while the need for security personnel even to consider making arrests arises rather infrequently in most businesses and institutions, this cannot be said of retailing. Although employees are responsible for significant losses, the fact remains that the very nature of retailing requires a public presence in stores. This, in turn, means that retail merchants also suffer from losses caused by shoplifters. It is because of this rather unique situation that virtually every state has passed laws designed to give merchants some protection against lawsuits filed charging them with false arrest and false imprisonment. At the same time, however, if a retail merchant, or anyone else for that matter, calls the police and asks them to make an arrest, and an officer does so without first getting a warrant, the general rule is that the private person requesting that arrest is not protected against legal action.[23]

Earlier in this chapter it was pointed out that the Fourth Amendment prohibition against unlawful searches and seizures does not to apply to private persons. Does this mean that no restrictions are imposed on searches by private persons? Not necessarily. First, of course, there may be limits agreed upon between employers and their employees in the form of either a union contract or an employment contract. In addition, however, state laws or court decisions need to be considered in terms of just how far security personnel can go in making a search. For example, while California's Merchants' Privilege Statute affords protection to retailers against being sued for false arrest and false imprisonment, its courts have held that the statute does not give security officers an unlimited right to make searches.[24] Thus it is important that security personnel not assume that because of their jobs they have a right to make searches and seize the property of others.

It is not at all unusual for security personnel who conduct investigations to interview the person or persons whom they suspect of having committed an offense. The object of such interviews is to get the persons being interrogated to confess or admit to having done that of which they are suspected. Before the U.S. Supreme Court decided the now well-known case of *Miranda v. Arizona*,[25] persons who were in custody and being questioned by the police about their alleged crimes did not have to be warned that they did not have to make a statement but that if they did it could be used against them in a court of law, that they were entitled to be represented by an attorney, and that if they could not afford an attorney, the court would appoint one for them. Now, although one constantly hears references to the so-called "Miranda warnings," it has also been held that private persons (including security personnel) are not required to give any such warning to persons whom they are questioning. Nevertheless, as with searches and seizures an awareness of what state courts hold in places where the employer has facilities is important. For instance, in New York, statements gotten by security personnel would be inadmissible unless they were made "freely, voluntarily, and without compulsion or inducement of any sort."[26]

As a rule, truly skilled investigators usually will not question a suspect in detail until they have completed or are near completion of the investigation. Neither do they approach the interview with the idea that unless they can get a confession, they have no case. Instead, they view it as an opportunity to get confirmation of what they already know. Despite the fact that security personnel ordinarily need not give a "Miranda warning," there is no reason why one cannot be given in a modified form, and doing exactly that can help avoid problems at a later date. As an illustration, suppose that a person suspected of wrongdoing is about to be questioned. If at the very outset they are told that the office door is closed to ensure privacy, not to restrict their movement; that any time they want to take a break for something to drink or eat, or to go to the toilet, they have only to say so; that they are not required to answer any of the questions put to them; and if the interviewer keeps an accurate interview log, he or she has minimized the risk of being accused of falsely arresting or imprisoning the person being interviewed and added weight has been given to the fact that if a statement is given, it was given voluntarily.

Closely related to the subject of false arrest, and of potential danger to security personnel and their employers, is the issue of libel and slander. Actions for libel or slander are based on a violation of public policy and a person's right to enjoy his or her reputation free of false statements.[27] What, then, are the differences between libel and slander, and on what basis might they create problems for security personnel?

A malicious publication that tends to hurt a person's reputation and expose them to public hatred, contempt, or ridicule is a libel, and "publication" can be in a printed or written form or by signs or pictures.[28] Slander occurs when the "publication" is by spoken words, gestures, or any form of communication other than those which would constitute libel.[29] If, therefore, a security officer accuses a person of having stolen something and takes the person forcibly into custody, the person might sue the security officer and the employer for slander, and the only defense would be proof that the person did in fact steal something from the employer. Assume that although the person did not steal anything, his or her name appeared in a newspaper article which gave the impression that the person had stolen something; this would be grounds for a lawsuit charging libel. Taking this into consideration, along with the fact that there are many cases which have held that any person who is falsely charged with stealing, whether orally or in writing, has a cause of action,[30] one can understand how libel and slander are issues that can affect security personnel in general, and those who work for retailers in particular. Protection given retailers against lawsuits for false arrest and false imprisonment do not necessarily protect them or their security officers against actions for libel or slander. This, then, is but another illustration of the importance of the law to security operations.

CRIMINAL AND CIVIL LIABILITY ISSUES

Having considered how laws and court decisions related to criminal and tort law can affect security operations, it is also necessary to consider how the issue of liability can affect security personnel and their employers. In other words, does the fact that what otherwise would be a crime or a tort was committed by security personnel mean that neither they nor the businesses or institutions for which they work cannot be held responsible for their misconduct, or for not having done something which they should? For those who may think this is so, nothing is further from the truth.

First and foremost, security personnel are not above the law; neither should they expect to be. If anything, they should be among those who are most obedient to and respectful of the law. Consequently, if they commit an act that is a crime, they can and should be prosecuted by the state. Furthermore, if what they do is an act related to the scope of their employment, the employer may also be held liable for the crime. To illustrate, suppose the law states that under no circumstances is criminal history data to be given to private parties, and that a violation of the statute is a crime. Nevertheless, an employer wants to know if people whom it might hire have arrest records, and makes this clear to its security manager. The latter then locates someone who has access to the data and is willing to make it available in return for personal payment. Subsequently, this arrangement becomes known, and both the security manager and the employer are prosecuted for violating the criminal history statute and the laws against bribing public officials.

As for civil liability, it is important to remember that, as pointed out earlier in the chapter, crimes can also be torts. While injured parties will testify for the state in criminal cases, if they want payment for their injuries in the form of money, they have to sue civilly in tort. When they do, they almost invariably will name both the employee, whom they allege was responsible, and the employer, as defendants, for two reasons. First, there are the laws of agency or master and servant which hold that principals or masters are responsible for what their agents or servants do within the scope of their employment. Second, naming employers acknowledges the fact that financially they have greater resources than do their employees. This commonly is referred to as the "deep pockets" approach.

For instance, assume that an incident occurred causing the plaintiff an injury or a loss. Assume further that this particular tort is also a crime. Nevertheless, if prosecuted as a crime and the defendants are found guilty, the employee might be punished by being jailed; the employer's punishment probably would be only a fine. However, since the plaintiff alleges that it happened either because of something which an employee did or failed to do, and which either caused or might have prevented the injury or loss, it is pursued as a tort action, with the plaintiff asking for $250,000 in damages. It is highly doubtful that the individual employee/defendant has personal assets amounting to that much if the plaintiff wins; it is quite likely that the employer/defendant has either assets or insurance which will cover that amount if the plaintiff is successful. Therefore, in the civil case both the employee and the employer are named as defendants, and theoretically both are liable to the plaintiff if the latter wins.

There may be occasions when an individual employee is required to pay a successful plaintiff more in damages than the employer is required to pay, even though both are named as defendants in a lawsuit. For instance, the May 10, 1983 edition of *The Boston Globe* carried a story about a Pine Manor College student who was raped and awarded $175,000 on the basis of the school's duty to protect its students from the criminal acts of others.[31] However, the actual report of the case reflects that the school had a maximum liability under Massachusetts law of only $20,000, since it was considered a charitable organization, but its vice president of operations, who had designed and supervised its security system and established security's patrol pattern and the school's lock network, was legally liable for the remaining $155,000.[32]

Of course, there are also times when businesses or institutions are sued in tort in security-related matters without individual employees being directly involved or named as defendants. As an example, in March 1992, a California jury awarded a student of the University of Southern California $1.6 million based on the university's failure to provide adequate security around an off-campus dormitory where she lived and where she was raped in 1988. Despite the school's defense that it did have adequate security, including escort services and round-the-clock patrols, the jury accepted the plaintiff's argument that the university was guilty of fraud and negligence by hiding information about crime in the neighborhood, and it was considering whether to assess punitive damages as well.[33]

By no means are these illustrations the only basis for security-related legal action being taken against businesses and institutions. Some of the more common incidents which may prompt people to bring tort actions can be traced directly to the ways in which security personnel discharge their duties, and have been discussed earlier in this chapter. Among them are assaults and batteries, false arrest and imprisonment, libel, slander, and defamation of character.

The foregoing examples offer some insight into the nature of criminal and civil liability as they can affect security operations. They also illustrate what improper conduct by security personnel can cost in terms of dollars. However, to try to measure what the hidden costs of such conduct can amount to as a result of damage to an organization's reputation is an impossible task. How does one measure the number of customers who will avoid shopping in a store when the news media carry a story about its security officers falsely arresting legitimate customers, or when a story appears about hotel security personnel defaming a guest or hospital security officers assaulting a visitor or patient?

INSURANCE CONSIDERATIONS
IN SECURITY PROGRAMMING

In many businesses and institutions, particularly those of any appreciable size, insurance matters are handled by a risk management department that is separate and apart from the security department. It will be the risk management department manager's responsibility to represent the organization in its negotiations with insurance companies to obtain the best value, any special services that an insurer may offer, and in trying to settle claims when the occasion demands.

That security's mission is to protect and conserve the employer's assets is one thing, but to recognize that security, no matter how efficient, cannot possibly prevent all losses is another. Consequently, some means must be found that will help minimize the dollar value of those losses that may occur. For this purpose insurance becomes an important consideration. However, there are three factors that cannot be ignored. First, as noted in Chapter 5, virtually all insurance policies have a deductible clause the size of which depends largely on how much the insured is willing to pay for its coverage. Second, it is naive to assume that since an organization has insurance it needs no security program. Third, it is shortsighted for any security director or manager to rationalize that since the employer is insured, the quality of the loss prevention program, and the training and supervision of security personnel, can be compromised. Therefore, security managers need to understand how insurance can play a role in security programming.

In essence, a deductible provision in an insurance policy means that the insured is prepared to take a calculated risk in terms how much money it can afford to lose without any expectation of reimbursement by a third-party insurer. Since the cost of 100 percent coverage would be almost prohibitive, the overwhelming majority of organizations have deductible clauses in their insurance policies. Therefore, if they suffer losses that are not covered because of this provision, it means that for all intents and purposes they are insuring themselves, and they absorb the cost of those losses.

The amount of the deductible may vary from one policy to another and from one type of insured organization to another. For a sizable business or institution a deductible of $50,000 for any one loss is by no means uncommon. However no organization, regardless of its size or financial stability, can afford to suffer multiple losses even in this range and expect to show what might be considered an acceptable margin of profit.

Therefore, this places a burden on security operations since it is under these circumstances in particular that effective loss prevention programs assume such great importance. Furthermore, they must be preventive in the true sense of the word. Physical protection, operating and security policies and procedures, executive support, and line management involvement must all come together to prevent as much loss as possible and to keep the scope and magnitude of unavoidable losses to an absolute minimum. Theorizing that identifying, apprehending, and punishing those responsible for losses is the best way to prevent them from again happening to a business or institution, even if some of the latter may be in the nonprofit class, is neither acceptable nor cost-effective from a management perspective. Of course, it goes without saying that to the best of its ability, security is also responsible for preventing any losses in excess of the amount of the deductible.

Organizations that have insurance, and consequently rationalize that either they need no security program or that at best only a minimal effort is required, are naive. Aside from those losses which they must absorb themselves under their policy's deductible provision, they lose sight of the fact that every time they have a loss for which a claim is filed they risk incurring additional expense. First, the insurer and the insured may differ on the value of the lost or stolen assets. For instance, the policy may pay for the lost assets but not for any lost profit. Depending on what has been lost, the insurer may figure depreciation in calculating the claim's value. When such things occur, insurers usually prevail, and it is the claimant who suffers the additional loss. A policyholder prepared to fight on this issue will also incur litigation costs but without any assurance of a victory in court. Then, too, even if the amount of the claim is undisputed, there is a good chance that if it is a substantial claim, the cost of the policy's premium will increase when the policy is renewed. It will make little or no difference that premiums may have been paid for years without payments having been made to the insured for claims. Simply put, no amount of insurance prevents losses completely, and in most cases even where there is extensive coverage an insured will have to absorb some loss.

When an organization has both insurance and a security program it is essential for its security manager to maintain the highest standards not only in terms of the basic program, but also with respect to the training and supervision of security personnel. To compromise in either respect is shortsighted and unprofessional. It is also critically important for security managers to make certain that their counterparts in risk management take into account the types of additional insurance coverage that may be necessary to protect the employer in the event that third parties file claims based on the conduct or misconduct of members of the security department.

By developing and maintaining high program standards the risk of loss, irrespective of the deductible issue, is or should be reduced greatly. This means that assets are less in jeopardy or at risk, thus making certain of their availability to the employer, whether for manufacturing, sales, research, or any other legitimate purposes. Furthermore, if few or no claims are filed with the insurer, the likelihood of disputes having to be litigated is lessened, and the cost of insurance premiums should remain fairly constant instead of increasing, thus benefiting the employer.

However, the very presence of security personnel, no matter how well trained or closely supervised, in and of itself represents a potential for third-party claims with which a risk department manager may not be completely familiar. Therefore, it is of the utmost importance that security directors or managers discuss the types of coverage in existence, and that when it appears that more is necessary, they make appropriate suggestions.

In considering this aspect, security directors dare not assume that simply because of the high quality of their personnel, training programs, and the supervision afforded them, the employer is immune from claims that may be filed by third parties. That security officers perform their duties in a highly professional way will not necessarily prevent someone from feeling that they have been victimized and suing the participating security officer and his or her employer. Should that happen, insurance can help avoid or at least minimize the defendants' legal fees; it can also help reduce the amount of damages to be paid by the defendants to a successful plaintiff.

For a better understanding of this subject it may be helpful to review briefly some of the torts mentioned earlier in this chapter. For example, for what offenses are security personnel and their employers potentially vulnerable and most likely to be sued? How would the right kind of insurance help to prevent or minimize both costs and liability? To answer the first part of this question, both security and risk management department managers must analyze the risks involved in security operations.

This analysis must take into consideration the type of business or institution by which security personnel are employed. Obviously, the risks to which the employer will be exposed because of security department operations will vary in relation to the organization's activities. To illustrate the point, the risk of exposure will be greater in activities that are likely to bring security officers into direct contact with the general public rather than with other employees. For instance, the likelihood of direct contact between security personnel and the general public is far greater in such fields as retailing, medical centers, transportation, entertainment, banking, hotels, and academic institutions than it is in a manufacturing, warehousing, or research environment.

While virtually all employers are exposed to certain types of torts, the exposure will not be as great in some types of activities as it will be in others. Therefore, either fewer claims may be filed or the damages sought may be less. For example, despite the fact that generally speaking, the Fourth Amendment has been held not to apply to searches by private persons, searches conducted in a relatively closed atmosphere such as a manufacturing plant, where there is little or no general public involvement, may lead to questions about the invasion of privacy being raised more often than they would be in a more open environment. On the other hand, allegations of false arrest or imprisonment, slander, and defamation of character can be made regardless of the degree of general public involvement, but they are likely to occur more frequently where an organization's exposure to the public is greater, as would be the case with retailers.

These differences would not justify any security or risk manager deciding that certain types of insurance coverage can be avoided in a particular type of environment. However, taking into account the likelihood of a tort occurring, the possible frequency of such an occurrence, the types of persons most likely to file claims alleging torts by security personnel, and projecting what such classes of persons might seek in the way of damages all warrant consideration relative to the amount of insurance coverage that would appear to be adequate for the employer's protection. For instance, a well-known person accused of shoplifting in a retail store that sells expensive merchandise, or a celebrity who had too much to drink in a hotel lounge and alleges that he was assaulted by a security officer, would be more likely to sue in tort and seek considerable sums in the way of damages than would an employee who alleges that his or her privacy was invaded. Nevertheless, to assume that only well-known or wealthy customers will sue for large sums is unrealistic, especially in our highly litigious society, where someone less fortunate might see such a lawsuit as a golden opportunity leading to early retirement.

Thus risk managers, once alerted by security managers to the types of claims most likely to be filed and the most likely types of claimants to be involved, will attempt to get insurance coverage for these torts which, if committed as alleged, will result in the filing of claims. In placing the necessary insurance they will also take into consideration the categories of persons most likely to be involved as either claimants or as employee-defendants. The former will provide some insight into the question of how much coverage is needed for any given offense; the latter may possibly give the risk manager at least some clue as to the frequency with which security personnel may be involved in the commission of torts that will become the basis for claims to be filed. Therefore, the underlying process is one designed to help reduce the risk of surprise and unanticipated losses and of litigation costs when an action is brought against the employer.

Working closely together, risk management and security managers can provide their employers with effective, realistic programs for the prevention and containment of losses. While the functions of these two departments are different, they are also complementary. If the security and risk management department managers consider their respective departments competitors, and if they see their departmental functions as mutually exclusive, in the final analysis it will be the employer who suffers.

SUMMARY

Truly professional security directors or managers who work for progressive, enlightened organizations soon learn that they need to know considerably more than the fundamentals of criminal law and the rules of evidence if they are to succeed in protecting their employers. While they are not expected to become lawyers (although some are), they are expected to be sufficiently familiar with other aspects of the law which can have a bearing on departmental operations. They need to have an appreciation of the difference between crimes and torts and of the criminal and civil liability issues that are inherent in security activities.

Furthermore, security directors and managers must be made to realize that the range of legal issues with which they may be confronted is wide, and that in some cases those issues may not arise with such frequency as to make them readily disposable without consultation. They have to understand how important it is to be able to avoid pitfalls by seeking the advice of counsel when in doubt and before acting.

Equally important is the need to appreciate the relationship between security and insurance. Although insurance cannot prevent losses in the sense that security can, it can minimize the loss in those cases where some losses may be unavoidable. Insurance can also help protect the employer against losses that may be the outgrowth of security operations themselves despite the quality of security personnel, their training, and their supervision. Security managers should not lose sight of the fact that well-conceived and executed insurance plans can make important contributions to security programming when there is effective and meaningful communication between security and risk management department managers.

REVIEW QUESTIONS

1. Should security personnel be concerned only with lawful behavior in performing their duties, or should they be equally concerned with behaving ethically and morally? Why?

2. For what reasons is it important for security directors or managers to be familiar with more of the law than crimes, torts, and the rules of evidence?

3. What is the difference between a crime and a tort?

4. Under what circumstances can a security officer make an arrest for a misdemeanor? For a felony?

5. A security officer's assault on a third person while on duty causes injury to that person and prompts a civil suit for damages. Can the injured person also name the employer as a defendant, or is the security officer the only defendant? In such a case can failure to train security personnel properly be introduced by the plaintiff as a factor?

6. Should the Fourth and Fifth Amendments to the U.S. Constitution apply to private security personnel? If so, why?

7. In what ways do security and risk management departments complement each other?

8. What is a deductible clause in an insurance policy?

9. Can insurance coverage alone prevent security incidents from happening?

10. Why does an organization need an effective security program regardless of the amount of insurance it has?

NOTES

[1]*Burdeau v. McDowell*, 256 U.S. 465, 65 L. Ed. 1048, 41 S. Ct. 574, 13 A.L.R. 1159.

[2]Employee Polygraph Protection Act.

[3]*The Report of the Task Force on Private Security,* National Advisory Committee on Criminal Justice Standards and Goals, Washington, DC, 1976, pp. 382–387.

[4]*John Church Co. v. Aetna Indemnity Co.*, 13 Ga. App. 826, 80 S.E. 1093; *Employers' Liab. Assurance Corp. v. Citizens Nat'l. Bank*, 85 Ind. App. 169, 15 N.E. 396; *Thomas & Howard Co. v. Am. Mut. Liberty Ins. Co.*, 241 N.C. 109, 84 S.E.2d 337; *S. Sur. Co. v. Austin* (Tex. Com. App.) 17 S.W.2d 774.

[5]35 Am. Jur. 2d 518, 519, §§ 23, 25.

[6]No distinction is to be drawn between the liability of a principal for the tortious act of an agent and the liability of a master for the tortious act of a servant. *Restatement, Agency*, 2d ed., § 212 *et seq.*

[7]*Safeway Stores, Inc., v. Kelly*, D.C. Appeals (D.C. App. No. 80-474).

[8]48 Am. Jur. 2d 702, § 863. Employer surveillance of union activities violates 29 U.S.C.S. § 158(a)(1) where it improperly interferes with the employees' right of self-organization (*NLRB v. Purity Food Stores, Inc. [Sav-Mor Food Stores]*, C.A. 1, 354 F.2d 926) or where the information obtained therefrom is used to interfere with union activity as by dismissing employees therefor (*Press Co. v. NLRB*, 73 App. D.C. 103, 118 F.2d 937, *cert. denied* 313 U.S. 595, 85 L.Ed. 1548, 61 S.Ct. 1118). It is not clear whether surveillance is an unfair labor practice per se. The 9th Circuit has declared that it is not unlawful unless it interferes with, restrains, or coerces employees in the exercise of rights guaranteed by 29 U.S.C.S. § 157, or dominates or interferes with a labor organization as prohibited by 29 U.S.C.S. § 158(a)(2) [*NLRB v. Nat'l. Motor Bearing Co.*, C.A. 9, 105 F.2d 652]. The 4th, 5th, and 6th Circuits disagree (*NLRB v. Collins & Aikman Corp.*, C.A. 4, 146 F.2d 454; *Hendrix Mfg. Co. v. NLRB*, C.A. 5, 321 F.2d 100; *NLRB v. Eaton Mfg. Co.*, C.A. 6, 175 F.2d 292).

[9]48 Am. Jur. 2d 703, § 864. Using labor spies or undercover operatives to spy on union affairs violates 29 U.S.C.S. § 158(a)(1) (*NLRB v. Calumet Steel Div., Borg-Warner Corp.*, C.A. 7, 121 F.2d 366; *Atlas Underwear Co. v. NLRB*, C.A. 6, 116 F.2d 1020; *Ohio Power Co. v. NLRB*, C.A. 6, 115 F.2d 839).

[10]48 Am. Jur. 2d 703, Section 865. Suggesting to certain employees that they gather information concerning union organizational activities violates 29 U.S.C.S. § 158(a)(1) whether the action is coercive or not (*Suburban Transit Corp. v. NLRB*, C.A. 3, 499 F.2d 78, *cert. denied* 419 U.S. 1089, 42 L. Ed. 2d 682, 95 S. Ct. 681, and later appeal C.A. 3, 536 F.2d 1018; *NLRB v. Assoc. Naval Architects, Inc.*, 355 F.2d 988; *Edward Fields, Inc. v. NLRB*, C.A. 2, 325 F.2d 754).

[11]One who maintains upon his premises a condition, instrumentality, machine, or agency which is dangerous to children of tender years by reason of their inability to appreciate the peril therein, and which may reasonably be expected to attract children of tender years to the premises, is under a duty to exercise reasonable care to protect them against the dangers of the attraction. *United Zinc & Chem. Co. v. Britt*, 258 U.S. 268, 66 L. Ed. 615, 42 S. Ct. 299, 36 A.L.R. 28; *Copfer v. Golden*, 135 Cal. App. 2d 623, 268 P.2d 90; *Ramsay v. Tuthill Bldg. Material Co.*, 295 Ill. 395, 129 N.E. 127, 36 A.L.R. 23; *Davoren v. Kansas City*, 308 Mo. 513, 273 S.W. 401, 40 A.L.R. 473; 62 Am. Jur. 2d 406.

[12]*Morison v. Moat*, 9 Hare 241, 20 L.J. (NS)513, 21 L.J. (NS)248.

[13]*Pollard v. Photographic Co.*, 40 Ch. Div. 345, 58 L.J. 251.

[14]*E.I. duPont de Nemours Powder Co. v. Masland*, 244 U.S. 100, 61 L. Ed. 1016, 37 S. Ct. 575 reversing the Circuit Court of Appeals, 3rd Circuit, in 224 F. 689.

[15]*Nat'l. Starch Prod., Inc., v. Polymer Indust., Inc.*, 273 App. Div. 732; *Rabinowitz & Co. v. Dasher*, 82 N.Y.S.2d 431, 437.

[16]*Smith v. Dravo*, 203 F.2d 369.

[17]*U.S. v. Coplan*, 185 F.2d 629, 28 A.L.R.2d 1041, *cert. denied* 342 U.S. 920, 96 L.Ed. 688, 72 S.Ct. 362; *Dorsey v. U.S.*, 174 F.2d 899, *cert. den.* 338 U.S. 950, 94 L. Ed. 586, 70 S. Ct. 479, 340 U.S. 878, 95 L. Ed. 639, 71 S. Ct. 116.

[18]*State v. Sutter*, 71 W. Va. 371, 76 S.E. 811; Restatement of Torts, § 119(c).

[19]An arrest is the taking, seizing, or detaining of the person of another (1) by taking or the putting on of hands; (2) or by any act that indicates an intention to take that person into custody and that subjects that person to the actual control and will of the one making the arrest; or (3) by the consent of the person to be arrested. *Comm. v. Kloch* (Pa. Super.) 327 A.2d 375; *Bey v. State* (1978, Fla. App. D. 3) 355 So. 2d 850; *U.S. v. Robinson* (1980, C.A. 5, Ga.) 625 F.2d 1211; *State v. Maxwell* (1978) 60 Ohio Misc. 1, 14 Ohio Op. 3d 44, 395 N.E.2d 531; *McAnnis v. State* (1980, Fla. App. D. 3) 386 So. 2d 1230.

[20]If the person arrested understands that he is in the power of the one arresting and submits in consequence, it is not necessary that there be an application of actual force, a manual touching of the body. *Lee v. State*, 45 Tex. Crim. 94, 74 S.W. 28; *Christ v. McDonald*, 152 Or. 494, 52 P.2d 655. If the party making the arrest professes to have the authority to do so and commands a person by virtue of that pretended authority to go with him, and is obeyed, the two going together in the direction pointed out by the one claiming the right to make an arrest, it is an arrest and imprisonment within the meaning of the law.

[21]A suit for false arrest or imprisonment is a proper cause of action where the aggrieved party is arrested without legal authority. *Colter v. Lower*, 35 Ind. 285; *Roberts v. Thomas*, 135 Ky. 63, 121 S.W. 961; *Coffman v. Shell Petroleum Corp.*, 228 Mo. App. 727, 71 S.W.2d 97; *Breck v. Blanchard*, 20 N.H. 323; *Kredit v. Ryan*, 68 S.D. 274, 1 N.W.2d 813.

[22]As a general rule, malice and lack of probable cause are not essential to a cause of action for false imprisonment. *Stallings v. Foster*, 119 Cal. App. 2d 614, 259 P.2d 1006; *Kredit v. Ryan*, 68 S.D, 274, 1 N.W.2d 813; *Smythe v. State*, 51 Tex. Crim. 408, 103 S.W. 899.

[23]It is generally held that if an officer arrests without a warrant solely at the request or instigation of a private person, the officer's authority does not protect that person and the latter's liability is determined as if he had made the arrest himself. *Porter v. Granech*, 136 Cal. App. 523, 29 P.2d 220; *Robinson v. Van Auken*, 190 Mass. 161, 76 N.E. 601; *Farnam v. Feeley*, 56 N.Y. 451; *Karner v. Stump*, 12 Tex. Civ. App. 460, 34 S.W. 656. The arrest by the officer must be so induced or instigated by the private person that the arrest was not made of the officer's own volition but to carry out the private person's request. *Grinnell v. Weston*, 95 App. Div. 454, 88 N.Y.S. 781; *Blackwood v. Cates*, 297 N.C. 163, 254 S.E.2d 7; *(Blue) Star Serv. Inc. v. McCurdy*, 36 Tenn. App. 1, 251 S.W.2d 139; *Davis v. Nadel*, 138 N.Y.S.2d 50.

[24]Security officers could search to recover goods in plain view, but any intrusion into defendant's person or effect is not authorized as incidental to a citizen's arrest or under the Merchants' Privilege Statute. *People v. Zelinski*, 594 P.2d 1000.

[25]384 U.S. 436, 16 L. Ed. 2d 694, 86 S. Ct. 1602, 10 A.L.R.3d 974

[26]*People v. Frank*, 52 Misc. 2d 266, 275 N.Y.S.2d 570.

[27]As a matter of public policy, individuals should be free to enjoy their reputations unimpaired by false and defamatory attacks. *Fairbanks Publ. Co. v. Francisco (Alaska)* 390 P.2d 784; *Short v. News-Journal Co.* (Del. Sup.) 212 A.2d 718; *Swede v. Passaic Daily News*, 30 N.J. 320, 153 A.2d 36; *Raineer's Dairies v. Raritan Valley Farms*, 19 N.J. 552, 117 A.2d 889; Restatement of Torts § 559. The gist of an action for libel or slander is injury to the plaintiff's reputation. Restatement of Torts § 559; *Altoona Clay Products, Inc. v. Dun & Bradstreet, Inc.* (C.A. 3, Pa.) 367 F.2d 625; *Gruschus v. Curtis Publ. Co.* (C.A. 10, N.M.) 342 F.2d 775; *Reed v. Real Detective Publ. Co.*, 63 Ariz. 294, 162 P.2d 133; *Van Horn v. Van Horn*, 5 Cal. App. 719, 91 P. 260; *Serge v. Parade Publ., Inc.*, 20 App. Div. 2d 338, 247 N.Y.S. 317.

[28]A libel is a malicious publication, expressed either in printing or writing, or by signs and pictures, tending either to blacken the memory of one who is dead, or the reputation of one who is alive, and expose the person to public hatred, contempt, or ridicule. 50 Am. Jur. 2d 514; *Time, Inc. v. Hill*, 385 U.S. 374, 17 L. Ed. 2d 456, 87 S. Ct. 534; *Cowper v. Vannier*, 20 Ill. App. 2d 499, 156 N.E.2d 761; *Lyman v. New England Newspaper Publ. Co.*, 286 Mass. 258, 190 N.E. 542, 92 A.L.R. 1124; *Collins v. Dispatch Publ. Co.*, 152 Pa. 187.

[29]Slander consists of the publication of defamatory matter by spoken words, transitory gestures, or by any form of communication other than those constituting libel. Restatement of Torts § 568(2); *Spence v. Johnson*, 142 Ga. 267, 82 S.E. 646; *Gambrill v. Schooley*, 93 Md. 48, 48 A. 730; *Little Stores v. Isenberg*, 26 Tenn. App. 357, 172 S.W.2d 13.

[30]Many cases establish the rule that it is actionable per se to falsely charge another, orally or in writing, with theft or larceny. *Holliday v. Great Atl. & Pac. Tea Co.* (C.A. 8 Mo.) 256 F.2d 297; *Conard v. Dillingham*, 23 Ariz. 596, 206 P. 166; *Wonson v. Sayward*, 13 Pick (Mass.) 402; *Jorgensen v. Pa. R. Co.*, 25 N.J. 541, 138 A.2d 24, 72 A.L.R. 2d 1415; *Laudati v. Stea*, 44 R.I. 303, 117 A. 422, 26 A.L.R. 450.

[31]*The Boston Globe*, May 10, 1983, pp. 21, 22.

[32]*Mullins v. Pine Manor College*, (Mass. 1983) 449 N.E.2d 331.

[33]*The New York Times*, March 29, 1992, p. 18.

Chapter 7

PERSONNEL SECURITY ISSUES

To think of personnel security issues only as they might apply to security department employees is comparable to looking at the tip of an iceberg and assuming that nothing more lies below what one sees. Put another way, to limit discussion of the subject to the security organization and exclude all other personnel considerations is unrealistic. This is true if for no other reason than the fact that it is people who cause security problems, and conversely, their cooperation is needed if programs to prevent security problems are to succeed. Furthermore, since employees should be seen as assets entitled to protection, particularly those who contribute most to the organization's success, more is involved in considering personnel security issues than merely thinking that good employee selection is the sole factor insofar as security is concerned. Therefore, in this chapter we consider various aspects of personnel matters with which security operations need to be not only concerned but also involved.

PREEMPLOYMENT SCREENING

In an ideal world employers would learn as much as they possibly could about those people whom they would like to hire. However, since we do not live in an ideal world it is necessary for employers to look for other ways in which to screen applicants for employment. Thus the responsibility for finding acceptable alternatives, and implementing effective preemployment screening programs, lies with an organization's human resources or personnel department.

118

True though this is, the fact remains that if the preemployment screening process is either inadequate, ineffective, or actually defective, whatever an errant employee does at work will affect the employer adversely. For instance, if an employee steals any assets, the organization for which he or she works is obviously affected. Less obvious is the fact that if one employee steals from another, and morale is affected, both the victim and employer suffer. The human resources or personnel manager who recognizes the potential problems that may result from defects in the preemployment screening process will also recognize the importance of calling upon security for assistance or advice. Neither are security directors or managers prevented from making helpful suggestions. On the contrary, since problems caused through lax personnel practices may well become matters requiring direct security department involvement, they should let their personnel department counterparts have the benefit of any ideas they may have for improved preemployment procedures. However, security directors also need to understand that no matter how close the cooperation with human resources, or how effective security's help may be, preemployment screening is not primarily a security function, nor should it be. With this in mind, one necessarily wonders what options are available to human resources departments in terms of the screening process, and how security can help.

A question that all employers would like applicants to answer deals with their possible criminal histories. As noted in Chapter 6, although it is permissible for prospective employers to ask whether applicants have ever been convicted of felonies or serious misdemeanors, they cannot ask about mere arrests for crimes. This, coupled with the fact that in many states criminal history information is not readily available to private persons or organizations, can create potentially serious problems for an employer. True, a prospective employer might ask applicants to submit a copy of their criminal histories, yet attempts to pry into an applicant's past for evidence of criminality may lead to charges of discrimination or invasion of privacy. On the other hand, failing to at least attempt to find out whether applicants had criminal histories prior to the time of their employment could also result in third-party litigation if an employee with a criminal history commits a crime against someone in the course of the person's employment.

Of course, the ability to obtain such data would not necessarily assure a prospective employer that an applicant had no criminal history. For example, suppose that a prospective employer in Nebraska was either able to ask a central repository whether a particular applicant had a criminal record, or asked an applicant to submit a copy of his or her criminal history. Inasmuch as the only positive means of identification are fingerprints, it is highly unlikely that the Nebraska authorities would even try to answer the employer's question without first getting a set of the applicant's fingerprints. Assume further that in this situation there was no information, with or without fingerprints. Since we live in such a highly mobile society, this would not necessarily mean that the person did not have a record in another state, neighboring or otherwise.

Thus the only way for an employer to have any reasonable degree of assurance that an applicant had no criminal history anywhere in the United States would involve sending the person's fingerprints and other identifying data to the Federal Bureau of Investigation's Identification Division for a search. Even if the FBI were authorized to honor such a request, it would be a costly and time-consuming undertaking for both the prospective employer and the FBI. At the same time, legal issues might be raised as to the propriety of such an inquiry. For example, unless the prospective employer could show a direct relationship between the job and an applicant's criminal history, such as one or more convictions for embezzlement by a person wanting a job as a bank teller, it is conceivable that the failure to hire because of a criminal history could result in a charge of discrimination against the prospective employer.

Despite this, concerns about privacy or the inability to have access to criminal histories does not excuse any organization's failure to at least make a good-faith effort to screen applicants properly. How can this be done? The answer does not necessarily lie in having all employees covered by fidelity bonds, or going to the expense of having the security department or an outside agency conduct detailed background investigations. This does not mean that no employees need bonding or that background investigations are never justified. Instead, it recognizes the reality that fidelity bonds do not guarantee an employee's honesty, nor are all applicants considered for positions of such sensitivity as to justify the time and cost that would be involved in subjecting them to background investigations.

The first step, and one of primary importance to the preemployment screening process, is the way in which applicants complete applications for employment, and the way in which they are examined by the personnel or human resources department. In some cases it is not unusual for completed applications almost to send a signal to interviewers cautioning them to be wary of the applicant. Neither is it unusual for interviewers either to overlook or to ignore defects in applications which at least should alert them to the fact that additional questions need to be asked of the applicant. If this opportunity is missed, it may result in hiring a person who eventually will prove troublesome.

Perhaps one or two illustrations will prove helpful. One case involved the employment of a person as a security manager who subsequently was a prime suspect in a case involving the theft of gold from the employer. The other concerned a service employee's failure to report for work because he was in custody, charged with being a party to an armed robbery.

In the first example the security manager was hired on the basis of his background in both policing and security. No attention was paid to, nor were any questions asked about, the fact that when he left policing because of an alleged job-related disability, he reportedly was in almost constant need of pain medication, there were unexplained extended gaps of time between each job subsequently held, and he never had a job that lasted for more than a few months. Furthermore, in each of those jobs he either had less responsibility or made less money than he had in his previous position. Whether or not he was guilty of the larceny, proper evaluation of his application might well have prevented his being offered the job of security manager in the first place.

As for the second illustration, although the employee's application showed a three-year period for which he listed no activity whatsoever in terms of either schooling or employment, the personnel interviewer made no effort to find out what, if anything, the person had done during that time. Asking the person what he had been doing during those three years, or where he had been, might have brought to light the fact that he had been in prison after having been convicted of robbery.

Under no circumstances should applicants be asked any questions that are in violation of law or which might be used to discriminate against a person. However, respect for the law and privacy do not excuse a failure to examine an application carefully and ask applicants questions that will clarify what they have written. In the first illustration above there were questions that obviously needed to be asked of both the applicant and former employers which were not asked. In the second example, there would have been nothing improper in asking for an explanation for the three years left blank on the application. True, the applicant might not have given a truthful answer, but at least personnel would have done its job properly.

A second critical part of the process concerns the importance of contacting both former employers and references. Again, fear of violating one's privacy is no excuse for not confirming prior employment, dates, job title, and salary. If former employers will not say why the applicant left because they fear possible litigation, at least they should be asked whether they would consider rehiring the person. The slightest hesitation in answering this question can be a signal in itself telling the caller that perhaps the applicant was an unsatisfactory employee.

With regard to references, human resources personnel often will not contact an applicant's personal references. The assumption is that no applicant will list as a personal reference anyone who might say anything unfavorable. This is true, yet there are times when personal references may provide information that is quite favorable from their point of view, yet it also might indicate to a prospective employer that the applicant may have certain weaknesses that could prove troublesome and which need to be considered before a job offer is made. For those under consideration for highly sensitive positions, it may also be worthwhile to contact neighbors.

For instance, suppose that an applicant has applied for a position as a purchasing manager. When personal references or neighbors are contacted, they volunteer information about the person's life-style which may suggest that the applicant is living well beyond his or her means. Bearing in mind the opportunities that purchasing employees have for either soliciting or accepting kickbacks from vendors, an effort certainly should be made to try to determine the source of the person's wealth before offering employment as a purchasing manager.

A company faced with precisely such a situation failed to look into the matter. It subsequently was very embarrassed when a vendor called the manager of the plant where the purchasing manager was employed to complain about what it called "extortion." Only thereafter did the employer learn that this problem could be been avoided altogether if the personnel representative had not ignored comments made by two personal references who had merely expressed envy about the types of vacations which their friend had been able to take. The vacations to which they referred, in relation to what the person had been paid by previous employers, at least should have aroused the personnel representative's curiosity.

If preemployment screening is not a primary security function, the obvious question is: What can security directors do to help their personnel department counterparts? However, before answering that question there is need to remember what not to do. First, they should not try to help by telling human resources managers just how they and their staffs should operate. That may well prove to be counterproductive, and understandably so. Instead, as pointed out in earlier chapters, since they have learned how personnel representatives handle applications and applicants, they need only suggest possible ways which might prove helpful in that respect. This approach is much more acceptable, and it is one that can be employed by security managers using as their entrée what they themselves have learned about fact-finding techniques based on their investigative work.

Naturally, the first thing is to make certain that all applications are complete in every respect. There should not be any breaks in time, regardless of where the person was or what he or she might have been doing during that period. If there is a question on the application about felony convictions, it should be answered. Under the heading of employment history, well-thought-out application forms will ask not only for former employers' names and addresses, but also for dates of employment, job titles, beginning and ending salaries, supervisors' names, and the reasons for leaving. Again, each item should be answered by the applicant. The names, addresses, telephone numbers, and positions of personal references should be noted, along with the number of years that they have known the applicant.

Whether the application has been received by mail or is presented in person, it should be reviewed carefully to make certain that it has been completed in detail. If accompanied by an applicant's résumé, the résumé and application should be closely examined for possible discrepancies. Furthermore, if there are unanswered questions on the application, the applicant should be asked to explain them. In the event that academic credentials are required for any position, transcripts offered by applicants should be refused. Instead, they should be told that official grade transcripts must be sent directly to the prospective employer by the college or university registrar's office.

In examining applications, with or without résumés, what are some of the things for which human resources representatives should be alert over and above complete data? Perhaps this question is best answered by using an illustration. A manufacturer of consumer goods advertised for an office manager. The application of the person who was hired, completed in every respect, on first reading appeared to indicate that she would be ideally suited for the position. She even listed a clergyman among her personal references. The personnel manager, senior vice president, and chief executive officer all agreed that she was the person for the job.

Among her responsibilities was the administration of the prize program for qualified sales personnel; some prizes were quite expensive. Six months after she started work the controller began to get calls from the companies from which the prizes were purchased asking why, for the first time, they had not been paid. The controller had no explanation, inasmuch as the checks had been made out for each supplier upon the office manager's presentation of approved invoices. However, he recalled that in each instance she asked that the check be given to her so that she could mail it to the vendors. The ensuing investigation revealed that she had opened a bank account under a fictitious name, and had endorsed and deposited all the checks in that account for her own use.

It was only then that those who had approved of her being hired regretted having ignored the advice of an experienced security consultant to whom they had shown the application before making the hiring decision. He noted several things about the application which caused him to suggest that they exercise caution and not offer employment before contacting previous employers and personal references. Among the items that prompted him to urge care were:

1. Although the application was completed in every respect, it also indicated that she changed jobs frequently. According to the information she herself provided, these changes occurred about every 12 to 18 months.

2. The reasons given for the frequent changes were "better opportunities." If job titles alone were the criteria used by the applicant, these statements appeared to be true. However, with each change her starting salary was less than it had been in the job she left.

3. In applying for the office manager's position, not only was the applicant willing to accept a lower beginning salary than she claimed to have been making in the job she was leaving, but the location of the new job would make commuting to work both more difficult and more time consuming.

4. Based on her claimed academic credentials, she was overqualified for all but her first two jobs.

The investigation which followed the discovery of her illegal activities revealed that she had been fired from all but her first two jobs because of suspected embezzlement or larceny. None of her employers had ever filed a criminal complaint against her, preferring instead to allow her to make restitution. She had only one of the two college degrees which she claimed, and it was not from the university listed on her application.

Equally noteworthy was the fact that the clergyman whose name she gave as a personal reference was not a personal reference; he was another of her victims. Asked why under the circumstances she dared to use his name, she said she knew from past experience that rarely were personal references contacted, and she felt that using a clergyman as a personal reference made her seem even more trustworthy when applying for a position involving responsibility.

The examples used above consist of situations that might have been avoided if human resources personnel had been more attentive and inquisitive. Many more could be cited. They proved not only to be embarrassing but also to be costly to the victimized employers, who in addition to the losses suffered (even if covered by insurance) again had to go to the expense of recruiting, this time properly screening, hiring, and training replacements. As has been pointed out in earlier chapters, security managers need to learn how other departments of their organization function. Perhaps if that had been done in these cases, and they had succeeded in establishing a close working relationship with the human resources department, some of these difficulties could have been avoided. However, one thing is clear. Although security has no direct involvement with preemployment screening, there assuredly is a very direct connection between preemployment screening practices and the security problems that can result if those practices are either nonexistent or defective.

EMPLOYEE ORIENTATION AND EDUCATION

The importance of proper training for security personnel, and how such training benefits employers, was discussed in Chapters 3 and 5. Nevertheless, as important as that training is, it must be understood by both security directors and their organizations' executives that security department employees alone cannot provide the level of protection required to safeguard and conserve all assets properly. Successful security programs are team efforts that need more than the support of executives and the involvement of line managers and supervisors. Such programs call for the cooperation and understanding of all employees, neither of which can or should be taken for granted. Employees in general have to understand why there is a security program, and how they, as well as their employers, can benefit from such a program.

To do this, organizations have to consider security's role in both employee orientation and ongoing educational efforts. Orientation sessions, usually held the first day of work to acquaint new employees with their surroundings, tend to focus on such things as when employees are paid, paid holidays, working hours, vacation policies, and fringe benefits. Some do not even mention the fact that the organization has a security program; in others, personnel representatives mention security in passing.

The most logical time to make employees aware of the existence of a security program is during the new-employee orientation sessions. The security part of the orientation is best given by a representative of the security department, preferably the security manager, not by human resources personnel. A proven method is either to have an audiovisual presentation or to show a film, followed by a brief discussion of the overall security program with time for the new employees to ask questions. During the discussion the security manager obviously wants to speak about security's importance to the organization. However, it is important to let employees know how a good program that benefits the employer also benefits them. This is not a detailed recitation of all the security policies and procedures; it is a general outline of the ground rules. The objective is to help employees understand how they can contribute to the security program's success.

In terms of both new-employee orientation efforts and other forms of security-related education, a pitfall that should be avoided is presenting everything in terms to which average employees find it hard to relate. For instance, an excellent vehicle for some forms of education, and certainly for helping to maintain security awareness, is an organization's newsletter or comparable form of internal communication. To illustrate further, telling employees that unexplained losses for a specified period represent a percentage of sales is not particularly helpful as a security message. On sales of $10 million, with losses of 3 percent, the employer's loss would be $300,000. Yet many employees, if not most, would find it hard to understand how this could affect them since everything has been expressed solely in terms of sales and losses. On the other hand, telling them that the $300,000 loss was equal to a given number of jobs or to certain fringe benefits would make it easier for the average employee to understand the problem's seriousness.

Of course, other forms of education should not be neglected or overlooked. For example, if well conceived, the audiovisual or film presentations used for new-employee orientation can be used for periodic refresher programs. Managers can be asked to discuss certain aspects of security at department meetings, or to invite security department representatives to do so. Other illustrations may also be helpful. A large company regularly held formal training programs for new or newly promoted supervisors and managers. For each program, blocks of time were set aside for the corporate security director to provide instruction on what they could and should do to help protect and conserve assets. In another company the security director was invited to the organization's annual joint conference of all its sales and service managers to help educate them in how to implement the organization's security policies and procedures. In yet another firm, the corporate security director was asked by his counterpart in purchasing to train purchasing managers in how to implement a new policy for the protection of proprietary information to make certain that there were no breaches of security when dealing with third-party vendors who supplied various items to the employer.

Suitably designed posters can also be used to help educate employees about the importance of various aspects of security. The challenge facing security directors in this regard is in designing posters whose appearance and message will be equally acceptable to employees at the top, middle, and bottom levels of the organization. In other words, they should not be so simple as to be laughed at by senior management, but neither should they be so complicated that lower-level personnel will not understand the message.

From the standpoint of employee education it is also important to remember that the effort must be repeated. Whether in the form of posters, audiovisual or film presentations, or discussions at meetings, a one-time exposure will not do much to educate personnel about security's importance and the importance of their individual contributions to the success of the loss prevention program. In other words, new-employee orientation should not be seen as the one and only time when personnel generally learn something about an employer's programs for the protection and conservation of its assets. The subject is one of which employees need to be reminded with some degree of regularity, and with cooperative, involved line managers and supervisors, this can be done without necessarily requiring the participation of members of the security department. In fact, not infrequently, employees can be made even more conscious of security's importance when the message is delivered by their immediate superiors instead of by security personnel, since they presumably have no special reason for trying to "sell" security to those who work for them.

EMPLOYEE IDENTIFICATION

Although no one can deny that employee identification is a personnel security issue, the question is not necessarily who is responsible for issuing such identification, but rather, one of having employees both identified and identifiable. For most organizations the principal form of identification is the photo identification badge prepared, issued, and controlled by the security department. In others, the badge is the domain of the human resources department. Regardless, it should be understood that badges are not the only form of identification used. Other popular forms of identification used by some businesses and institutions are uniforms and name tags, either in addition to or in lieu of photo identification badges.

Even in organizations that function in a relatively closed environment, such as a research and development operation or a manufacturing plant, which have few if any visitors, the fact remains that employee identification is needed. This is not just a matter of better controlled access to a facility. It also relates to controls within a building because an effective security program is not feasible if employees assume that because of their employment, they are automatically entitled to enter any and all areas of the employing organization, no matter where they are or what purpose they serve.

Just as organizations need to impose limits or restrictions on which employees may have access to sensitive information, so should limits be placed on specific locations or areas in terms of employee access. For instance, in hotels or medical centers there is no real justification for housekeepers to be in food preparation areas, retail salespersons working in clothing departments should not be allowed in fine jewelry department stockrooms, and manufacturing production employees have no reason to enter shipping, research, or finished goods areas. Nevertheless, without a suitable form of identification they may be inclined to do so. Equally important is the likelihood of their succeeding if supervisory or managerial personnel cannot easily or readily determine whether unauthorized persons are in their respective areas because of a lack of identification. This obviously can result in a range of problems with which security managers in particular are concerned. At the same time, it can lead to employees wasting time and to needless disruptions that can affect productivity, quality, and service.

In some types of businesses or institutions it is also important for members of the general public to be able to identify employees other than security personnel. Therefore, whether to require employees to wear their badges at all times while on the premises, or merely to insist on their being shown to gain access to a facility, is a management decision that often is influenced by the type of organization involved. Employee identification can be quite helpful to retail customers in search of salespeople; it is especially useful in hotels and medical centers. However, in the latter two types of organizations, the fact that personnel may wear uniforms, and even name tags, does not always offer guests or patients the level of assurance that they need when dealing with staff.

For example, in most hotels and medical centers there is nothing particularly unique or distinguishable about engineering or housekeeping department uniforms. Their unauthorized duplication is neither difficult nor cost prohibitive. What assurance do hotel guests have that a person who knocks on their door and says that he or she is the maid or from engineering really is an authorized employee of the hotel? When someone in a white uniform, with or without a name tag, tells a mother holding a newborn infant that he or she has come to return the baby to the nursery, how does the mother know if that person is a nurse or a kidnapper?

Photo identification badges are not an absolute guarantee that the badge is authentic, even when color coded, but they are among the more reliable means of visual identification. They can be used by employees to help them recognize other employees. They are also useful to the general public when they feel in need of assurance that persons with whom they are in contact, or upon whom they are relying, are in fact who they profess to be.

There are ways in which to increase the reliability factor when photo identification badges are used. Regardless of whether such badges are issued by an organization's security or human resources department, certain safeguards need to be put in place and adhered to. First, since the unauthorized duplication of any badge that has been designed thoughtfully and properly and made with the right kind of equipment can be both difficult and expensive, it is imperative that all forms of validation and blank badge stock be secured at all times. In addition, badges should have numbers for accountability; employees' payroll numbers are often used for this purpose.

Employees should sign receipts for their badges, and all badges should be returned to the employer when employment is terminated, regardless of the reason. If color coding is used in connection with badges and employees are assigned new duties that involve a change of code, the old badges should be recovered and destroyed and new badges should be issued. In the event that an employee reports a lost or stolen badge, security personnel at all access control points should be alerted, to minimize the risk of an unauthorized entry. If identification badges are used in connection with computerized access control systems, all badges of terminated personnel and all reported lost or stolen must be deleted from the system immediately.

EMPLOYEE PARKING

Not all businesses or institutions provide employee parking. For those who do, however, there are four principal issues that security managers need to address: controlling access to the parking facilities, the safety of persons who use those facilities, the protection of parked vehicles, and compliance with the organization's parking policies.

In some cases access control is a factor because there simply are not enough spaces to accommodate everyone who would like to drive to work. In others, space is not necessarily a problem, but parking by trespassers may be. For example, during 1956–1961 an east coast academic institution provided free parking in several lots for faculty, staff, and students. There were between 2500 and 3000 spaces; faculty, staff, and students who drove to the campus daily numbered approximately 7500. Until reassigned to a newly appointed security manager, parking was the province of the buildings and grounds department. Their philosophy was that parking permits were nothing more than a "hunting license": for all practical purposes there was no limit on the number of permits, in the form of decals, issued. The problem was complicated by the fact that only the three largest lots were policed, and since the school was in an urban area, there was nothing to prevent trespassers from parking in the lots while shopping or working in the neighborhood.

The competition for space, and the way in which the parking program had been handled, posed a significant public relations problem when the decision was made to have security become responsible for parking administration. The security manager was of the opinion that those to whom decals were issued should have at least a reasonable chance of finding a parking space. Among the things done were the following:

1. A survey made of the existing facilities indicated that realigning and restriping the spaces in the three largest lots into separate sections for compact and full-sized automobiles would increase capacity by an average of 20 percent.
2. There was an incentive for carpooling, but the plan precluded all vehicles in the pool from being driven to the campus on the same day.
3. Department heads were given the responsibility for determining to which members of their departments decals would be issued.
4. Security personnel continued to control access to the three principal lots; physical access controls were installed for the remaining, smaller lots.

The protection of employees who use an organization's parking facilities, as well as of their vehicles, is but another security issue related to employee parking. Depending on jurisdiction, there may be legal differences between what an employer owes its employees in terms of their personal safety as distinguished from what might be owed with regard to protecting their vehicles and contents. The fact remains, however, that whether any legal duty is or is not owed to employees, morale, employee relations, and even reputation can be adversely affected if at least a reasonable amount of security is not provided.

Imagine the impact on morale, employee relations, and an organization's reputation in the community if an employee is the victim of a robbery, assault, or homicide in an unprotected parking lot or garage. On the other hand, reputation may not suffer if employees find that their vehicles have been vandalized, stripped, broken into, or stolen while parked in an unprotected facility, but morale and employee relations surely will. If employees are victimized in this way with any frequency, with morale and relations adversely affected, the probability of both turnover and an impact on productivity cannot be ignored.

Organizations that provide employee parking, even when there is sufficient space and trespassers are not a major problem, still need to have policies governing the use of those facilities and must ensure compliance with those policies. As an example, at a large manufacturer's corporate headquarters a number of spaces for the use of visitors were set aside. The company's policy was that no employees were allowed to park in visitors' spaces. Nevertheless, there were times when some employees, including some corporate officers or employees at headquarters from outlying locations, would park in the visitors' area. To ensure compliance, the policy also stated that a violator's car would be towed at the owner's expense. On those occasions when the policy was violated by any employee, including the executive vice president, automobiles were towed. The same was true whenever vehicles were parked in either fire lanes or handicapped spaces.

This is not to say that there are no organizations that provide reserved parking for executives. That, of course, is also a matter of policy. However, having policies that are not enforced is tantamount to having no policies at all. This is no less true when the issue relates to employee parking. For optimum effect, policy compliance, regardless of what that policy may be, must be required of all personnel, and enforcement needs to be applied objectively and uniformly.

CONFLICTS OF INTEREST

Another personnel security issue with which security managers are involved and with which they need to be concerned relates to conflicts of interest that may arise in different ways and under different circumstances. Three illustrations may help to clarify some of these differences. In one, a purchasing manager places orders on behalf of his or her employer with a business in which he or she, or a member of his or her immediate family, has an interest and from which the purchasing manager personally will gain or otherwise benefit financially. In another, an employee has a personal interest in or provides help to an organization that is in competition with his or her employer. On occasion there are also employees who have a noncompeting business of their own for which they work, but they do so on their employer's time and using the employer's resources.

That conflicts of interest per se are not necessarily crimes does not mean that they cannot be both costly and embarrassing to employers. There is an assumption that when a person accepts a position with an organization, he or she does so with the understanding that they will devote all of their working hours, and attention, to furthering the employing organization's best interests. Certainly, they are not expected to do anything that will in any way be harmful to the employer. True, employers may well have a cause of action in a civil court against employees who have conflicting interests, but the fact remains that having to resort to a lawsuit suggests the likelihood that no effective preventive measures were in place to begin with.

To help minimize conflict-of-interest problems from arising in the first place, all new employees should be required to sign agreements dealing not only with actual conflicts of interest but with anything that gives the appearance of such a conflict. Since the agreement has legal standing, it is best prepared by the law department. By the same token, as a matter to be disposed of during new-employee orientation, the agreement's purpose and the employer's policies for dealing with those who do not comply logically are items that should be handled by the human resources or personnel department. Therefore, although preventing conflicts of interest is a personnel security issue of legitimate concern to security, the fact remains that it is not one which is or should be considered within the exclusive province of the security department; neither should any employer expect it to be. Rather it is a responsibility that security departments share, or should share, with the employer's human resources and law departments.

With this in mind, what is or should be security's role? Should it be limited to investigating suspected policy violations, or is there room for involvement in other ways? No one would question the propriety of security looking into allegations of conflicting interests on the part of employees and objectively gathering and preserving evidence for use by the law and human resources departments. However, based on security's experience, the director or manager may be able to alert the law and personnel departments to those areas where the greatest risks exist, and he or she may also be in an excellent position to help educate employees generally, and department heads particularly, about the dangers and telltale signs of possible conflicts of interest. Of course, despite the fact that security directors would like to be able to assure their employers that measures to prevent conflicts of interest can be put in place, experience has shown that this is an unrealistic expectation.

The following illustrates not only an investigation involving a conflict of interest, but also how various departments in an organization in which security was integrated rather than isolated worked together under the corporate security director's guidance and direction. The victim was a multinational Fortune 300 corporation; employees in four different countries and at corporate headquarters were suspected of involvement.

A Far East Regional internal audit manager on a routine visit to an office in one of the four countries found a questionable-looking purchase order. The response to his question about it seemed to implicate both a local employee and one at the regional headquarters. Upon returning to regional headquarters he questioned the named employee, who admitted his role and implicated employees in two other countries. The internal audit manager then called the corporate director of internal audit, who immediately advised the corporate security director. Since all of those implicated had access to computer terminals, the corporate security director arranged through his counterpart in management information systems to have the computer files of all of the known suspects "dumped" and sent directly to him. He then found evidence implicating a corporate headquarters employee. Because time was of the essence for various reasons, including the need to develop and preserve evidence, and the distance from corporate headquarters was so great, he asked the company's Far East Regional attorney to assist with the overseas aspect of the investigation while he concentrated on the one at corporate headquarters and coordinating the inquiry. With the investigation's completion and admissions of guilt by all of the parties involved, and because of the level of some of the participants, the corporate headquarters personnel department was informed of the outcome and it then became involved in the administrative and disciplinary action taken.

While the entire organization learned an important lesson from the foregoing in terms of how to improve the administration and oversight of international operations, this case also shows how invaluable good interdepartmental relations can be to a successful security program. Without the prompt and unquestioned assistance of the internal audit, legal, and personnel departments, the problem might never have been discovered, or once discovered, it might have been too late insofar as obtaining evidence of participation was concerned. Without such evidence, any action by the company to protect itself would have been almost impossible.

WHITE-COLLAR CRIME

Closely related to, but different from conflicts of interest, is the subject of white-collar crime. Although both offenses can be harmful to employers in a variety of ways, unlike conflicts of interest, white-collar crimes are precisely that—crimes.

An early definition of white-collar crime, offered by Edwin H. Sutherland, would be considered quite narrow by today's standards. He described such activity as "a crime committed by a person of respectability and high social status in the course of his occupation."[1] Neither high social status nor an offender's sex are now considered essential characteristics of a white-collar criminal, although socially prominent persons do commit white-collar crimes. However, being a person of apparent respectability and committing the offense in the course of one's employment remain valid parts of the definition.

It is precisely because white-collar crimes are criminal offenses that they may be prosecuted, and often are. In the early and middle 1980s there were occasions when corporate officers were prosecuted, some by the federal government and others by state governments, for their participation in crimes that would satisfy Sutherland's white-collar crime definition. In the late 1980s and early 1990s, others, also considered respectable and of high social status, were prosecuted by the federal government, found guilty, and jailed for their involvement in "insider trading" schemes.

Although many of these cases have received widespread publicity because of the people involved, there are countless other prosecutions involving employees who do not necessarily satisfy the "high social status" characteristic but who have, nonetheless, committed white-collar crimes. They are persons of respectability who have committed offenses during the course of their employment.

For instance, a purchasing employee who asks for or accepts a bribe for an order, or a salesperson who offers a bribe in order to get one, may be guilty of commercial bribery. Bookkeepers who embezzle from their employers are white-collar criminals. The same can be said of bank employees who set up dummy bank accounts, then through the use of computer technology, transfer funds from customers' accounts to their own. Employees who sell proprietary information to their employer's competitors are guilty of white-collar crimes.

Here, as with other aspects of an organization's operations, knowledgeable security directors and managers can work closely with their employers' legal and human resources departments in an effort to prevent white-collar crimes from occurring. This, of course, is the ideal solution to the problem. Nevertheless, there is always the risk that someone will conclude that he or she either is too clever to get caught, or occupies a position within the organization which, in the person's opinion, gives them some form of immunity. However, when any crime, white collar or otherwise, has been committed or is suspected, security directors are obliged to look into the matter.

On such occasions security directors who have to deal with white-collar crime may find themselves on the horns of a dilemma. They have no great difficulty in proceeding with an investigation if the known or suspected employee is a person whose position is below executive level. However, they may well have a real problem when they are confronted with a white-collar crime involving a corporate officer. This puts the security director in the awkward position of having to deal with more than the crime itself; he or she now has to deal with ethical and moral questions. To do the right thing by proceeding with the inquiry, and when appropriate bringing it to the attention of other corporate officers, possibly members of the board of directors, and to the proper authorities, may not always be appreciated by one's superiors. In fact, this might result in loss of the job.

Some would argue that under such circumstances the only ethical and moral course of action would be to proceed regardless of the cost. Although correct in principle, in our rather complicated world, this answer may be too simplistic. Suppose that the security director has a family to support. Is an ethical and moral obligation owed to them? If so, to which set of ethical and moral values should a security director give higher priority? Although there are no easy answers to such questions, the fact remains that they cannot be ignored. Adding to the difficulty is the realization of the effect that prosecution can have on former associates, now turned criminal, and the knowledge that white-collar criminals' personal backgrounds may be such that they do not lend themselves readily to "rehabilitation."

EXECUTIVE PROTECTION

The *New York Times* for June 24, 1992, had an article captioned "Businesses Take Steps to Prevent Kidnappings."[2] Among other things, it cited the April 29, 1992, kidnapping of Sidney J. Reso, an Exxon executive, to whose body the authorities subsequently were taken by one of the kidnappers. It also noted some of the precautions being taken by corporations and executives in an effort to minimize the risk of kidnapping. This article, and the Reso incident, served to illustrate the vulnerability of organizational executives and the need for their security directors to try to protect them.

Not mentioned, however, were three challenges that security directors occasionally must face in discharging their duties in the executive protection field. One is an executive's lack of interest in the subject, another is the importance of extending executive protection to families as well as to the executives themselves, and a third is ego. Illustrations may be helpful.

A multinational corporation's newly hired security director was cautioned by his immediate superior during his first day on the job against even mentioning the words *executive protection* to the company president. Despite a rather high profile, the latter reportedly refused to believe that anyone would think him to be important enough to consider kidnapping. Furthermore, much later the security director's suggestion that there be a company policy prohibiting large numbers of key executives from traveling together on the same aircraft was rejected by the president, who refused to recognize the impact that the loss of a number of key personnel might have on the organization's ability to survive.

One of the greatest challenges for security directors insofar as executive protection is concerned will arise when they have to confront an executive who simply is not interested in the subject and does not even want to discuss it. If ever there was a need for security directors to use their sales skills to the fullest, this is it. They need to be able to convince disinterested executives of the subject's importance not only to themselves, but also to their families and the organizations for which they are responsible.

From time to time security directors will encounter executives who will admit a need for executive protection and be cooperative, yet either fail to take into account the importance of extending protection to their families or hesitate to do so for fear of frightening family members, particularly children. An unwillingness to provide protection in such cases is more than unrealistic; it suggests naivete on the executive's part. A person or group who want something of importance from an organization, whether in the form of cash or the performance of an act by that organization, might easily rationalize that holding a wife or children hostage would bring far quicker results than kidnapping the executive. Once again, when security directors encounter reluctance on the part of executives to extend protection to their families, they must call into play all of their skills as salespersons in the hope that they can convince executives of the need to protect their families as well as themselves.

Executive ego will also challenge security directors on occasion. Overcoming this particular type of problem may be even more difficult in some respects than dealing with executive protection per se or protection for families. The more progress one makes moving up the executive ladder, the greater the number of perquisites to which one becomes entitled. A luxurious office and one or more private secretaries aside, this often includes an expensive, chauffeur-driven, or otherwise attention-grabbing automobile, perhaps with vanity license plates; air travel in first class or possibly by company or chartered aircraft; and suites in the best hotels. Furthermore, the higher the position, the greater the likelihood of being interviewed or photographed by the media or of becoming known to members of the general public through other means.

As an example, at one time the president of a large hotel chain not only was given a driver but also a silver gray and black Mercedes kept spotlessly clean by the driver. Its license plate consisted of the letters by which people generally referred to the company. In addition, when at corporate headquarters, the president was a creature of habit in terms of his departure times from both home and office and routes taken between the two. Two other factors further complicated matters insofar as his protection was concerned: his photograph and a personal message appeared in every copy of the chain's directory of hotels, one of which could be found in every room in every hotel; and the chain was a subsidiary of a much larger organization whose political activities attracted a good deal of unfavorable publicity.

These considerations, which gave him a high profile, also increased his vulnerability as a potential kidnap victim. Security directors, on the other hand, would much prefer to see the executives for whose protection they are responsible maintain a low profile. Fortunately, in this particular illustration the chain's president did not allow his ego to overrule his common sense. Once the security director explained how by altering his habits and modifying his life-style the president could enhance his personal safety, and that by doing so he, his family, and the company all would benefit, he readily agreed to the changes recommended.

Of course, it is also important to remember that executive protection is not confined to their personal safety while at work or away from home on business. To provide optimum protection for executives and their families, it may also be necessary to consider the security of their homes. Since one expects executives to be well paid and to live accordingly, it is shortsighted for security directors to think only in terms of kidnapping or extortion. A burglary or an armed robbery can be a traumatic experience for all the victims and leave them with the feeling that they have been violated. Such an experience can be particularly unnerving to the family of an executive whose job involves considerable business travel. Therefore, in providing executives with a complete approach to protection, security directors cannot afford to ignore the installation of home security systems.

Without doubt, one of the many important roles that security directors must fill for their employers involves the safeguarding of the organization's executives. Nevertheless, no matter how much they want to do a good job in this regard, or how conscientious they are in carrying out their duties and responsibilities, they must realize that in the final analysis the entire question of executive protection rests not in their hands but in the hands of those to be protected. Put another way, security directors have to accept the fact that executives can be protected only to the extent to which they are willing to accept protection.

CRISIS MANAGEMENT

Closely allied to the subject of executive protection is the matter of crisis management. Even some major corporations fail to appreciate the fact that they could be confronted with a crisis in the event that something befell one or more of their key personnel. Suppose, for instance, that one or more executives were seriously injured or killed in an accident, and they would be unable to function in their normal roles for an extended period of time. Or imagine getting a demand for several million dollars in ransom to rescue a kidnapped board chairman or company president.

Incidents of this sort can and do happen. When they do, the choices are possibly to risk the very existence of the organization by virtue of administrative and operational paralysis, or to have a crisis management plan and team in place capable of continuing the business with little obvious disruption or affect. It is unlikely than anyone would deny that the latter is the preferable choice, yet the former may come to pass because those who normally control an organization simply cannot conceive of a time when they personally would not be able to make all of the major decisions.

No organization wants to have to deal with a true crisis based on the loss, temporarily or otherwise, of key personnel. Nevertheless, those which are among the best managed do not ignore the possibility that they might have to, and they prepare and plan accordingly.

They understand that in a crisis, decisions have to be made, emergency funds may have to be made available, the news media and victims' families have to be dealt with, and close and effective liaison will have to be established and maintained with the public safety authorities.

In fact, the work being done by the authorities may in some ways influence some of the decisions that have to be made by the crisis management team. It is only natural, therefore, that an organization's security director or manager be a member of any crisis management team, and that he or she will play an important role should the team be activated. Neither is it uncommon for security directors or managers to be called upon by their employer's executives and asked for guidance in organizing a crisis management team both in terms of its composition and the functions to be performed by each team member.

It should be noted that there are organizations that are willing to pay the premiums for insurance coverage to help them deal with certain types of crises, primarily cases involving either the kidnapping of key personnel or their families, or extortion. Insofar as this can be done, insurers will usually require that the insured business or institution have a crisis management team and plan in place, and that the existence of such coverage is not disclosed beyond a very few key personnel. To maintain insurance coverage for this purpose can be helpful, especially if the crisis is one that involves a demand for a large sum of money, such as the $18.5 million ransom demanded by the kidnappers of Exxon executive Sidney J. Reso, mentioned earlier, or extortion. Nevertheless, as was pointed out in Chapters 5 and 6 in discussing risk management and insurance considerations in security programming, important though insurance may be, coverage by itself will not prevent problems from arising. Consequently, despite whatever insurance they may carry, it behooves businesses and institutions to plan for crises and be organized to cope with them should they occur, at the same time hoping that activation of the crisis management team and plan will never be necessary.

PROTECTING EMPLOYEES IN GENERAL

Executive protection, and the accompanying need for a crisis management program, obviously are of great importance to any organization. What should be of equal importance to any business or institution is the need to provide protection to those employees who are not in the executive category. In previous chapters it has been said that security is responsible for the protection and conservation of all of an employer's assets, and it was noted that among those assets are an organization's employees. Although they do not require the same types of protection afforded to executives, the fact remains that they, and what few items of personal property they may elect to keep at work, need to be safe.

Good employee morale in all likelihood will result in increased loyalty, less turnover, and better productivity. At the same time, however, if employees are adversely affected by an organization's inadequate or nonexistent security program, morale may suffer. Employees who are victimized by virtue of thefts of personal property or invasions of their privacy, assaulted enroute to or from employer-provided parking facilities, or harassed because of their race, creed, color, sex, countries of national origin, or religious beliefs cannot feel good about where they work. The fact that an employer may be observant in terms of equal employment opportunity laws does not necessarily mean that some of its employees will avoid all forms of harassment where fellow workers are concerned.

Certainly, security has a role to play in providing for the personal safety of all employees and in investigating complaints of harassment even though the resolution of harassment complaints necessarily is a personnel department function. When employees complain of their victimization, security has an obligation to conduct an inquiry in an effort to determine who was responsible. More important is security's obligation to try to help employees avoid problems in the first place, some of which can be done with little or no expense or inconvenience to the employer.

Faculty members and staff at a well-known university felt uneasy, and understandably so, when such things as small change from desk drawers, and bills from wallets, mysteriously disappeared from their offices. The security manager began a campaign which consisted of his leaving handwritten notes on doors to open but unoccupied offices reminding those who worked in them to secure the offices whenever they left, even if only for a few minutes. The result was a marked decrease in the number of such incidents.

Another illustration of what can be done to improve employee protection involved a large medical center in a less than desirable neighborhood. Its very limited daytime parking was restricted to the medical staff despite the fact that for all practical purposes the parking area was unused after hours. At the same time a matter of genuine concern to nursing personnel working between 3:00 P.M. and 7:00 A.M. was fear of being assaulted while walking to or from their automobiles, which they had to park on city streets surrounding the institution. The security manager suggested that the nursing staff be permitted to use the doctors' parking area on condition that nurses not park their cars there before 2:45 P.M. and that they would be out no later than 7:15 A.M.; the medical staff agreed. As a result, security for nursing personnel working at night was greatly improved with no expense to the hospital or inconvenience to the doctors.

EMPLOYEE TERMINATIONS

Whenever any employees are terminated, their departure should be considered as a potential personnel security problem. This is true whether the termination is for cause, voluntary, due to a reduction in force, or retirement. It would be unfair to imply that all terminated employees invariably cause security-related problems for employers; it would be unrealistic and imprudent to deny that some do. Therefore, while the termination process clearly is a matter for an organization's human resources staff, security personnel cannot afford to assume that no risks are involved when employees sever their relationship regardless of the reason for their leaving.

Employees terminated for cause, and those affected by a reduction in force, may pose the greatest risk from a security perspective. Employees who are discharged for cause obviously have done something sufficiently serious to warrant such drastic action. They may have committed a crime or been guilty of violating a major policy. In these instances it is quite likely that security either was instrumental in their apprehension, or it was involved in investigating allegations made by others which resulted in a decision to terminate. Therefore, those terminated for cause may already have caused the employer damage.

Depending on the nature of the offense, security may be called upon to help in trying to obtain some form of reimbursement or compensation. As an example, in one company a finance department employee's curiosity about another employee's expense reports prompted an investigation by security. A substantial fraud was uncovered. The result was a decision to prosecute and with security's help the entire sum fraudulently obtained was recovered.

Termination as part of a reduction in force can be a traumatic experience. No matter what an employer may offer in the way of salary and benefits continuation, or outplacement services, the fact remains that affected employees see themselves, and in many cases their families, without a job and a steady income. There is understandable concern about being able to provide food, shelter, clothing, and perhaps even adequate medical care. As a result, even when reductions in force are processed with great care, there may be some terminating employees who show their resentment over their loss of employment by doing things that may be harmful to the employer. Such acts may be relatively minor, or possibly significant.

One of the many high-technology companies forced to reduce its size as the result of a general recession found it necessary to have a series of terminations. Because both the personnel and security departments shared a concern about protecting the employer, there was close cooperation throughout. During the early stages the only damage suffered was a single act of vandalism—an outside rear view mirror was torn off a company truck. Much later, however, it was determined that a former computer programmer had inserted a virus into a program that he had developed for a manufacturing process. Fortunately, the discovery was made before any damage was done, but if this had not been the case, the result could have significantly affected the plant's manufacturing capability even if only temporarily.

Although there may be less risk from a security point of view, the fact remains that employees who leave voluntarily or retire may also represent something of a risk to an employer. Again, to reduce these risks to the greatest possible extent, there has to be close cooperation between the human resources and security departments, and help from line management. Not only do there have to be policies intended to minimize problems from occurring in the first place, but security has to be closely supported by line managers and the personnel department in terms of implementation. Losses of this kind may not be eliminated, but they need not reach any appreciable magnitude.

One might assume that employees who voluntarily leave one employer for another would have no reason to do anything to harm the former. Unfortunately, this is not always true even though in some instances they do not knowingly intend to do anything wrong. Nevertheless, the organizations they are leaving may be victimized in one way or another.

To help illustrate what can happen, a small business anxious to expand aggressively recruited personnel from a much larger competitor. In addition to offering high salaries and good fringe benefits, they provided automobiles. However, there was a quid pro quo. As a condition of employment all new hires were required to bring their copies of the latest technical manuals put out by their former employer. In another instance, involving a newly started company, employees being recruited from an established competitor were asked to bring their copies of their old employer's telephone directory so that additional sources for recruitment would be available. Since many had decided to take their directories anyway to enable them to keep in touch with old friends, it never occurred to them that what they were being asked to do was wrong.

Although retirees may represent the least likely source of a threat, the possibility cannot be ignored. The risk may be greatest to the extent that they keep in touch with old friends at work; it may also be one of the most difficult to handle. Certainly, trying to avoid problems in this category will require the utmost tact and diplomacy on the part of both security and the human resources department.

It is not at all uncommon for retirees to visit their former place of work occasionally, call old associates, or socialize with former co-workers. There certainly is nothing wrong with them doing this. However, human nature being what it is, when such contacts do occur, it is likely that there will be at least some discussion about what is going on at the workplace. Many retired employees have an interest in how things are going where they used to work, and those currently employed see no reason not to tell them. Herein lies the danger since the current employees then are in the process of providing proprietary information, the retirees are the recipients, and none of the parties necessarily knows where the information will ultimately come to rest. It may go no further than the retiree to whom told, or it is conceivable that it could end up in the hands of a competitor of the former employer, inadvertently or otherwise.

It is assumed, and rightly so, that employees are to be trusted. For the most part, this is true, and the same can be said of retirees. However, it is also possible that even the most trustworthy person may say or do something unintentionally. If this happens, the potential for problems exists. How, then, can the human resources and security departments minimize the risk in tactful, diplomatic ways?

First, all terminated personnel, regardless of category, should be subjected to an exit interview. Among the items covered should be the organization's policy for protecting its proprietary information. Terminating employees need to be reminded of any employee agreements that they may have signed when hired and which should have included a provision covering the need to maintain the confidentiality of proprietary information even after leaving the organization. It is also important to utilize line managers and supervisors whenever terminating employees are clearing out their offices or workstations, to minimize the risk that any of the employer's assets are taken at the same time. Most persons would consider their presence during the process less offensive than that of a security officer.

From a security viewpoint, as part of any ongoing security education program there is a need to remind personnel that proprietary information is to be made available only to those with a legitimate need to know, something that former employees, retirees included, do not have. Furthermore, since good loss prevention programs control access to both facilities and internal locations, there is no reason why former employees, whether retirees or otherwise, should be given unrestricted access to the facility or any parts thereof.

SUMMARY

Although personnel matters are the primary responsibility of an employer's human resources department, which is as it should be, the fact remains that some matters are properly the province of the security department. True, nonexistent or lax preemployment screening may add an element of risk insofar as crimes or other forms of misconduct are concerned. On the other hand, even the most comprehensive and thorough procedures cannot guarantee that such incidents will not occur. When they do, whether they are actual crimes such as thefts, assaults, fraud, or white-collar crimes, or policy violations such as the unauthorized disclosure of proprietary information or conflicts of interest, it becomes security's job to take appropriate action to protect the employer.

However, to limit security's role to dealing only with crimes or policy violations shows a lack of understanding of its proper place in the scheme of things. The security function is, or should be, much broader. If security's purpose is to help protect and conserve an employer's assets, and if it is expected to deal with situations when those assets are either in jeopardy or have been lost, surely it has a role to play in orienting and educating employees about their responsibilities in preventing incidents and in the overall security program.

Employees' personal security, whether in the form of executive protection or the protection of employees generally, is important to morale. Their sense of security, whether at the workplace, enroute to and from the organization's parking facilities, or while traveling on business, can be important factors insofar as the employer's success is concerned. Nevertheless, security directors also have to be realists and understand that despite their best efforts there may be occasions, no matter how rare, when executives, as victims of accidents or crimes, cannot perform their duties. Consequently, security directors not only have to be members of crisis management teams and help formulate crisis management plans, they also on occasion may have to serve as catalysts in the development of crisis management programs.

Employee terminations, regardless of reason, can contribute to security-related problems. Some examples have been cited; countless more could be included. While the termination process is a personnel department function, knowing what can happen requires security and human resources departments to cooperate and have good communications before, during, and after the process has been completed if the employer really is to be protected properly. The termination process is another good illustration of the importance of the security organization and function being integrated into all aspects of the employer's operations.

REVIEW QUESTIONS

1. Are there, or should there be, any legal, ethical, or moral restrictions based on the preemployment screening process?
2. Should security departments play a more active role in the preemployment screening process? If so, in what way?
3. What should be the purpose of employee orientation and education efforts?
4. Should orientation and education programs be offered only to new employees, or should old-time employees be included as well?
5. What purpose do employee identification programs serve?

6. What is the difference between a conflict of interest and a white-collar crime? Give examples of each.

7. Should employers be concerned with the protection of all of their employees or only with that of their executives? If yes, why?

8. What may be one of the most difficult things for security directors to do in terms of providing executive protection?

9. Should executive protection programs be extended to include executive families, and if so, why?

10. If an organization has an insurance policy to cover possible executive kidnappings and ransom demands, does it still need a crisis management team and plan? What purpose would they serve under these circumstances?

NOTES

[1] EDWIN H. SUTHERLAND, *White Collar Crime* (Hinsdale, IL: Dryden Press, 1949), p. 9.

[2] *The New York Times*, June 24, 1992, sec. D, p. 2.

Chapter 8

ORGANIZATIONS AND ACTIVITIES IN NEED OF SECURITY

Chapter 1 introduced the reader to the overall subject of security and the distinctions between policing and security. In Chapter 2 we discussed career opportunities in security, while in Chapters 3 through 7 we acquaint students with a range of subjects with which all security directors and managers not only must be familiar but also with which they must deal. Reference has been made throughout to the challenges that confront truly professional security executives, but only in a rather general way.

Nevertheless, even persons who are somewhat familiar with the subject of security often do not appreciate the different types of businesses, institutions, and activities that either have or need effective security programs. Furthermore, just as all security directors or managers must face challenges that might best be described as generic in nature, so are there more specific or unique challenges to be found in connection with the various types of organizations that have security programs.

Since this book's primary purpose is to introduce the reader to security, any discussion of security's application to a given type of organization or activity necessarily must be brief rather than detailed. At the same time, however, an introduction to security would be incomplete without at least some mention being made of our economy's multiple needs for sound loss prevention programming. Therefore, what follows is a synopsis of those businesses, institutions, and various activities that find themselves either in need of or having security programs.

RESEARCH AND DEVELOPMENT

Research and development activities are not confined to college and university campuses. They may be found in any number of businesses as well as in some institutions. In fact, for some organizations, research and development may be their lifeblood, for without the constant search for and development of new products, they might cease to exist. Good examples of some organizations to which this applies are the automobile, computer, and pharmaceutical industries. To remain competitive and survive, they maintain research and development operations that will allow them to offer new or better products to consumers. Research and development have resulted in smaller and less polluting motor vehicle engines and powerful personal computers. The pharmaceutical industry, working closely with medical centers and universities, has produced medication that can help prevent, or in some cases even cure, diseases.

If research and development may be called the lifeblood of some businesses and institutions, information is the lifeblood of research and development. The information may be transmitted orally, in hard copy, or electronically. It may also be stored in different forms of media. In any event, its use, transmission, and storage have to be protected. Once research and development have been completed, decisions have to be made as to whether the end result is something that can be patented or copyrighted, or if it is best treated as a trade secret.

From a security viewpoint the data have to be protected from misuse or theft by employees as well as against acts of industrial espionage perpetrated by either foreign or domestic competitors. In some cases foreign governments have reportedly used their intelligence services to try to obtain business information. For instance, the French government's activities in this regard was noted in Chapter 1. Others suspected of acts of industrial espionage through the use of either their intelligence services or former intelligence personnel reportedly include the Japanese, British, Argentinians, and Egyptians.[1] On the domestic side, private investigators, professional recruiters (also known as headhunters), sales personnel who call upon certain types of industries, and competitors' human resources departments may be used for the purpose of obtaining useful information.

In the event that acts of industrial espionage have been committed by either domestic or foreign competitors, the victim may have to resort to litigation. However, even if successful, it has suffered some loss. Another security and legal concern arises when an employee leaves an organization to go to work for a competitor, and the latter subsequently offers a new product very much like one on which the person had been working in his or her former position. Although this case, too, may be litigated, the difficulty lies in the fact that proving ownership of data that are in some form of media is one thing; trying to prove it when, figuratively speaking, the data are stored in someone's memory is another.

Security directors or managers responsible for protecting research and development operations must meet two different challenges. First is the challenge inherent in the need to protect the information. The other challenge lies in designing the security program for the protection of that information in a way that will not prevent employees from doing their jobs in the most efficient and effective ways. In other words, while access to data should be limited to employees who have a legitimate need to know, the interpretation of this standard should not be so restrictive as to inhibit research personnel from working with colleagues who may be able to contribute to the project's expeditious completion. Security managers must remember that it is not just a question of getting new products to market; they must be gotten there ahead of the competition.

MANUFACTURING

Although it is not uncommon for manufacturers to have research and development programs, and as important as they may be to an organization's success, the fact remains that with or without research and development, security concerns exist and need to be dealt with. Like any other form of business or institution, manufacturers need to have good preemployment screening and continuing educational programs to minimize their risks and losses. Like other organizations, they need to have effectively supervised and controlled purchasing departments. This is needed to combat the susceptibility to kickbacks and bribes sometimes associated with buyers.

In earlier chapters it was said repeatedly that for optimum results, security programs not only need to be fully integrated into all aspects of an organization's operations, but also that the most effective security directors or managers must learn how the business or institution functions. As applied to the manufacturing process security directors have to recognize the breadth and variety of the assets for whose protection they are responsible. They soon learn that there is far more to securing a manufacturing operation than having security personnel monitor alarm systems, control access, and make patrol rounds.

Regardless of the existence of a research and development facility, information needs to be protected. This would include, among other things, such diverse data as those found in the organization's personnel files, customer lists, bills of materials, expansion plans or those for major alterations, budget information, and contemplated advertising campaigns. To protect information there also is a need to protect the company's communications in whatever form they may be.

Manufacturers make products which, in turn, are sold either to wholesalers, distributors, or directly to consumers. Regardless of the way in which sales are made, deliveries have to be made to the businesses or individuals who buy directly from the manufacturer. Those deliveries have to be made in timely fashion and in ways that will not damage the product. Insofar as security directors or managers are concerned, there is need, directly or indirectly, to be concerned with transportation matters. Of course, security's involvement will be much greater if the manufacturer has its own fleet of trucks, aircraft, or vessels. Should that be the case, the means of transport as well as the merchandise being moved have to be protected. Transportation security issues as such are discussed in another section of this chapter.

Manufacturers do not rely only on what information they have and a wave of a wand to have a product appear. Buildings and equipment obviously are needed, but so are the utilities that keep the buildings lighted and warm, and the equipment operating. However, nothing can be manufactured without the raw materials that go into the product. Whether they happen to be steel, glass, plastic, and rubber for the manufacture of automobiles; cloth, zippers, buttons, and thread to make clothes; chemicals for the pharmaceutical industry's use in making medicines; or precious metals and integrated circuits for the manufacture of computers, the fact remains that without raw materials nothing can be manufactured. Buying raw materials in the right amounts is purchasing's responsibility, but once those amounts have been received into the employer's inventory, protecting them against loss or theft is security's responsibility.

Unless a manufacturer works three shifts a day, seven days a week, there inevitably will be only partially finished goods on the production line when the plant is closed or possibly staffed by a skeleton crew. To make certain that the manufacturing process is not disrupted when work resumes, it is necessary to protect work in process. That means preventing the theft of raw materials or components, and acts of vandalism. For instance, if a computer manufacturer's production line is about to start work on a Monday morning only to find that one or two printed circuit boards have disappeared, the process would be disrupted. This would result in the manufacture of fewer units, deliveries to customers might be delayed, and the manufacturer's reputation and future sales could be affected. Consequently, security's responsibility must be extended to include the protection of work in process.

Rarely in manufacturing does a finished product go directly from the production line to shipping. Even if the interval is a relatively short one, most finished goods usually go into inventory preparatory to shipment. The loss or theft of inventory could have the same effect on a manufacturer's ability to make deliveries to customers as would a disruption to a production line. Whether the ensuing damage to the company's sales and reputation ranges from relatively mild to disastrous, the fact remains that it would suggest a weakness in the security program.

Goods awaiting shipment must be protected. Even when ready to be moved, steps have to be taken to ensure that only those units consigned to a particular transporter are picked up by it. Whether goods are loaded in error, or there is collusion between a shipper and carrier, this could mean a potential loss to the manufacturer much the same as if production had been disrupted or inventory had been stolen. Making certain that things of this sort do not happen is but one of security's many duties.

What has already been said about security's role in a manufacturing environment would apply regardless of what is being made. However, since not all manufacturing is the same, neither will all of security's concerns be the same. Although competent security directors and managers should be able to move from one type of organization to another without discomfort, they nevertheless will find variations as they move from one industry to another. Some of these differences are best illustrated.

Manufacturers of expensive clothing are constantly concerned with the problem of "knock-offs." This happens when the original manufacturer makes a garment which, because of very limited and tightly controlled production, is to be sold in a few exclusive stores or specialty shops for one price, and another manufacturer then makes copies that are sold to far more stores and in far greater quantities for considerably less money. This is not illegal, but it tends to lessen the value of the originals, makes sales more difficult, and means less profit.

Over the years those who make some other garments, and manufacturers of some accessories and even some watches, including expensive ones, have found themselves confronted with problems stemming from counterfeiting. This is also true of those in the record business. Although counterfeiting often involves a patent infringement or copyright violation, and the tendency is to pursue such matters in court, the fact remains that not all countries afford patents and copyrights the same degree of protection as they have under U.S. law. Consequently, if the counterfeiters make their products in other countries and the laws there are not the same as they are in the United States, the victim finds it much more difficult to cope with the problem.

Although computer manufacturers may also have problems of copyright violations or patent infringements, and like jewelry manufacturers they use precious metals, they have a number of other concerns which are more directly attributable to the nature of their particular industry. Examples of such concerns include a willingness by some companies, which compete directly with them in the maintenance field, to upgrade printed circuit boards without authorization and to pay for customer lists; the laxity of some field engineering personnel, which results in the theft of spare parts and tools; and the unauthorized copying of diagnostic software by competitors in the service aspect of the industry.

A customer list's value to a competitor is relatively easy to understand and needs no further elaboration. The other examples cited need to be expanded upon, however briefly. Most, if not all, computer manufacturers can provide service to customers who have purchased their products. This is another legitimate source of revenue. They can also help their customers upgrade existing computers from a less to a more powerful system through an exchange of printed circuit boards, with the customer paying for the new board. Assume for a moment that a new board bought from the manufacturer sells for $100,000. A competing maintenance firm has a machine that can burn the details of a copyrighted integrated circuit onto a blank—admittedly in violation of the copyright laws—and does exactly that, then offers to sell its board for $50,000. This is obviously injurious to the manufacturer.

There is no reason to suspect the honesty of most field engineers. Nevertheless, there occasionally are some who will decide to leave their jobs and go into competition with their former employers. Because of their work experience they intend to provide service on those computers with which they are familiar. They know that they can compete without the formality of an office or staff; they cannot compete, at least initially, without access to both spare parts and some equipment. Knowing, too, that they cannot buy spare parts from the former employer, and that some equipment, such as an oscilloscope, can be quite expensive, prior to the time of their resignation they will go through the motions of reporting an alleged theft of company assets from their unlocked vehicles. They will feign embarrassment over having left the car or van unlocked, but in the interim they have secreted away the allegedly stolen parts, tools, and other equipment.

The manufacturer has devoted resources to the development of diagnostic software. Its purpose is to facilitate the provision of service to customers who report operating problems. Because of the software's value from both a service and a monetary point of view, diagnostic software is tightly controlled. However, there may be relatively rare occasions when, because of the size of an installation at a customer site, the manufacturer and customer will enter into an agreement under which a copy of the diagnostic software can be left at the customer's place of business to minimize downtime if a problem should arise. The customer's data processing operation may be so large that it also uses another manufacturer's computers, serviced by a so-called third-party maintenance organization.

There now exists a risk that one of the latter's employees may copy or attempt to copy the diagnostic software so that that organization can offer to service all of the machines for less money.

By no means are computer manufacturers the only ones with special concerns. The pharmaceutical industry may make products that help immunize people against diseases, but the industry itself it not immune from unique security concerns of its own. Again, like other industries, especially those with substantial resources devoted to research and development, information is critically important and needs to be protected. At the same time, once new products are ready for market there has to be a sales effort, which may involve a two-pronged approach. One, for which the industry is well known, involves direct advertising in newspapers, magazines, and on television. This method is effective when the products are of the nonprescription variety. The other, less well known to the general public, uses sales representatives who call on doctors and hospital pharmacies with samples of prescription drugs, urging their use in the treatment of patients. The object is to familiarize physicians and hospital pharmacies with the product in the hope that thereafter it will be prescribed when appropriate.

Doing this makes it necessary for the manufacturers to provide their sales representatives with adequate supplies of samples and the accompanying literature. The volume of samples, the prospect for their misuse by salespersons, and the risk to the public if samples are stolen and improperly disposed of or ingested by the wrong person represent a significant security concern for the industry. As with computer industry field engineers, most pharmaceutical industry salespersons are honest and hard working. Nevertheless, occasionally there are a few who are either dishonest or lax in terms of how they protect the samples for which they are responsible.

There have been manufacturers who have learned, much to their chagrin, that some salespersons will trade some or all of their samples at a neighborhood drugstore for candy, cosmetics, or a host of other personal necessities. On occasion they have also learned that samples not properly safeguarded have been stolen, and at that point their concern is heightened because of the uncertainty of their disposition. There is a loss, but probably little or no other danger for the manufacturer if they simply ended up being flushed down a drain. On the other hand, if taken by someone who may be allergic or suffering from an ailment that will react negatively to this particular drug, that person may become seriously ill, or die, and if the cause of the problem is identified as the manufacturer's new product, it suffers damage to its reputation as well as embarrassment.

Pharmaceutical manufacturers, as well as those who process foodstuffs, also worry about someone, whether an unhappy employee or a complete stranger, poisoning or otherwise contaminating their products. If this occurs, illness or death may result, while trying to identify the perpetrator may be almost impossible. Consequently, added precautions must be taken by both industries from the moment the manufacturing process begins through packaging and distribution to guard against anything that could taint the end product. Failure to do so can result in bad publicity, embarrassment, a loss of public confidence in the manufacturer with an attendant loss of sales, and the likelihood of litigation, with all of the costs that that entails.

Contamination is not the only worry of those who manufacture and process foodstuffs. They have other security concerns, arising largely from the theft of merchandise for personal use or subsequent sale by employees. They also risk losses due to spoilage of merchandise if both raw ingredients and finished items are not handled carefully. Insofar as theft is concerned, food processers are keenly aware of the fact that what they make and sell are products that can be used in virtually anyone's home. Therefore, employees may steal for personal use or, knowing that there is a ready market, to sell directly to their own "customers." The individual thefts may not be in large volume, but over time their value can amount to a sizable sum of money. In either case, the manufacturer or processor suffers a loss. At the same time, once processed food items have been removed from their packaging, it may be extremely difficult, if not almost impossible, for any manufacturer to identify the items as being theirs. As a result, the emphasis on loss prevention is heightened in this particular industry.

The negligent or untimely handling of raw ingredients used to make foodstuffs can result in spoilage. For example, a delay in transferring materials to suitable storage facilities or coolers, or failure to follow a first in–first out precept in putting those materials into the production process, can mean that some will no longer be usable as intended. This represents a dual loss for the manufacturer. First, it has paid for raw materials that cannot be used; second, fewer units of an item will be produced and available for sale. Furthermore, if spoilage is not detected before materials go into production, or it is ignored, contaminated products may be sold to unsuspecting customers. From the manufacturer's point of view the end result will be the same as for any contaminated products insofar as adverse publicity, embarrassment, and litigation are concerned.

Like all manufacturers, those who make both ground and air transportation products have concerns that are common to all manufacturing organizations, and others that are more or less special to their industries. For instance, no organization can afford to tolerate corruption in its purchasing department that may result in either paying more for materials of a lesser quality, or in getting less than it should for the amount charged. Neither does any manufacturing organization want to buy defective components, but should any be received, go into production, and end up in a finished product, the maker will suffer a loss. However, if this does happen, nowhere is the potential for disaster as great as in the case of an automobile or aircraft manufacturer. Here the defect can cause serious injury or even death to those using the particular vehicle.

Of course, the receipt and use of defective parts does not necessarily mean that someone in purchasing is dishonest or incapable of doing their job. Buyers may do their jobs and do them well, yet those responsible for the manufacturer's quality control program may have been less than attentive in doing their work. Security certainty has, or should have, a role to play in helping to preserve the integrity of the purchasing process. At the same time, although security is not involved in either the quality assurance or manufacturing process, if problems arise and the consequences are costly, there is a strong probability that the security organization will be called upon to help determine the source of those problems and how they arose in the first place.

Inasmuch as the purpose of this book is to serve as an introduction to security, the foregoing examples of some of the many variations that can be found should suffice. One can see how all manufacturers have certain security concerns in common, yet each type of manufacturing activity has certain challenges for its security personnel which clearly are distinguishable from those in other businesses. Truly professional security directors and managers realize that they must integrate their departmental activities into all phases of the manufacturing process if they are to help protect and conserve assets. They also understand the importance of being knowledgeable about their employer's business operations if they are to do their jobs well.

At the same time, increasing numbers of manufacturers are becoming aware of the potential for loss that exists if they have no security, what they have is inadequate, or their existing programs lack leadership for the tasks that lie ahead. Those who are interested in and determined to professionalize their security operations are coming to realize that prevention, not detection and apprehension, is essential for survival. This can be accomplished only through employing competent security directors and managers who can help integrate the security function into the total operation rather than allowing it to remain isolated, as has so often happened in the past.

WHOLESALING AND WAREHOUSING

Not all manufacturers sell directly to consumers; they sell to wholesalers, who, in turn, sell to retailers, who then sell to consumers. Wholesalers buy in bulk from manufacturers and need places in which to store their inventories. Then there are others who, needing storage space above and beyond what they may have on their own premises, will avail themselves of warehouses. Of course, warehouses are not used only by wholesalers or other types of businesses in need of storage space. They also offer their facilities to the general public when anyone in that category needs space in which to store property for either a short or a long term.

Although wholesaling and warehousing are different, they also have some common security concerns, which justifies considering them together. For example, unlike manufacturers or food processors, neither has need for much equipment other than that which is necessary for the safe movement of materials on their premises. However, in common with other types of organizations, both wholesalers and warehouses have legitimate concerns with the physical protection of their facilities during both working and nonworking hours. They also share a concern with making certain that when wholesalers buy, they receive the correct quantities, and that what the general public says it is entrusting to a warehouse is in fact what is being deposited for safe storage.

Again, like manufacturers and food processors, the nature of wholesaling is such that there is little or no need for persons other than employees to be on the premises. Although this may limit exposure on one hand, it also exposes assets to a group that not only has the greatest opportunity to steal, but also knows most accurately the value of the assets and potential markets to which they might be sold. Warehouses, on the other hand, are more exposed to the general public since anyone renting space is entitled to access to their property. Nevertheless, the lessees tend to select a particular warehouse because they assume that their goods will be protected properly, thus prompting many to do business only with bonded warehouses.

For both, then, concern with honest employees and effective physical security measures are of great importance, although these alone are not the only things to which they must pay attention in order to protect themselves. Illustrative of some wholesaling and warehousing problems are the three examples set forth below.

A large grocery wholesaler, with its own warehouse, received deliveries by railroad freight cars in such quantities that more times than not it felt obliged to leave cases of canned goods and sundries on its 150-yard-long shipping–receiving dock at day's end. Despite the fact that the warehouse was well inside its fenced property line, the theft of from one to three cases at a time was not unusual. The losses mounted and affected profit margins. As a result, it was prepared to spend a sizable sum of money for rolling steel doors with which it could fully enclose the dock. However, it retained the services of a security management consultant, who showed them how the dock could be cleared on a daily basis at no cost. The solution lay in merely staggering the working hours of two forklift operators.

A warehouse open to and used by the general public was faced with a different problem, but one that nonetheless was becoming both expensive and embarrassing. On occasion, individuals who used its facilities would remove items from storage, then file claims alleging either that some things had been stolen or that they had been damaged while in storage. The lessee would pass the claims on to its insurance company, but the dollar value of many came within the policy's deductible clause. As a result, it either had to risk having a dissatisfied customer by refusing to pay on the claim, or it had to absorb the loss. Until the problem seemed to be getting out of hand, persons placing property in storage were usually allowed to put sealed boxes into storage without inspection by the warehouse. The latter merely acknowledged the receipt of a given number of containers; the procedure basically was the same when property was removed. However, the increase in filed claims prompted the warehouse to change its policy by requiring the examination of all containers in the owners' presence both as they were being put into storage, and again as they were taken out. This was followed by a marked decrease in the number of claims filed.

By no means are private organizations the only ones liable to be victimized by warehouse thefts. Government can also be a victim. For instance, in May 1991, the District Attorney for the Borough of Brooklyn announced the arrest of a storeowner accused of illegally having in his possession three dozen cribs owned by New York City; he also acknowledged that his office was investigating allegations that city workers had stolen other city-owned property from one of the city's warehouses, which was filled with items destined for the poor and shelters and worth $11 million.[2]

It becomes evident that even such activities as wholesaling and warehousing, whether owned by private organizations or government, are not immune from security concerns even though their operations are quite different from those of manufacturers and processors. There are assets that need to be protected.

RETAILING

Retail stores can be found in a wide variety of categories and sizes. The term includes such operations as department, discount, drug, and grocery stores; men's and women's clothing and accessory shops; home centers; and specialty shops. These stores or shops may be part of a large retail chain. They may also be relatively small, neighborhood, family-owned businesses. Many of them share the same concerns as those applicable to other businesses or to other retailers. Some also have special problems that may be attributable to either their size or the nature of their activities. However, one characteristic of retailing that distinguishes it from research and development, manufacturing, or wholesaling and warehousing is its dependence on public access to the premises. In other words, without customers entering the stores, whether to buy or merely browse, retail merchants cannot exist. This, in turn, means that their security programs must be designed to protect assets against loss or theft by either apparent customers or by employees.

Courtesy of Bloomingdale's, New York City

"Shrinkage," the expression of choice for those in retailing, is usually reflected as a percentage of gross sales. This problem, which has confronted retail merchants for years, at one time was considered to be due primarily to shoplifting by third parties. Shoplifting continues to be a major concern for retailers. At the same time, there was, and still is, great reluctance even to think of employees as possible contributors to losses even though their access to assets, and opportunities for wrongdoing, far exceed the access and opportunities that are available to the general public. This attitude also tends to ignore the ways in which employees can contribute to reduced profit margins without necessarily being guilty of outright larceny. In any event, the employer may still suffer losses.

Shoplifters, posing as customers, and employees can and do steal with an inevitable loss to the merchant. In trying to cope with shrinkage problems, security directors and managers are challenged by a host of factors, all of which may contribute in varying degrees to the losses suffered. In doing their jobs, however, they also need to be cognizant of the fact that the overriding need to sell in order to stay in business may have to take precedence over security considerations. What, then, are some of the factors that may contribute to losses of which retail security directors and managers need to be aware?

Insofar as trying to cope with third-party thefts is concerned, the ways in which merchandise is displayed, employee attitudes, and the nature of the operation itself can all contribute to the problems or their solution. It is assumed that persons other than employees who enter a store are prospective customers. Whatever is available for sale must be displayed for their benefit. People like to be able to see and feel what they think they may want to buy. In some types of stores they will want either to try on or try an item before buying. This is not unreasonable.

However, when merchandise is displayed in such a way that for all intents and purposes employees are prevented from observing what people are doing, the opportunity for shoplifting is increased while the risk of detection is decreased. There are some stores where merchandise is displayed on racks or shelves in such a way that a salesperson's or cashier's line of sight is blocked. Can the security and merchandise managers come to an agreement that will satisfy both of their needs, or will it be necessary to buy and install some type of security hardware in order to reduce the risk of shrinkage?

If the goods being sold are of a type where customers would like to try them on, what is there to minimize the risk of having a person hide merchandise for removal from the store while in a dressing room? Are there limits on the number of garments that one person can take into a dressing room at one time? Is anyone responsible for making certain that for each garment taken into a dressing room one comes out, including the one being bought; is there a hanger recovery and count policy? If the sale involves expensive jewelry, does the salesperson remove only one item from the case at a time and return it immediately after showing it unless it is sold to the customer? Are salespersons cautioned about being distracted while showing things to customers?

Bad and costly as it is, the mere theft of merchandise by shoplifters is not the only shoplifting-related security problem confronting retail stores. Another aspect of shoplifting of which both retail sales and security personnel must be made aware is a secondary tactic used by some shoplifters with considerable success. The first stage consists of the larceny of merchandise normally associated with shoplifting. The second stage occurs when shoplifters return to the victimized merchant, or to a similar store, with the stolen goods, allege that they received the items as gifts to explain the absence of sales slips, and say that since they already have something similar, they would like to return the merchandise and get its cash value. It is not unusual for cautious shoplifters to attempt the return at the victim's place of business knowing that the brand is actually sold there. That minimizes the risk of anyone suspecting shoplifting. However, other shoplifters concerned about possibly being recognized by the victim's security staff prefer to return stolen goods to a store other than that from which they were taken. Although they are uncertain as to whether the second store actually sells that particular product or brand, they are willing to gamble that customer service personnel with whom they will deal will not be so familiar with the store's inventory that they will refuse to accept the items. When this tactic succeeds, either the original merchant is twice victimized or two different stores will incur losses.

Employee attitudes and the nature of an operation can also have an effect on a store's shrinkage. Over the years various types of products have been developed for the retail market to help reduce losses due to shoplifting. Stores have bought them. Nevertheless, too often the safeguard fails not because of a defective product but because of employee attitudes. For instance, a merchant tags items so that an alarm will sound if the tag is not properly removed and someone tries to leave the store with that item. A person carrying a tagged item passes a detector while leaving the store, the alarm sounds, yet salespeople ignore it. Although the store has spent money for a product designed to protect its assets, its employees' attitudes counteract the system's effectiveness.

Of course, even the most conscientious employees will find it difficult to prevent losses if there are not enough of them. The advent of self-help stores, which are largely discount operations, meant that retailers needed fewer employees. However, some soon learned that there were people who thought that self-help really meant help yourself. Shrinkage increased. Some department stores even reduced their sales staffs, with the same results.

Of course, shoplifting is not the only way in which retailers lose money to third parties. Fraud also takes its toll whether perpetrated through the use of forged or stolen credit cards, the issuance of checks for which no funds are on deposit, or the purchase of goods for which the customer has no intention of paying. Modern technology has made advances that can help merchants reduce losses involving the use of credit cards if the customer is physically present and is asked for his or her card. However, the salesperson who makes a credit card sale in response to a telephone call from a customer may not always be so lucky as to avoid a loss.

Without in any way minimizing the seriousness of problems caused by third parties, whether in the form of shoplifting or some form of fraud, the fact remains that employees are also major contributors to losses. There are a number of ways in which employees can be responsible for significant losses of profits if not always of merchandise. Of course, like other organizations, retailers can suffer losses traceable to dishonest employees, whether they work as shipping or receiving personnel or as cashiers. The former can steal, pack, and ship goods to themselves, relatives, or friends without the risk of being caught by a parcel inspection program when they leave work at day's end. Receivers can be careless in checking in deliveries, or they can be in collusion with truckers or possibly even with local vendors and sign for short shipments as if they were complete. Cashiers can steal cash from register drawers.

These forms of larceny are quite obvious. At the same time, others may be far less evident, and consequently, much more difficult to detect. For instance, another form of stealing occurs when employees "borrow" goods with the idea of returning them. However, since the borrowing was without anyone's permission, when the time comes to return the items the employee becomes concerned lest he or she will be seen. If that should happen, the result may range from embarrassment to dismissal for stealing. Therefore, the employee decides that perhaps it is best simply to forget about bringing the "borrowed" merchandise back to the store.

A far more subtle form of misconduct occurs when employees see things which they would like to have but cannot afford, even with their employees' discounts. These employees would never think of stealing outright, yet they devise ways to buy the merchandise at prices which they can afford even if it results in lost profits to their employer. They will manage either to soil softgoods or to damage hardgoods slightly. They will then approach the department manager, noting that the soilage or damage means that the particular item cannot now be sold at its established price. In many, if not most cases, this will result in a markdown. The markdown, plus the employee's discount, now has brought the price within an affordable range for the employee. Some employees see no harm in doing this, on the theory that they really are not stealing. After all, they are paying something for the items.

There are other employees who abuse the discount privileges that retailers give their personnel. This, too, means less profits for the merchant. They ignore the fact that employee discount policies tend to limit strictly exercise of the privilege to members of the employee's immediate family. Even the most liberal employers do not extend the discount privilege to all of the employee's relatives, and they certainly do not extend it to their friends. Nevertheless, employees who engage in the practice of discount abuse will not hesitate to buy for relatives who do not qualify for the privilege under the employer's policy, and for friends. Once again, these employees will rationalize that there is nothing wrong with what they are doing inasmuch as there is payment for the goods purchased. They fail to understand that in their own way they are stealing from their employer by depriving the company of the margin of profit that it would earn if the merchandise was sold at the listed price.

Of course, rank-and-file employees are not the only ones who may be guilty of misconduct. Managerial personnel can be equally guilty in their own ways. Perhaps one of the more common offenses is the submission of fraudulent expense reports by department managers or buyers. To illustrate, assume that an employee in this category works for a store in Cleveland, Ohio. He or she plans a trip to New York to buy merchandise for an upcoming season. In the interest of seeing what is available in the most expeditious way, visits are scheduled in advance with those manufacturers in whose lines the buyer is interested. One of these manufacturers is prepared to do more than merely display its merchandise. In an effort to make certain that it will get a large order from the buyer, it not only entertains him or her while in the New York area but also pays the person's hotel bill. However, when the buyer returns to Cleveland and submits an expense report, he or she includes the cost of the hotel and even of meals paid for by manufacturers.

In all fairness to retail employees it should be noted that the submission of fraudulent expense reports is neither unique nor exclusive to retailing. It is an activity with which all organizations must cope and where failure to do so can be quite costly. Illustrative of the problem was a March 25, 1992, item in the *Boston Globe* which stated that according to an internal memorandum of the Digital Equipment Corporation, expense account abuse was costing about $30 million a year, with policy violations covering such things as football tickets and liquor.[3]

Thus it becomes apparent that there is so much more to the subject of retail security than dealing with shoplifting. At the same time, the inherent nature of retailing, which is an extremely competitive business, makes merchants increasingly dependent on their reputations for value and service. This, in turn, makes it imperative for security personnel to perform their duties in ways that will help to protect and conserve the employer's assets but without jeopardizing good customer or other public relations.

TRANSPORTATION

In thinking about security needs in transportation, the airline industry usually is one of the first things that comes to mind, primarily with regard to passengers. However, all forms of transportation, land, sea, or air, whether by rail or truck, to move people, cargo, or both, need security. It is immaterial whether the form of transportation is one available to members of the general public, such as most airlines, railroads, ships, buses, or trucks, or whether it is proprietary, as would be the case for a large company that uses its own fleet of trucks to transport merchandise. Satisfying their security needs involves not only the protection of the means of transport, regardless of what form it may take, but also the protection and conservation of those assets that are necessary to keep the means themselves operational.

The idea of transportation security is not new. In Chapter 1 we noted that one of the earliest examples of the use of private security in the United States occurred in 1855 when the railroads contracted for protection during the course of their westward expansion. As they continued their development across the length and breadth of the country, they began to employ their own personnel, primarily to protect both freight and passengers. Despite the fact that railroads no longer are as widely used as they once were, they still provide most of their own security.

One might also say that a forerunner of cross-country bus company operations were the stage coaches that carried both passengers and light cargo, particularly in parts of the country as yet untouched by the railroads. It might even be said that their use of a person to "ride shotgun" to protect stage coach drivers, passengers, and freight was comparable to the use of "sky marshals" on aircraft to combat skyjacking and terrorist problems that plagued airlines during the 1960s and 1970s. These different but similar situations are illustrative of the fact that in addition to providing security for both passengers and cargo, transportation companies that serve the general public must also be concerned with protecting one of their very important but tangible assets—their reputations. This is not to suggest that companies that use proprietary transport systems need not be concerned about their reputations. Late deliveries, or delivery of damaged goods, can be embarrassing and costly.

Courtesy of American Airlines

Courtesy of American Airlines

Thus concerns about protection are no less true today than they were when the railroads saw a need for security in 1855, or when a principal means of transportation was the stage coach, or during the time when skyjacking and terrorist attacks against aircraft were quite commonplace. People who use some form of public transport either to go from one place to another, or to move personal or business assets, usually make their selection based on a carrier's reputation. Once they determine that a transporter goes to the place or places in which they are interested, they tend to focus on its reputation for providing safe, on-time delivery. Those who do business with companies that use their own transport are equally interested in being assured that once an order is placed, the merchandise will be delivered on time and in good condition.

Therefore, to satisfy customers' needs, organizations involved with moving people, cargo, or both, must be ready to provide security for passengers and cargo from the start to the end of the service. This necessarily translates into having secure passenger and freight terminals, safe passage, and making certain that the means of transport offered are protected at all times against any acts that might make their use unsafe. Furthermore, since timely departures and arrivals, whether of passengers or freight, are also important to persons and organizations that rely on transportation services, protecting the assets needed to keep the very means of transport operational assumes increased importance.

Not surprisingly, the type of transportation involved and the nature of what is being transported have a bearing on the nature of an organization's security concerns. However, whether one is a security director or manager for some form of public transportation, or works for an organization that uses its own aircraft or vehicles, the mere fact that where transportation is concerned their employer is not necessarily burdened by security-related problems does not justify an assumption that they enjoy immunity.

For instance, some airlines that have suffered from terrorist activity, skyjacking, or both, occasionally have been the victims of armed robberies of their cargo terminals. Other airlines, which have not had to worry about terrorism or skyjacking, nevertheless have suffered from cargo terminal robberies. All airlines are concerned about the safe, undamaged arrival of passengers' luggage. Long-distance bus companies rarely have any particular security concerns. However, when during the course of a strike by employees of a major carrier there was violence, protecting passengers, terminals, and equipment became matters of great importance.

Operators of streetcars or buses worry about personnel being robbed or even killed. Equally troubling is the thought of passengers being molested, injured, or killed by gangs while awaiting transportation or enroute to their destinations, or simply being injured or killed by a stray bullet as a vehicle passes through some inner-city neighborhoods. Oceangoing passenger vessel operators have learned that it is possible for terrorists to take over a ship. In one case they terrorized passengers and killed one before throwing his body overboard. In some parts of the world, smaller vessels may be victimized by pirates, as has happened off the coasts of Singapore and Hong Kong.

Those who move freight by truck are ever mindful of the potential for hijacking. This is especially true of those who are known to carry valuable cargo for which there may be a ready market. Railroads no longer fear the same types of problems which prompted them to employ security personnel during the years of their expansion, but even now they are concerned with the theft of freight and in avoiding derailments or other accidents which might injure or kill passengers, or damage freight, and which might be caused by switch or engineering personnel performing their duties while under the influence of drugs or alcohol.

If the foregoing are not enough to satisfy a security director's need for challenges, another remains. It concerns the protection and conservation of those assets that a transporter must have to keep its equipment operational. Days when vehicles cannot be used represent lost revenue for the transporter. It makes no difference whether the transportation system involved is public or proprietary. If spare parts, tools, fuel, lubrication, or tires are stolen by maintenance employees, the employer's loss may be doubled. First, it must buy replacements. Second, if it is unable to operate any of its vehicles because they need service or repairs which cannot be provided due to a lack of maintenance materials, it loses the income it would have derived from their use. Therefore, the question that has to be answered deals with how security can assist the organization's maintenance managers in devising ways designed to protect all of the many assets required if safe, usable equipment is readily to be available.

HOSPITALITY

The hospitality or lodging industry, as it generally is referred to, is composed primarily of hotels and motels, both of which may encounter a wide range of security problems. Some of their problems are attributable to the fact that unlike most other organizations they are open for business 24 hours a day, seven days a week, 52 weeks a year. Like retailing and public transportation, hotels and motels must rely on public acceptance and use if they are to make a profit and stay in business. Also in common with retailing, the industry may suffer losses caused by customers or guests, as well as by employees. Like some aspects of public transportation, particularly airlines, hotels or motels can find themselves in dire circumstances if their reputations are hurt by bad publicity.

The industry's security concerns and needs have undergone a good deal of change over the years. Today, much more is expected of security managers than keeping burglars and prostitutes out of hotels and preventing fights among drunks in the bars. The job has become quite complex and demanding. For a better understanding of the rather unique nature of lodging industry security, it may be helpful to distinguish between those concerns that are guest related and those that involve employees. Of course, a further distinction must be made with regard to the guest aspects of security. This is due to the fact that while guests obviously are a source of income, they can also be responsible for losses. What has to be done to protect guests against loss or injury will be considered initially, as it should be, not only because they are a property's primary source of income, but also because the nature of some guest-related security problems may be such as to damage a hotel's reputation severely. That, in turn, can affect sales.

Hotels and motels function around the clock. Guests are free to come and go at all hours. Larger hotels usually have multiple entrances and exits. This is also true of some motor hotels, where guests can go directly to or from their automobiles without passing through a lobby. Guests at many older and smaller motels can park their automobiles right outside their rooms once they have registered. Although around-the-clock operations, and the relative ease with which people can enter and leave hotels, motor hotels, and motels, are by no means solely responsible for guest-related security problems, it is unwise to ignore the possibility that they do contribute to some of those problems. In any event, among other things, guests have been murdered, raped, assaulted, robbed, died as a result of either an accidental or arson fire, become ill and died because of an ill-conceived housekeeping policy, been seriously injured by virtue of a property's negligence, or had valuables stolen from their rooms.

Not surprisingly, cases of this sort will usually mean a lawsuit. Security will be a key issue with layout, design, locks and locking devices, control over keys where there has not yet been a conversion to electronic or computerized systems, the ease in general with which rooms can be entered, the security department's size, training, duties, supervision, the frequency of patrol rounds, and the property's history of any form of criminal activity being examined closely. The combination of physical security and a security department's effectiveness can make the difference between a hotel winning or losing a case in which a guest, or a guest's estate, is the plaintiff. In either event, there will be publicity of a sort best avoided, whether it is transmitted via the news media or by word of mouth. Depending on the circumstances, even a successful defense may not be enough to overcome any negative publicity generated by the original incident.

Problems of this sort can and do arise. Therefore, suitable programs must be undertaken to prevent them from happening to the greatest extent possible. Fortunately, for the most part they do not happen with such frequency as to be the focal point on which lodging industry security must concentrate.

However, there are allied issues that also need attention. The hospitality industry has become increasingly concerned with the matter of patrons in a bar or cocktail lounge

Courtesy of The Boston Park Plaza Hotel

who appear to be inebriated, insist on having more drinks, and who then may attempt to drive. In many jurisdictions the hotel could be held liable if it continued to serve that person and he or she were involved later in an automobile accident that resulted in death or serious injury to third persons.

As more and more women travel alone, whether on business or for pleasure, a higher level of protection may be called for to prevent their being victimized or unduly disturbed while on the premises. In addition, as increasing numbers of people with physical disabilities travel, thought has to be given not only to protecting them against problems that could affect any guest, but also to the matter of their safe evacuation in the event of an emergency such as a fire. How does one make certain that a guest with a hearing problem knows that a fire alarm has sounded, or that a guest who is blind or who uses a wheelchair or crutches gets help in evacuating?

Liability understandably is an issue of legitimate concern whose importance cannot be underestimated. However, if it becomes an obsession to the exclusion of all other security-related matters, it can result in the loss of substantial sums because of inattention to other aspects of operations that relate to security matters which occur almost daily. Among these is the question of losses that can be attributed to guest behavior. Some may even be related to injuries or thefts alleged by some guests to which they themselves contributed. Dealing with these possibilities can be among the most challenging tasks facing hotel security managers. In all cases where there is concern that a guest may be the source of a security problem, security managers must be ever conscious of the fact that whatever they are called upon to do to protect and conserve their employer's assets, they must do it in a most diplomatic way.

The industry has long been aware of the fact that some guests will steal. Those who do usually fall into one of two categories. Those who are souvenir hunters tend to limit themselves to taking keys, a shoeshine cloth, an ashtray, a sewing kit, shampoo, or soap.

In first-class or luxury properties, some will go so far as to take one or more towels or terrycloth bathrobes. Other guests will take almost anything that they can carry, including bed linens, drapes, lamps, furniture, and unsecured television sets. Properties with parking facilities that guests can reach without passing the front desk tend to be the most vulnerable. In any case, whatever is stolen must be replaced by the victim hotel or motel. That, of course, directly affects the inn's profit picture.

By no means are thefts of this sort by guests the only way in which they can contribute to losses. Guests who leave without paying their bills are obviously contributors. The same is true of those who during their stay run up very sizable bills only to confess at checkout time that they have no money with which to pay or who try to pay with stolen or counterfeit credit cards.

There are also some guests who may try to have the cost of their stay made complimentary by alleging that they were injured, have had something stolen, or both, as a way of explaining their misconduct to their employers or families. For instance, there is the salesperson who spends all of his or her expense cash advance drinking with a stranger. He or she then complains to the hotel that although the cash was left in the room for safekeeping precisely because he or she planned on going out, upon waking up the next morning the money was gone. The inference is that a hotel employee stole the money.

If the guests succeed in such cases, the inn is the loser. Consequently, it is imprudent to assume that all allegations of this sort are true. However, unlike a trial where the burden of proof is on the plaintiff, here the burden of either proving or disproving the guest's complaint really rests with security. Like all guest-related issues, these matters must be handled by security personnel with the greatest tact, diplomacy, and skill.

Turning to the role of lodging industry employees with regard to losses, certainly they have far more opportunities to steal, and access to assets and facilities, than do guests. They also have access to guest rooms. Not to be overlooked, however, is the fact that they can also contribute to an inn's losses simply by being inattentive, careless, lazy, or by ignoring the employer's policies, or perhaps a combination of all four.

Examples of employee dishonesty would have to include bartenders who occasionally bring their own liquor bottles to work, serve drinks from those bottles, charge customers the set bar prices, and pocket the money. There may be some members of the housekeeping staff who see no need to buy bed linens, towels, furniture polish, or soap for their homes when they can take them from the hotel, just as some members of the kitchen staff will from time to time take food for home consumption. Other not uncommon acts of employee dishonesty are bellpersons who use a master key to steal from guests' rooms, front office clerks who accept payoffs from prostitutes for placing keys in the key rack in a way which lets them know which rooms are occupied by lone males, or the engineering employee who takes home light bulbs, tools, and engineering supplies rather than going to a store to buy them.

Each such case represents a loss to the employer and thus is a security problem. However, these are not insoluble problems if security managers have learned how the lodging industry functions, and if they are able to work closely with various department heads, such as the food and beverage director, executive housekeeper, front office manager, and chief engineer in developing mutually acceptable programs to reduce losses resulting from employee dishonesty. Nevertheless, reducing losses, even when attributable to dishonesty, must be done in ways in which the solution of one problem will not lead to others of the labor relations variety.

Another aspect of lodging industry security revolves around the need to devise methods to help reduce losses that are caused not by dishonesty but by human failures. Conceivably, losses of this sort could prove more costly to an inn than those which are the result of deliberate misconduct. Here, too, a few typical examples may best serve to illustrate some of the more commonly encountered problems.

Food and beverage cost controllers who do not take the time to weigh deliveries of orders where purchasing is by weight, or to check the quality of what is delivered, can contribute to losses by allowing their employers to pay for what they may have bought but did not in fact receive. Unless permitted by policy, employees who do their personal laundry on the inn's time and who use its resources help reduce profit margins. Receiving and kitchen personnel who do not follow a first in–first out principle in food handling, particularly where perishables are concerned, contribute to spoilage and waste, both of which mean losses to the hotel. Failure to screen garbage carefully may result in table settings being thrown out and having to be replaced. Housekeeping personnel who, when making up rooms, do not take time to make certain that all bed linens, towels, drapes, lamps, clothes hangers, and furniture are in place, are derelict. Those who see used room service trays sitting in hallways but do not notify room service of their presence and location so that they can be picked up, are guilty of contributing to a property's poor reputation. This, in turn, will affect sales and revenues. Bartenders who ignore policy and free-pour liquor instead of measuring drinks cost their employers money.

The foregoing synopsis of the hospitality industry's security concerns makes it quite obvious that a great deal more is involved than merely having security officers monitor employee access, patrol hallways, help with lounge guests who may have had too much to drink, and respond to emergencies. Protecting everyone lawfully on the premises, both guests or employees, and making every effort to secure their property as well, are important aspects of hotel security. No less important is the need to protect the employer against losses, whether caused by dishonest guests, dishonest employees, employees who simply do not perform their jobs as they should, or vendors who are prepared to risk being caught making deliveries that are either short in weight or not up to the hotels's quality standards.

HEALTH CARE

There are a number of similarities between the hospitality industry's security concerns and those that confront hospitals or medical centers. Some of these shared concerns are due to the fact that like hotels, hospitals function around the clock throughout the year. Of course, there also are significant differences in terms of their populations, access, and the nature of their basic operations. For instance, people usually stay at particular hotels as a matter of personal choice; they are usually admitted to particular hospitals because their doctors have staff privileges there or recommend them. Hotel guests can come and go as they please; hospital patients cannot, and even visiting hours are limited. Hotels serve guests, while hospitals provide patients with care and services that presumably will help them recover from their illnesses.

Similarities and differences aside, even today there are people who do not fully appreciate the scope and magnitude of the security problems that hospitals face. The director of hospitals for a large municipal hospital system once observed that as far as he could tell, the only two things that never disappeared from any of the city's hospitals were "bodies and bricks," to which he then added that by no means was he all that certain about the "bodies."[4] Despite the seeming humor, he was concerned about the impact that losses could have on his hospitals' operations, particularly on the quality of patient care, feelings that are shared by hospital administrators in general. Neither nonprofit health care facilities nor those in business to make a profit can sustain their operations indefinitely if they have continual losses. Both government and private hospitals have closed their doors because they lack financial resources.

Most, if not all of the security-related problems found in hotel purchasing, receiving, food operations, housekeeping, laundry, and engineering can be found in health care facilities. It is immaterial whether hospital employees or members of the medical staff are dishonest, negligent, lazy, or unconcerned. The result is the same insofar as it affects the institution. Employees who solicit or accept kickbacks from vendors; are too lazy to make certain that quantities ordered are received or that perishables are used on a first in–first out basis; steal food, housekeeping, or engineering supplies; or do their personal laundry at the hospital contrary to policy are guilty of contributing to a hospital's losses. The occasional house officer or attending physician who borrows something from a floor, ward, or operating suite and forgets to return it also contributes to those losses.

Of course, employees and staff are not alone in this respect; patients may also be contributors. However, when they are, it most often occurs with the help or suggestion of personnel and under circumstances where neither party considers what it will cost the hospital for replacements. For example, it is not at all unusual for patients who are being discharged to ask for, or simply be given, such things as plastic wash basins, hand lotion, or talcum powder which could be used for other patients. Individually, the per unit cost may seem inconsequential, but if this happens with any frequency, the annual replacement costs can be quite substantial.

By no means are these the only significant security-related concerns facing health care facilities. Like any organization, protecting reputation is critically important. However, a failed reputation can be injurious to a medical center in ways that do not necessarily apply to other types of activities. To illustrate, if a hotel's reputation is damaged, occupancy will decrease and so will profits, but with the passage of time both occupancy and profits may return to an acceptable level. If a hospital's reputation is damaged, it can result in an investigation by the state licensing authorities, the bodies that accredit hospitals, or both, and if its license is revoked or its accreditation is withdrawn, it may have no choice but to shut down.

There are other significant security-related concerns that are distinctly different from anything encountered in the hospitality field. Among them are the effect that visitors can have on patient care, whether provided on a patient care floor or in an emergency room setting. In addition, the inherent nature of hospitals involves pharmacies and prescription medications, narcotics included, the risk of infant kidnappings for those with either obstetric or pediatric services, and the risk, no matter how slight, of someone with fake credentials passing themselves off as physicians or nurses and being permitted to care for patients. Problems can also arise when patients either are or become psychotic, and last, but by no means least, is the way in which toxic or otherwise contaminated waste is handled.

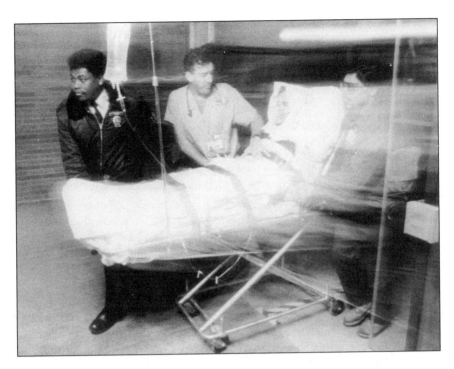

Courtesy of Mount Sinai Medical Center, New York City

Hospital patients are traumatized by the very fact of their injuries or illnesses. Their visitors may also be somewhat traumatized by a combination of their concern for the hospitalized relative or friend whom they are visiting, and the hospital setting itself. If a patient's admission is the result of an emergency, he or she may not even be aware of what is happening, but if that person is accompanied by a friend or relative, the degree of the latter's trauma may be elevated. In either case, visitors may pose problems that can affect the patient's care, although visitor behavior may be based on the best of intentions.

Suppose, for example, that a patient's illness is such that the attending physician prescribes, among other things, a low-salt or no-salt diet. The patient is unhappy and complains about the hospital's food to a visitor, who meaning only the best, on the next visit brings the patient a sandwich whose contents are high in sodium. Suppose that the patient has been seriously injured in an accident and is brought to an emergency room by ambulance. While awaiting evaluation for treatment by a triage nurse, the patient's next of kin arrives. Out of genuine concern the relative tries to do something in a well-meaning attempt to ease the patient's pain, but in doing so gets in the way of the emergency room staff. These illustrations are by no means uncommon in a hospital setting.

Medical centers have their own pharmacies. The pharmacies, in turn, dispense both prescription and nonprescription medications based on orders written by patients' physicians. Controlling the dispensing of medications in either category is a matter of concern to hospitals since an error may have an adverse effect on a patient if the patient happens to be allergic. Neither aspirin, sulfa, nor penicillin is a narcotic; therefore, a dispensing error is not likely to cause a patient to develop an addiction. However, this does not alter the fact that if a patient is allergic to any of them, erroneous administration can result in a significant reaction. Then, of course, among prescription drugs are those that are considered controlled substances because of their narcotic content. The way in which they are given to patients obviously is critical.

Granted that the administration of medication is not itself a security issue, the fact remains that the way in which all medications are handled, from the time they are received by the institution until they are actually dispensed to patients, can have security overtones. If shortages occur at any stage of the process, the probability that the hospital's security department will have to become involved is quite high. At one time it was quite common for a supply of narcotic drugs, however modest, to be kept in a "narcotics locker" on each floor or ward, with the key in the care and custody of the charge or head nurse. A narcotics count was supposed to be taken with each change of shift. Because of what hospital administrators rightly perceived to be risk of misappropriation, many hospitals altered this practice. Where this has occurred, all medications are controlled by the pharmacy, and those prescribed for each patient are identified accordingly and sent directly to the floor. Despite this, a risk still exists when pharmacies, unaware of patient discharges, send narcotics to a floor and instead of being returned they are appropriated by personnel for personal use or sale. As a result, a close working relationship needs to exist between a hospital pharmacy and its security department in order to have effective controls over medications and to minimize the risk of misappropriation.

Perhaps one of the most traumatic experiences that can be had in the health care field involves the kidnapping of a newborn child from a hospital nursery or of an ill child who is a pediatric patient. From time to time one reads of such an event. The kidnappers who have been apprehended in these cases usually have not asked for ransom; neither are they criminals in the normally accepted sense of the word. They often are women who for one reason or another want a child of their own. Nevertheless, the impact on the victim and its parents can be devastating, and the effect of the negative publicity that such an incident generates does the institution's reputation a great deal of harm. While access control to the hospital, its nursery and floors, and an employee and staff identification program can help reduce these risks, security directors need to work closely with all aspects of administration in developing additional preventive measures for the protection of all patients who happen to be children.

The importance of preemployment screening for all organizations has been discussed in earlier chapters, but nowhere is this task as important as it is in the health care field. Dishonest employees can do employers financial harm for which they may have some form of protection and from which they may recover. However, even the gravest act of dishonesty in a business setting cannot compare to the harm that can be done to a patient if unqualified or incompetent persons are hired or granted staff privileges by a hospital.

However infrequently it may happen, the fact remains that from time to time the news media will report cases of persons with fake credentials practicing medicine and performing surgery in hospitals, or of nurses whose incompetence has resulted in multiple questionable deaths at institutions where they have worked. In either case the hospital's reputation suffers, the community that it serves loses faith in it, and there may be costly losses if litigation follows. As is the case with dispensing medications, the primary responsibility for preventing such occurrences rests with human resources departments, directors of nursing, and physician screening committees that grant staff privileges. Nevertheless, if the security department is fully integrated into the organization, it can help minimize the risks to the hospital by working with these constituencies in helping them design and implement meaningful procedures to detect fake physicians' credentials or questionable nursing behavior before rather than after incidents affecting the quality of patient care occur.

Hospitals need not be classified as so-called "mental institutions" before they encounter problems with psychotic or delirious patients. Such encounters may occur not only in emergency room settings, but also on patient care floors. When they do, security assistance may be crucial. Psychotic or delirious patients may become violent. If so, they may pose a threat to the personal safety of those who are trying to care for them as well as to other patients. Should this be the case, the likelihood exists that security will be asked to help the professional staff subdue the patient. That security will be called upon to help becomes even more probable if a violent but conscious patient professes to be suffering from a fatal disease, such as AIDS, which can be transmitted by mixing body fluids, as might be the case if the patient bit someone hard enough to puncture the skin. This is another illustration of both the need for security assistance and proper training for security personnel.

The inherent nature of hospitals is such that they cannot avoid generating toxic, hazardous, or contagious waste. By the same token, what they generate must be disposed of in ways that will not result in any of that waste affecting or infecting those who may come into contact with it either as part of the disposal process or accidentally. Despite the best efforts of hospitals in collecting and disposing of this waste, the news media occasionally will report that a health care worker has become infected through an act of carelessness on the individual's part or that of a co-worker, or that evidence of such waste has been found dumped somewhere away from the hospital itself.

All hospital personnel need to be educated and constantly reminded about the risks and what they must do to protect themselves against injury or infection. Security departments can help implement the institution's program by making certain that suitable containers for the waste are available in patient rooms and other parts of the hospital where any such waste might be generated, and that great care is exercised in its disposition if that is done on the premises. However great this challenge is, an even greater one arises when disposition is done off site by a third party under contract. To protect itself, the generating hospital needs to be certain that the waste is picked up, the contractor transports it in an approved type of vehicle to a licensed facility for incineration or some other approved form of disposition, and that it actually is disposed of in a safe and suitable way. Following up on this phase of the process is a task well within the role that a hospital security department can and should play.

FINANCIAL INSTITUTIONS

The mere mention of "financial institutions" usually brings to mind banks and banking. However, the term is also used to encompass stockbrokers and insurance companies. Unlike many other activities, such as retailing or manufacturing, financial institutions are regulated by various government agencies. For example, most banks are subject to regulation by the U.S. government; those which are not are regulated by state banking commissions. Stockbrokers are regulated by the Securities and Exchange Commission, a federal agency, and state insurance commissioners regulate insurance companies that do business in their states.

Like all other organizations, financial institution security directors and managers must deal with the generic concerns that can result in losses for their employers. Among these are all dishonest acts that can be perpetrated by employees, regardless of their level of importance within the organization, and scandal affecting any financial institution's reputation conceivably can have an impact of such significance as to effectively put it out of business. No matter how important reputation is to other organizations, a loss of public confidence is rarely as disastrous as it is for a financial institution.

To illustrate, suppose that executives of a government contractor are defrauding the U.S. government and are found guilty. They may be imprisoned, fined, or both. Depending on the circumstances, the company may also be fined. It may even be prohibited from doing further business with any government agency for a specified period. However, rarely will it be forced out of business. On the other hand, assume that a bank officer's arrest for embezzlement is publicized. The resulting publicity causes a sizable number of customers to lose confidence in the institution and prompts them either to withdraw funds or to close their accounts altogether. This, in turn, may cause a run on the bank and make it impossible for it to keep its doors open.

But the problems common to virtually all organizations are not the only security-related issues with which financial institution security departments must deal. Neither are they the same among the three categories of such institutions. Banks, brokerage firms, and insurance companies all have different concerns which are uniquely theirs.

Banks always have been targets of bank robberies and of burglaries in some cases. Robberies may be perpetrated by one or more people, many of whom are armed, while others profess to be armed as a way of expediting their mission and escape. In all instances of this sort bank personnel must assume that the robbers are armed. This, in turn, represents a possible threat to the safety of both employees and customers since armed robbers who fear apprehension may elect to hold those present hostage and threaten to or actually injure or kill one or more people if not allowed to escape.

Bank robbers also have been known to hold a bank manager's family hostage as a way of forcing the manager to get them into his or her branch, open the vault for them, and permit them to get away. There have also been instances when burglars have entered a closed bank and cleaned out safe deposit boxes, which often contain valuables in the form of jewelry, cash, or other negotiable instruments.

Distasteful as these offenses are, banks have made an effort to minimize their risks and losses. Great strides have been made over the years in the improvement of the types of alarm systems they use. The use of closed-circuit television and time-lapse surveillance cameras has also helped to reduce the risk of acts of violence or hostage taking, and they have been very useful to law enforcement agencies for purposes of identification, apprehension, and conviction.

The banking industry's increasing competitiveness has caused banks to search for ways in which they can attract new customers. However,this has also added to their security-related concerns. One of the problems about which bank security departments must worry is credit card counterfeiting and fraud. The other is the safety of customers using automatic teller machines (ATMs).

Courtesy of Bankers Trust
Company, New York City

Unlike the American Express card, which is independent and not bank connected, MasterCard and Visa credit cards are issued by various banks. Although they are a service to customers, they are also a source of income to the issuing banks. As a result, banks actively solicit people to become users of their particular credit cards. In doing so, it is not unusual for the solicitation to tell prospective customers that their applications have already been approved. The fact that written applications may have to be completed and returned to the soliciting bank does not necessarily guarantee that all of the data provided by applicants are accurate. If it is not, and dishonest persons then use the card to the extent that they have been given a line of credit, the bank may well suffer a loss. In an attempt to minimize the risk of credit card abuse, establishments willing to accept credit cards in payment can now run them through a reader. Thus the amount of the purchase, whether for goods or services, can be approved before the customer or hotel guest leaves the premises. However, in those situations where a credit card is used to buy something by telephone, this safeguard is unavailable and the risk remains.

In many respects credit cards are like currency. As a result, it is not surprising that just as from time to time where are attempts to counterfeit paper money, so are there people who will try to counterfeit credit cards. To combat this problem it is necessary to secure the blank card stock on which data are imprinted, and card designs are modified periodically in the interest of better protection. Despite these measures, counterfeit credit cards still appear occasionally.

Neither the issue of credit card fraud nor of counterfeiting pose a threat to the physical well-being of people. The same cannot be said with regard to bank customers who use an ATM. Occasionally they are robbed; sometimes they are injured or killed in the course of a robbery. The question of whether banks are or should be held liable in such cases is one for the legal system to decide. However, in the interest of good customer relations one might think that banks cannot afford to have people feel unsafe if they use an ATM. Liability aside, a challenge for banking industry security directors and managers is whether customer safety can be improved beyond what now exists and whether it can be done reasonably from an expense standpoint.

A story in the *New York Times* of July 8, 1992,[5] captioned "Council Backs Security Steps for A.T.M.'s," concerns the New York City Council's Public Safety Committee's approval of a bill that would force New York City banks to improve security at automatic teller machines. The bill, which reportedly would be even more strict than similar laws in California and Nevada, was prompted by publicized crimes at such machines during 1991, including one in which an assistant district attorney was shot at a cash machine, and another in which an off-duty police sergeant was killed while trying to stop a robbery at an ATM. The story indicates that the bill, if passed, might well be overturned by the federal courts on the premise that federal laws preempt local bank regulations. Should this be the final outcome, it is highly unlikely that the entire issue will be forgotten. Instead, something like the California and Nevada laws, which are less strict, might be adopted. In either event, this understandable concern with customers' personal safety while using ATMs is another security issue for banks.

Stockbrokerage operations are distinguishable from those of banks and other financial institutions in several ways. Despite being regulated by the Securities and Exchange Commission and having personnel who are responsible for compliance, they have security concerns that need to be addressed. Among them is the fact that while so many transactions are computerized, they still deal on a daily basis with stock certificates and bonds, many of which are payable to "bearer" rather than a specifically named person. Another distinguishing characteristic is their access to sensitive information about organizations whose stock is traded on the market. Then, too, they are frequently designated by corporations as the recipients of proxy votes when stockholders need to vote on issues at a corporation's annual meeting. The nature of some of these very issues does not always lend itself to regulation. When this happens it is not uncommon for security to have to become involved with oversight to try to prevent incidents from occurring that could prove to be both costly and embarrassing to the employer.

As for the high volume of negotiable instruments that are handled by brokerage houses daily, perhaps government regulation, which includes procedures for screening "registered representatives," has contributed to a sense of false security and a degree of unjustified confidence in employees who actually handle stock certificates and bonds. As an example, a personnel manager for a major Wall Street securities company once admitted that his organization's preemployment screening practices did not extend to messengers since the job was considered a rather menial position. This, despite the fact that every working day messengers were handed briefcases filled with thousands, possibly even millions, of dollars worth of negotiable instruments and sent out on the streets of New York City to deliver some while picking up others. In another like organization, where computer room security was extremely tight, virtually anyone dressed in a business suit could enter the "back room" where employees processed stock certificates and where they were permitted to keep personal bags, briefcases, purses, and so on, at their desks. In still another securities organization it was an acceptable practice for employees to leave unfinished work, including completed stock certificates or bonds to be mailed to customers, on their desks when they left work for the day. The risks simply were not fully appreciated.

Notwithstanding the understandable worry about problems such as those cited, stockbrokerage firms are very concerned about one of the more insidious forms of white-collar crime: namely, insider trading. The very nature of their business makes it necessary for them to be privy to a good deal of information in order to best serve the interests of their customers. They have on their payrolls employees who specialize in analyzing certain industries and evaluating the performance of individual organizations within those industries so that the registered representatives (their sales personnel), in turn, can make recommendations about buying or selling certain stocks to their customers. In addition, the analysts are invited to attend briefings given by organizations whose stock is traded publicly, at which time they may be told about otherwise unpublicized developments, and they customarily are present at corporate annual meetings.

For securities employees to attend briefings and annual meetings is a legitimate activity as long as those who become privy to data that are not otherwise generally known do not take advantage of their roles to benefit themselves, their families, or friends financially. Despite this, however, there are some brokerage house personnel who will use this "insider" information for personal gain and who will share what they know with family and friends. To illustrate this point, assume that the employee attends a pharmaceutical manufacturer's briefing and learns that a cure for cancer has been found, the necessary approvals for sale have been received, and that an announcement offering the product for sale will be made in 60 days. Based on this information, the employee buys 1000 shares of the company's stock at $10 a share. The day of the announcement the stock sells for $25 a share, and as a result of the information that had been received at the briefing but which was not known to the general public, the broker's employee has made a $15,000 profit.

Conversely, another employee has a friend who is the vice president for human resources for a large computer manufacturer. Because of the latter's reputation and size, the broker's employee has bought over time 1000 shares of stock at an average price of $25 a share. It is now worth $50 a share. The friend reports in confidence that the as yet unannounced results for the quarter just ended will show an unexpected loss instead of the profit originally anticipated. Consequently, the manufacturer will be laying off 500 employees. Upon hearing this the employee immediately sells his 1000 shares, having made a $25,000 profit on the original purchase. A week later the quarter results are made public, and the value of the stock drops to $35 a share. As a result of the confidential information given to the employee, the latter avoided what could have been a substantial loss.

Despite the fact that trading on the basis of insider information is a crime, and that the news media report prosecutions, findings of guilty, and penalties, there still are some people who, just as they are prepared to take their chances with the stock market, are also prepared to gamble that they can engage in insider trading practices and not get caught. However, when the practice is indulged in and those ultimately involved are apprehended, identified, and prosecuted, people who buy and sell stocks tend to lose confidence in that broker's organization. As with any other type of business its reputation is hurt, sometimes so critically that it cannot recover and stay in business.

As pointed out earlier, another thing that distinguishes stockbrokers from other financial institutions is the role they frequently play in collecting proxies for businesses in anticipation of the latter's annual meetings. Inasmuch as stockholders are entitled to vote on certain matters that may arise at an annual meeting, yet many cannot for one reason or another attend the meeting, the notice they get informing them of a melting to be held is accompanied by a statement of issues to be voted on, and a proxy. The proxy gives stockholders who cannot be present the option of voting their wishes on the proxy form, or of authorizing someone, usually the officers of the corporation, to vote in their behalf. In either case the completed proxy forms frequently are to be returned to a designated stockbroker, who then tallies the votes of those who have elected to indicate their wishes, and it also reports on the number of stockholders who are willing to let the corporate officers make the decision. Imagine the impact on a corporation if in circumstances such as these, proxies received by a broker were lost or stolen prior to the annual meeting date, if the tallies reported were manipulated by dishonest brokerage employees doing the count, or if the count simply proved to be inaccurate.

Like their financial industry counterparts, insurance companies are not immune from security-related issues. However, many of those that affect them are distinguishable from those of other financial institutions. Although this is true regardless of the type of insurance the company sells, it is that type of coverage which may, in and of itself, pose different problems for the company. Although insurance companies write policies covering a wide variety of risks, many people tend to think of the subject largely in terms of automobile, life, health and accident, and casualty insurance. All forms of insurance sold generate income for the selling company, but they also represent a potential for the payment of large sums of money to claimants who allege that they have suffered a loss covered by their policies.

The very nature of the business offers perhaps more opportunities for dishonest employees to steal than might be the case in other types of organizations; at the same time it leaves insurers vulnerable to the filing of fraudulent claims by policyholders. Just as one occasionally finds stockbrokers' employees being far too casual about the way in which they protect stock certificates, largely because the volume is so great that they may not fully appreciate the need for security, so can one find insurance company employees who prepare checks in payment of claims becoming less careful than they should be in order to protect their employer. The volume can be so great, and their work so routine, that they may not exercise the degree of care which they should for the protection of such things as blank check stock or check-writing signature plates.

One major insurance company almost lost over $2 million because employees at several levels, and in several departments, simply failed to do their jobs in ways that would have minimized the risk of such an occurrence. Accountability for blank check stock used in paying claims was lax, the counter on the department's check writing machine was rarely used, the signature plate was not secured properly when not in actual use, and instead of the company's internal auditors regularly auditing the department for policy compliance, they performed audits only when asked to do so by the department head.

Another internal security concern relates to the protection of policyholder information. Irrespective of the type of policy, the insurance company necessarily needs to have a good deal of information about the policyholder and the risks covered by the policy. Every potential insured applies for the coverage sought, and on the basis of the data provided on the application the insurer decides if it will issue a policy. Applications obviously need to include the policyholder's name and address, but beyond that they need to set forth details about what is covered. On the basis of these data, insurers determine both whether they will write the requested coverage and the premiums they will charge for it.

For example, an insured covered by life or accident and health policies will first have been given a physical examination by a physician. This means that the person's entire medical history to that point becomes a part of the file and needs to be protected. A homeowner seeking insurance for a residence and its contents is obliged to provide information relative to their value. Suppose that a home, assessed at $1 million, has among its contents paintings and sculpture by such well-known artists as Rembrandt, Chagall, and Rodin valued at $2 million, plus a good deal of expensive jewelry. The artwork and jewelry have to be described in detail. Imagine the serious consequences for both an insured and an insurer should any information of this kind fall into the wrong hands. For instance, what might be the impact on a political campaign if a candidate's medical history shows occasional depression and becomes known to voters, or if a burglar learns of a home's valuable contents and steals them, because both an opposing candidate and a burglar got the information from an insurance company employee?

EDUCATIONAL INSTITUTIONS

Educational institutions are unique in that they, perhaps more than any other type of activity, require a combination of security and policing if assets, people included, are to be protected. Where schools, from kindergarten through university level, once were rather serene settings respected by students and the general public, they are now more a reflection of what goes on in the daily life of their neighborhoods and cities. The relative ease with which students of almost any age can get their hands on weapons of one sort or another has made it necessary for school officials to use magnetometers to screen grammar, middle, and high school students upon entering buildings. It is not unusual to find security officers employed by urban public school systems. Many colleges and universities have come to the conclusion that to protect their facilities, faculties, staffs, and students properly, they need their own police departments, despite the existence of public law enforcement agencies.

Campus police forces function as would any law enforcement agency. In many cases their personnel have been given some form of governmental authority for that purpose with the realization that in the final analysis both the college or university and the community benefit. For the most part, today's campus police are trained. Their personnel deal with thefts of all sorts, assaults, rapes, vandalism, burglaries, robberies, muggings, drunkenness, drug use, and even occasional homicides. They try to prevent crime by patrolling campus buildings and grounds on foot and in marked cars. When crimes are reported to them they investigate using modern police methods. They work closely with all public law enforcement agencies on matters of mutual interest.

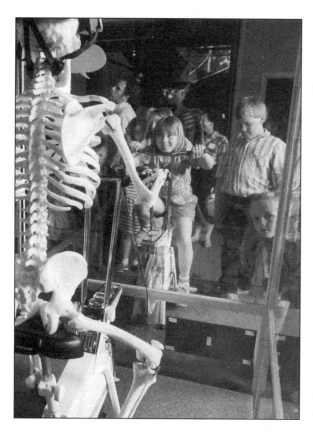

Courtesy of Museum
of Science, Boston, Ma.

Although campus police do provide security to their schools, they normally do not become involved with the concept of the overall protection and conservation of assets, which increasingly has become associated with security operations. If, for instance, allegations are made that a buyer is accepting bribes in return for placing orders with a particular vendor, or that someone has stolen blank transcript of grade forms from the registrar's office, they will respond and investigate. However, in anticipation of the fact that such things might occur, the campus police chief is not likely to learn how purchasing works so that he or she can suggest ways of preventing kickbacks. As for transcript form thefts, aside from recommending physical security to the registrar, procedures to prevent a recurrence will rarely originate with the head of the campus police.

Nevertheless, boards of education and college and university administrations are not immune from many of the same problems with which security directors and managers, and government inspectors general, must deal on a daily basis. For example, in addition to their professional qualifications there are issues related to the moral and ethical behavior of teachers. No public school system can risk laxity in preemployment screening if doing so can result in hiring a teacher with a history of child abuse or sexual molestation, or of a football coach with a reputation as a sadist. Imagine parents' reactions to the employment of a school nurse who is addicted to drugs, or of a janitor who has been involved with child pornography. Here there is more need for a person with a security rather than a police orientation, one whose approach to prevention is based on an understanding of how all departments function so that he or she can work closely with other department heads in minimizing risks.

At the college or university level some of the problems encountered are more subtle and complex. They are also much more akin to some of the concerns found in a business environment, particularly where there is a research and development organization. From time to time, problems of patent rights and conflicts of interest may arise if they are not guarded against initially. That these things can happen is due in part to three things: the mistaken belief that things that happen in the business sector simply cannot occur in academe, the fact that faculty members routinely are allowed time for outside activities, and the time-honored acceptance of the notion of academic freedom.

Most academics know that to be granted tenure and to be promoted through the ranks from assistant to full professor, they must achieve recognition on the basis of their research, writing, or both. This, in turn, will prompt them to apply for research grants to get the funding necessary for their projects. In the overwhelming number of such cases the work is done in accordance with the terms of the grant. Where the grant is for research that may lead to the filing of a patent application and subsequent granting of a patent, the ultimate beneficiary may be the organization that provided the funding, the person to whom the grant was awarded, the school, or a combination of all three.

However, in the event that the faculty member to whom the research grant has been awarded is also engaged in an outside business activity, and the research results are patentable, it is important for the school to have a mechanism in place to ensure that all the research, and the results thereof, are handled in strict accordance with the terms of the grant itself. One major academic institution discovered that a senior faculty member, who also was a partner in a business, was not averse to conducting research under grants at the university, using its facilities and materials, until he felt that he was nearing the desired results. At that point he would transfer the balance of the research to his outside business. Upon its completion he would file the patent application in that organization's name. Consequently, once the letters patent were issued, it was his organization, not the university or the original grantor, which benefited financially. This case illustrates the need for effective security programs to help protect colleges and universities from losses that can be attributed to conflicts of interest and to their failure to have procedures to help prevent the diversion of sponsored research activity.

Another aspect of security normally not encompassed by campus police responsibilities relates to work done at colleges and universities under contract to various agencies of the federal government. By no means are all institutions of higher learning involved with work for federal agencies, but those that are may be engaged in research for such varied agencies as the Department of Defense, Nuclear Regulatory Commission, Department of Transportation, and Central Intelligence Agency, among others. Whether the initiative for this research originates with the institution or the government, the fact remains that the contracts will require that information related to the work be protected. Since government contracts can mean considerable research income for the schools, and added prestige in some cases, it is not at all surprising that in many cases these awards are welcomed.

In some respects implementing security programs for government research is relatively easy. This is due to the fact that the awarding government agency sets forth clearly not only what must be done, but how it must be done. On the other hand, there invariably will be some faculty members who will react unfavorably to the restrictions imposed by the agreements on the ground that they infringe on academic freedom. If the terms of a contract are breached, the university may lose the work and associated income, and its reputation may suffer. If the faculty resents the security aspects of the program, morale will suffer. Conceivably, there even may be some orchestrated security breaches. Consequently, college and university security directors at those institutions engaged in government research are confronted with challenges best met through the combined use of patience and diplomacy. They must be able to convince the faculty of the work's importance at the same time that they help them understand that their academic freedom is not in jeopardy.

To illustrate a case of faculty reaction, in the mid-1950s a major academic institution was under contract to three government agencies, all of which had strict security requirements. The combined work represented an annual research income of from $65 to $70 million. Chronologically, this not only was during the Cold War between the Western powers and the Iron Curtain countries, but it was at a time when government agencies generally, and the U.S. State Department and Department of Defense were particularly sensitive to security issues resulting from McCarthyism, which lasted from 1946 to 1957. The name was derived from Senator Joseph McCarthy, who made accusations, often unsubstantiated, to the effect that both departments were riddled with Communists or Communist sympathizers.

At this time it was possible for certain types of unclassified information to be sent to Western European countries under a particular Department of Commerce license which, in fact, required no license. It merely required that all envelopes containing such material be marked to show that they were being exported in accordance with that Commerce Department provision. To assist rather than hinder faculty who might want to send material to colleagues in permitted countries, the school's librarian distributed a memorandum informing the faculty of the procedure and providing the number of the license to be used. Shortly after its issue, an internationally famous member of the faculty approached the security manager. In a belligerent tone of voice he threatened to resign if this meant that he had to get a license every time that he wanted to correspond with a friend in Switzerland. He had interpreted the word "license" as meaning a formal document rather than as meaning "permission." Once he was calmed down and this was explained to him, he not only appreciated the need for security but became one of the security manger's greatest supporters.

When one considers the nature of museums, whether of art, natural history, commerce and industry, or aeronautics, to name but a few types, it does not seem at all inappropriate to consider them as educational institutions. However, their needs are more in tune with the broad concept of security as expressed thus far in this book.

Museums are confronted with many of the same problems that are encountered by any organization. At the same time, they have concerns that are uniquely theirs. As a rule, museum exhibits are based on assets owned by the organization or loaned to it. Not surprisingly, those that it owns may be of such magnitude that they cannot all be displayed at the same time. Works on loan may be owned either by other museums or by individual owners. Consequently, museum security revolves around three primary factors: first, the source from which owned works are obtained; second, their protection while in storage; third, the protection of all works on display against acts of vandalism, theft, or destruction.

Courtesy of the Museum
of Science, Boston, Ma.

The source of owned works generally is through purchase or donation. In either case there may be a twofold question of legitimacy, one based on the work itself and the other on the ownership of the work being offered for sale. Counterfeit artworks are by no means unknown. In some instances the work may have been done with such skill that even experts may be misled. The detection of counterfeit art is not a security department function, but once it has been determined that the item is not authentic, security may well have a role to play by working with law enforcement authorities in trying to identify and locate the person responsible for the forgery and sale, and by helping the museum's attorneys collect evidence for a civil suit in an attempt to recover money paid for the work.

Another way in which security can play a role is in connection with the offer for sale of an authentic piece of art or sculpture by someone with whom the museum has no long-standing relationship. Just as forged or counterfeit artwork is not unknown, neither is the sale of stolen work. The country's best known museums, both private and government sponsored, have built their reputations on the quality of their exhibits. To maintain that quality, and their reputations, they cannot afford the embarrassment and publicity that inevitably accompanies the purchase of either a counterfeit or a stolen piece of art. In these cases while the legitimacy of the work itself may be unquestioned, there may be questions about how and from whom the seller acquired title, and security may well be positioned to help provide the answers.

If security is the protection and conservation of all of an employer's assets, it stands to reason that a museum's security department needs to be involved when owned assets are in storage. Issues related to temperature and humidity controls to prevent the deterioration of artwork almost invariably will be considered by the curator's staff, but they may not always be as well tuned to the need for physical security for the stored works as they should be. They may even labor under the impression that once a record is made of what is consigned to storage, periodic inventories are unnecessary. Certainly the physical security and inventory control aspects of stored assets are legitimate areas of concern for the security director's staff.

The protection of displayed works, whether owned or on loan to the museum, undoubtedly is of extreme importance. Knowledgeable museum security directors have access to some of the most sophisticated physical security devices available for the after-hours protection of their facilities and their contents. They have to be equally knowledgeable about devices that can be used to protect artworks when the museum is open to the public. From time to time one learns from the news media of paintings or pieces of sculpture that have been vandalized by visitors, or stolen when the museum is closed.

Museum security during visiting hours has to be both effective and discreet. The overwhelming number of people who go to museums do so for educational purposes and to enjoy the beauty of what is on exhibition; they do not go to damage or destroy. Therefore, the security system must be able to protect what is on display without inhibiting the pleasure to be derived by those who come to see it. The question of discretion in terms of physical security need not be considered for after-hours protection, but the training of security personnel does. There occasionally have been successful after-hours robberies during which valuable paintings have been stolen because of an apparent lack of good judgment on the part of museum security personnel. As with academic institutions, museum employees, guards included, often are inclined to accept what they are told without question. In some respects this is an outgrowth of the environment in which they work. Consequently, they may be more receptive to a ruse used by robbers to gain after-hours admission for the purpose of stealing valuable paintings and other artwork. Thus among the many challenges confronting museum security directors is the need to educate both their own personnel and employees generally about the importance of being ever alert to unusual requests that may presage a theft from the museum.

PUBLIC UTILITIES

For purposes of this section public utilities are companies that provide sources of energy and telephone communications. Like financial institutions, they are known as regulated industries. As a general rule they are subject to regulation by the public utility departments of the several states. However, those companies that own and operate nuclear reactors to generate electricity are also regulated by the Nuclear Regulatory Commission, which is an agency of the U.S. Department of Energy.

In considering the security needs of public utilities, one must also think about the sources from which they acquire materials, so that they, in turn, can sell their services to the public at large. In some cases those sources will be company owned; in others they will be purchased from independent third parties. Among the assets that public utilities

Courtesy of Maxus Energy Corporation

need to protect are their material sources, their facilities, which include both their generating plants, substations, and offices, their transmission lines, vehicles and allied equipment, and of course, the product or service itself.

The uninterrupted provision of power and telephone communications are of critical importance to both the general well-being of people and the nation's economy. Individuals need power sources for heat, food, and light; they need to be able to communicate with relatives and friends for their own peace of mind. Businesses and institutions need power sources and communications to operate effectively and efficiently. If there is a power failure of any kind or a disruption to telephone communications, there is an adverse impact on virtually every person and organization in the community or area affected.

It is relatively easy to understand the importance of protecting facilities and equipment. The cost of constructing a public utility company's facilities can run into millions of dollars; therefore, they are worth securing. Vehicles, tools, and other equipment needed to maintain operations and service to customers are also expensive and deserving of protection. In many respects these requirements are comparable to those of all other organizations, and public utility company security directors approach them in ways that are familiar to all security executives. Nevertheless, there are three aspects of public utility protection that differ from concerns in other types of activities: there are unique concerns for those involved with nuclear power; there is a need to protect transmission lines, which may run for hundreds, or even thousands, of miles, some overhead and some underground; and there is a need to prevent from theft the services they sell, bearing in mind the fact that gas, electricity, and telephone communications are intangibles.

Nuclear power plants are worrisome even under the best of conditions. Their construction plans must be approved by the Nuclear Regulatory Commission. The same is true of their plans for evacuation of the plant, and of people living and working within a given radius of the plant, in the event of an emergency. Their owners use sophisticated equipment to monitor constantly for possible radiation leaks or core meltdowns. These concerns, based on possible operations-related incidents, are safety oriented.

Unfortunately, these are not the only source of worry for plant owners and the Nuclear Regulatory Commission. Almost since the first nuclear power plant was under construction, thought has been given to the need to protect such facilities against the dangers of sabotage or willful destruction by terrorists or possibly by disgruntled employees, without regard to the impact that a release of radiation could have on innocent people. These legitimate concerns were, and continue to be, based on recognition of the fact that domestic terrorist organizations of one sort or another do exist in the United States, and of the uncertainties and frailties of human nature when employees feel they have a grievance against an employer and the employer is ignoring the problem.

An outgrowth of this has been the issuance by the Nuclear Regulatory Commission of detailed directives dealing with nuclear power plant security. Responsibility for their implementation, and any expansion that the owner and operator feels will further enhance security, rests with the latter. The directives even include training and equipment requirements for security personnel. Of course, there are also operational considerations. One is the exclusion from the facility of persons who use controlled substances. To comply, employees are subject to testing. However, in furtherance of this requirement it is not uncommon for nuclear power plants to include a provision in contracts with companies which supply them with either goods or services to ask that vendor employees submit proof that they do not use controlled substances.

Protecting transmission lines is another major security concern. The use of modern technology to monitor transmission will alert operators to a problem's existence, but it may not always identify the problem clearly, and it assuredly will not prevent one from occurring. In the 1960s an electrical transmission problem on the east coast of the United States resulted in a blackout of several major cities, Boston and New York included. The problem's source was operational, and corrective action was taken within a matter of hours. However, imagine the impact on the economy, and public safety and health, if a transmission problem was due to a deliberate act of sabotage. It could cause businesses to shut down, an increase in crime if alarms were inoperative and there was no light during hours of darkness, streetcars and subways would be unable to move, and hospitals would have to rely on emergency generators for even their minimum electrical needs. While this scenario focuses on an electrical transmission problem, the need to protect transmission lines is a concern shared by all organizations that offer their customers either energy or communications.

Courtesy of Maxus Energy Corporation

Public utilities have also been victimized by those who would steal from them. In some cases the loss will be money, but in others it will be a theft of the service the public utility sells to consumers. Money losses may be due to a variety of reasons. Utility companies are no more immune to robberies and burglaries than are other types of organizations. Also, some utility company employees who process receivables may not be above manipulating payments, wholly or partially, for their own benefit. Still another source of money losses is attributable to customers who simply fail to pay their bills.

Most money losses are relatively easy to detect. However, the same cannot always be said of losses suffered by public utilities when their products are stolen. One may wonder how it is possible for persons to steal an intangible product such as gas, electricity, or telephone communications, yet such thefts are problems with which public utility company security personnel must deal.

Insofar as gas and electricity are concerned, it is not so much a question of someone tapping directly into a transmission line and stealing as it is a matter of activating a dormant connection. For instance, service may have been discontinued to a location either because the consumer no longer exists or has moved, or because it has not paid its bills. Nevertheless, since the connection itself remains, someone will find a way to reactivate it without the utility company's knowledge or authorization.

Where telephone companies are concerned, in addition to fighting the problem of vandalized pay telephones and the theft of their equipment, such as instruments, they have the problem of stolen services. The use of "blue boxes" or "black boxes" by persons who know how to use the instrumentation to avoid paying for calls is not new, but the theft problem has increased with the use of 800 numbers and mobile telephones. Thieves have learned how to access an 800 line, then place calls to anywhere, with the 800-line customer being billed for the calls. A similar process can be used to identify a mobile telephone's access code number so that calls can be placed by the thief with the person or organization having the access code being billed. If when either of these situations occurs the consumer has a high volume of telephone use, it is possible that it may not be aware of the fact that it is paying for unauthorized calls, but if it detects and reports the problem to the telephone company, the latter almost invariably will authorize the customer to deduct the cost of those calls, and the utility then absorbs the loss. Of course, there may also be occasions when a subscriber will allege that one or two calls on its invoice were not authorized, even though this may not always be true. Once again the telephone company will absorb the loss.

The significance of the theft of telephone services was highlighted in a news item which stated that according to Telecommunications Advisors, Inc., the 1991 total for telephone fraud amounted to $2233 million. According to their data, the six most costly categories of telephone fraud involved long-distance calls, 800 number charges, victim management and staff time, victim consultant and staff fees, carrier and vendor management and staff time, and carrier and vendor consultant and attorney fees.[6]

When organizations not regulated by government have losses of any kind, they have the option of simply raising the cost of their product or service. However, this option is not readily available to some regulated industries, public utilities included. For them to increase rates they must first apply to the appropriate agency, and justify not only the request but also the amount of increase for which they are asking. In these situations there may then be hearings on the request, and only after the prescribed process has been completed will a decision on the request be forthcoming. Although utility company requests are usually granted, in many instances the full amount of the increase requested will not be. Therefore, the need for effective security to prevent losses increases.

REAL ESTATE MANAGEMENT

Whether a person or a business is responsible for managing real estate, whether they manage one or many properties, and whether they are residential, commercial, or industrial, there is a need to protect the real estate, the property's tenants, and invitees. Of course, one should recognize that while in many cases real estate managers have such a need, the responsibility for security by no means is theirs alone; it is more of a shared responsibility. However, to clearly and logically delineate the sharing, several factors often need to be considered. Among them are whether the owner is also the manager or if the latter is an independent organization. Is the property leased to tenants? If so, for what purpose, as a residence or as a place of business? If a multioccupant building is not leased, is the property in the nature of a cooperative or a condominium?

Protecting the real estate itself is an owner's legitimate concern, but implementing a security program for this purpose may be left to those responsible for the property's management. In either case, this aspect of protection relates primarily to physical security. The task is one of preventing a loss by fire, explosion, or through acts of vandalism. Building codes, particularly in larger cities, will require the installation of certain fire or life safety equipment, including sprinklers, smoke detectors, and standpipe. In those parts of the country that are earthquake prone other requirements may be imposed by local building codes. Efforts to deal with vandalism may focus on a combination of access control and surveillance equipment, with physical security supplemented by security personnel.

The issue of protecting occupants and invitees is not always as clearly defined. Initially there are two realities that must be recognized. One deals with whether occupancy is under the terms of a lease, or if it is in the nature of a cooperative or condominium. The other makes it necessary to distinguish between public and private use space. If occupants lease their space, the terms of their agreement with the property's management spell out the terms of their occupancy. This includes not only the length of the lease and rent to be paid, but also to what extent, if any, tenants can alter their space. Since it is a generally recognized rule of law that anything that becomes permanently attached to real estate becomes a part of that real estate, tenants may well be limited insofar as the installation of certain physical security measures are concerned. Nevertheless, the rental space occupied is viewed as for private use, and tenants occasionally will take steps to protect that space in ways that are not inconsistent with their leases. By the same token, landlords, be they owners or real estate managers, know that security problems can affect a property's reputation, and with it, rentals. Inasmuch as no landlord wants to have vacancies or a high rate of tenant turnover, they may well be amenable to tenant requests for improved protection.

Of course, the lease limitations imposed on tenants, coupled with the fact that multitenant properties all have public space, means that landlords are responsible for security in the public areas. This is based on the principle that only the landlord, rather than any tenant or group of tenants, controls public spaces such as lobbies, fire towers, elevators, hallways, and in commercial buildings, the rest rooms. Illustrative of some of the problems that may be encountered in public areas are cases of women being raped in office building elevators and being robbed of money and jewelry in mall rest rooms. Consequently, landlords have become increasingly aware of the need to take steps to minimize security problems in properties which they own or manage.

These same public space problems can arise in residential properties. This is equally true of properties that are either cooperatives or condominiums. However, there are two major differences in that where cooperatives and condominiums are concerned, the occupants are in a far better position to do whatever they feel is reasonably necessary to secure their private space, and their approval must be given for any significant steps to be taken to protect public space. Although there are legal distinctions between cooperatives and condominiums, for all practical purposes units are owned, not leased. Therefore, while the rules that govern the property must be respected, owners are not precluded from making improvements to their space, including those intended for protection.

The very ownership principle that makes cooperatives and condominiums attractive to many people can also have its drawbacks from the manager's viewpoint where security is concerned. The real estate manager is expected to do what it can to make certain that the property is well protected, but unlike rental property management, it cannot arbitrarily set standards; they must be approved by the shareholders or owners. This may make it necessary to sell the idea of security to the very people for whose benefit a program is intended, especially since some of them may see this as an attempted infringement on their property rights.

For example, a prestigious cooperative apartment in New York City, home to celebrities in the entertainment and corporate worlds, experienced problems with a series of small thefts from apartments as well as unexpected and unannounced visitors. A thorough security survey clearly indicated the existence of some glaring deficiencies and resulted in a number of recommendations being made for improved protection of both the building and its occupants. All of the recommendations were accepted by the property management firm, but despite the fact that the cost of implementation was negligible, it could not be undertaken without a vote of the members of the cooperative, which fortunately for them, was affirmative.

Regardless of the type of property, those who manage it also have an obligation to all of the occupants to try to avoid any use of private or public space that poses a potential security or safety threat to them. Although this task understandably is more difficult where private space is concerned, it is one that must be faced. This responsibility is of particular importance in commercial and industrial real estate. To illustrate the point, a condominium in Hong Kong that combined commercial and industrial activity included several occupants who leased their space from the actual owners. Among the businesses were jewelry manufacturers, sales organizations, high-technology companies, and makers of softgoods products. There were some who used open flames in their work, and others whose need for storage space prompted them to store packing materials in the fire towers. It was not unusual for a small fire to be started in the space of one of the organizations that used an open flame, and the obvious threat to everyone was evident. Despite this, the real estate manager tolerated these conditions until an unexpected inspection of the property occurred. The building manager was summoned to appear in court, was heavily fined, and escaped imprisonment on the basis of a successful plea that this was a first offense.

Increased litigation against real estate management organizations, particularly for failure to protect public spaces, with resulting losses or injuries to building occupants and their invitees, also has resulted in an increasing awareness of the need for protection. Whether buildings are used for residential, commercial, or industrial purposes, people who live and work in, and visit them, need to feel that they are at least reasonably safe and secure against harm.

CONSTRUCTION

The construction industry enjoys no exemption from security concerns. Again, like all of the activities mentioned earlier in this chapter, it suffers from many of the same problems. Once again, like those already discussed, it has to deal with matters that tend to be different because of the nature of the industry itself.

While damage to or the theft of equipment and materials may affect any organization, such losses may be more costly to contractors than in other types of organizations. This is due partially to the way in which many construction industry contracts are written, especially those involving major projects. In construction contracts it is not at all unusual to have a provision stipulating that the work is to be completed by a certain date and that the contractor will be penalized so many dollars a day in liquidated damages for every day completion is delayed unless it can clearly be shown that the delay was not the contractor's fault.

True, manufacturers do not relish the idea of having tools or raw materials stolen, but they know that since such losses can occur, it is prudent to have backup materials in inventory to keep a production line working. Retailers rarely allow their inventories to become so depleted that the theft of one item would materially affect operations. Although the losses have to be absorbed by the victim, and the damaged or stolen equipment or materials have to be replaced, there may be some reimbursement from insurance, and the amount of the loss is not multiplied by a time factor.

Contractors, on the other hand, may be penalized for an extended period of time, with the daily penalty rate running into several thousands of dollars a day. As an illustration, imagine a company under contract to build a new highway that includes construction of a bridge. In submitting its bid the company calculated a before-tax profit of $500,000. Liquidated damages will be assessed at the rate of $20,000 a day. Equipment for the job involves bulldozers, heavy-duty trucks, and at least one crane, among other things. Since the distance from the job site to the nearest town is 35 miles, and flatbed trailer trucks used to haul the bulldozers travel at a speed of 10 miles an hour when loaded, it is impractical to move the equipment for safekeeping at night and over weekends. Upon arriving at the site one Monday morning the job superintendent finds that a bulldozer has been stolen. This causes a five-day delay and reduces the contractor's calculated profit by $100,000.

Some contractors have been slow to recognize the impact on profits of equipment theft. However, as thefts of construction equipment have become increasingly common, and liquidated damages can prove costly, the importance of security has taken on new meaning. Delays caused by damage to or the theft of equipment or materials because they have not been protected properly are not considered excusable where liquidated damage penalties are concerned.

Many material thefts from job sites are not of such magnitude as to delay completion seriously, but they can further reduce the contractor's margin of profit. There are too many variables in calculating the cost of a construction job for any contractor to know exactly what the profit will be. For instance, no matter how experienced the contractor is, it is a practical impossibility to figure labor costs with precision. As a result, the bid submitted to the owner is at best an educated guess.

Construction jobs tend to involve more than one trade. There may be general construction personnel, steam or pipe fitters, carpenters, plumbers, sheet metal workers, electricians, insulation people, steel workers, and brick layers all on one project. Generally speaking, each trade is handled by a different contractor, but the need for coordination and close cooperation to complete the job on time usually results in a developing closeness among the various mechanics. This, in turn, may lead to petty but costly theft of construction materials. A pipe fitter will give copper pipe to an electrician who is doing some work at home, a sheet metal worker provides ductwork for a steamfitter remodeling a home, and a bricklayer gives brick to a carpenter for a patio. These thefts will not have a major impact on the job's completion, but over time they will affect the employer's profit picture.

Among the legal considerations mentioned in Chapter 6 was the subject of the attractive nuisance theory. Failure to secure construction sites and construction equipment properly can prompt children to play on or around the equipment when the site is inoperative. The family of a child injured or killed while playing at an unprotected construction site may well have a cause of action against a contractor.

Yet another security concern affecting this industry lies in the fact that for the most part mechanics employed at job sites are paid weekly in cash. This is not a new practice but may be risky. The financial instability of some contractors has prompted unions to insist on employees being paid in cash. To pay employees with the least amount of wasted time it is not unusual for job or project superintendents to be given the entire payroll for their job in cash. They, in turn, distribute the pay envelopes at the site every payday. The fact that considerable amounts of money may be involved, coupled with established patterns, puts job superintendents and payrolls at risk.

From time to time, all organizations may be faced with questions of ethics and morality. Contractors are no different, but they may have to deal with these issues more often and under pressures that others may not feel so readily. In fact, occasionally it is a question of illegality, not merely of ethics or morality. Sometimes questions such as these may be related to a particular contractor getting a job; at others the problem may assume added importance because of the fear of having to pay liquidated damages for completion delays.

Perhaps each of these points is best illustrated. In one case a prominent general construction company built a new home for the vice president of administration and operations for a large financial institution while it was erecting a 300,000-square foot addition to the institution's corporate headquarters. Some time after both projects were completed, moral and ethical questions arose when the financial institution's new security director made two interesting observations: that this was the first time that this general contractor ever was involved with residential construction, and that the vice president whose new house was built was the person whose job it was to approve all requests for additional monies submitted by the contractor.

In another situation a mechanical contractor was to erect a central heating plant and install a distribution system for a city-based university; the contract had a liquidated damages provision. The distribution system work required the contractor to open a number of city streets in order to lay piping. That, in turn, made it necessary for the contractor to get certain permits from the city before any street could be opened. After filing an application for the permits but before they were granted, a city inspector visited the site. He informed the job superintendent that because his office was way behind in its work he had no idea how long it would take before the permits would be issued. However, he also indicated that he was quite certain that if he could get $100 for every street opening he could get some extra help in the office; this would ensure that the permits would be issued without any delay. That from time to time the news media carry stories about the arrest and conviction of officials in different cities for similar acts of extortion indicates that the practice is neither new nor necessarily limited to one city.

Both illustrations are indicative of certain practices that tend to plague the construction industry from a security perspective. In addition to being ethically and morally wrong, when engaged in they can affect a contractor's profits and reputation. In the first, more questions were raised based on the premise that perhaps the company achieved its prominence not necessarily because of the quality of its work but by virtue of bidding low for major projects and making its profits by doing favors for clients. In the second, although the inspector was finally prosecuted, the contractor's reputation was hurt by those who ignored the extortion aspect of the case and remembered only the contractor's willingness to pay a bribe.

ENTERTAINMENT

In discussing retailing earlier, note was made of how diverse the field is. The same can be said of entertainment. It covers such activities as concerts, theater, sporting events, movies, radio, television, made-for-television movies, records, tapes, and compact discs. Also included are the security needs required for the protection of physical plant, such as a stadium, concert hall, or theater. There is also a need to protect the products, such as tapes, movies, records, compact discs, or tickets required for persons to attend an event.

Not to be overlooked is the importance of providing security for persons attending events and for the celebrities who provide the entertainment by their performances, whether they are stage, motion picture, radio, television, concert hall, or opera personalities or baseball, football, basketball, soccer, tennis, or hockey players. Furthermore, in professional sports there is also concern about athletes using drugs or gambling. That this is important is evidenced by the fact that major league baseball, the National Football League, the National Hockey League, and the National Basketball Association all have security directors or security representatives in the cities where teams are located.

That there is need to secure entertainment-related products is unquestioned. Movies, tapes, records, and compact discs are a major source of income to those who are responsible for their production. As a result, motion picture and recording studios know the importance of taking suitable measures to prevent the loss or theft of their ideas or products. However, they also know that they at least can take some comfort from the fact that, generally speaking, what they produce lends itself to being copyrighted. Therefore, if their works have been copied without permission and the payment of royalties, they have legal recourse in both civil and criminal court.

Closely allied to product is the importance of protecting tickets. This is not just a question of thievery or ticket scalping. It also relates to ticket manipulation in ways that will reduce the revenue paid to an owner, producer, or film distributor. This can happen in any form of entertainment, but it appears to occur most in the theatrical field, where revenue due, in whole or in part, is often based on the number of tickets sold for a performance.

An illustration of the problem can be found in a news item describing both the nature of the problem and how, even with the supposedly tighter controls offered through computer use, manipulation resulting in sizable losses can occur. According to the story, the Manhattan County New York District Attorney's Office was investigating allegations made by a producer to the effect that more than $300,000 had been stolen over a period of months, but it had not yet been determined whether box office or count-up-room (where ticket stubs are matched against tickets sold) operations or the computerized ticket inventory-scrutiny system had been compromised, with the computers used to control tickets having been manipulated.[7]

As to protecting facilities, it is no less important to those offering entertainment than it is to any other type of activity, and not surprisingly, many of the problems are similar. Assets need to be protected, and without a secure physical plant there can be no performance. However, unlike other types of activities, there are some performers who by the very nature of their performance or activity may cause an audience reaction that could cause damage to a facility. For instance, one aspect of security involves access control to make certain that only ticket holders or other authorized persons can enter.

In entertainment, access control is a form of crowd control; unruly crowds can mean vandalism. Of course, even if access control does not pose a problem, there is no guaranty that once admitted, people will behave. Injuries and even deaths have been attributed to unruly soccer fans celebrating a victory or mourning a defeat of their favorite team. Audience reaction to certain musical groups or individual vocalists can also be a source of worry to theater owners. The threat of fire in a crowded theater, nightclub, concert hall, or sports stadium is a constant source of concern to owners and program sponsors.

The need to protect both those attending performances of sporting events and those performing are high on the list of priorities where security is involved. A distinction must be made between those attending sporting events and those attending other forms of entertainment. Although there may occasionally be one or more unruly persons at a theatrical or musical performance, their behavior usually consists of being noisy or of trying to interrupt the performance. They can often be contained or escorted from the premises with minimal difficulty. Persons who attend concerts, the live theater, or movies are not likely to bring alcoholic beverages or become engaged physically with other people in the audience.

Sporting events pose a different problem for security. Even at stadiums where alcoholic beverages cannot be brought in by ticket holders, who are screened as they enter to prevent their doing so, there may be an inclination to drink alcohol before entering, whether at a "tailgate party" or elsewhere. It is also true that while hard liquor may not be sold at a stadium, beer usually is. This, in turn, can lead to rowdy behavior, possibly even to fights among spectators. If this happens and other patrons are disturbed, the lack of security may influence a decision whether or not to attend another event. Furthermore, inasmuch as it is not uncommon for parents to bring children to certain types of sporting events as a form of family outing, a failure to make them feel relaxed, comfortable, and safe can result in their not buying tickets for future games. The impact on sales, attendance, and the resultant loss of profits that may be the fruit of a failure to provide adequate security is not lost on team owners.

Without performers there can be no entertainment. Celebrities—whether athletes or other types of entertainers—have followers and fans but they can also have enemies. Unless they feel safe, they cannot perform at their best and therefore need protection. There are certain common concerns applicable to the protection of all entertainers. At the same time it is important to recognize that there are some security concerns that affect professional athletes which may be somewhat different from those affecting others who perform.

The generic concerns that apply to all performers involve protecting the person, the person's property, and the person's privacy. Celebrities appreciate the need to please their admirers, for without them they no longer have celebrity status. To avoid displeasing fans at the same time that they try to protect themselves from unwanted intrusion, some employ their own bodyguards. This is because there are times when all classes of entertainers find themselves the victims of an admiring public. Some members of that public may be satisfied with a handshake or an autograph, while others may be intent upon acquiring as a souvenir something of a personal nature.

Many entertainers and professional athletes spend a good deal of their time traveling to fulfill an engagement or to play a game. Time away from home adds to their vulnerability, and consequently, to their need for protection. For example, when a professional sports team finishes a game in one city and travels to another, arriving around midnight with an afternoon game scheduled for the next day, they need to be able to get to their rooms and to bed as quickly as possible. They should also not have to worry about fans awaiting their arrival at a hotel to ask for autographs or perhaps hoping to steal something from a player's luggage while the person is registering.

There is also the matter of protecting against possible enemies, whose threats can affect a performer's peace of mind. Should this seem to be the case, extra care in protecting the person may become necessary. As an illustration, before baseball's 1974 All-Star Game in Pittsburgh, threats were made against the life of Lou Brock, an outfielder for the St. Louis Cardinals who was scheduled to play. Because of this the director of security in the office of the Baseball Commissioner worked closely with the Pittsburgh Police Department, the hotel's security staff, and security personnel at the stadium to prevent anything from happening to Brock during the course of his stay in Pittsburgh, not just while on the playing field. Happily the game was played without incident. Of course, something of this sort is not limited to professional athletes. Threats could be made against any performer, and suitable steps would have to be taken to reduce the element of risk to the lowest level possible.

In addition to security issues of the sort outlined above, it was noted previously that there are two matters of particular concern with regard to professional athletes. One involves drug use; the other, gambling. Although drug use does not seem to be widespread, it is worrisome for various reasons. Although a team owner may be wholly unaware of the fact that a player uses drugs, once such use becomes common knowledge the team's integrity may be at risk. Because drug use can shorten a player's playing life, result in injuries to the user and possibly to others, and contribute to lost games, professional sports teams know that in addition to health there are economic considerations.

Perhaps nothing so affects the integrity of any sport as much as the knowledge, or even the suspicion, that players gamble. This applies equally to collegiate and professional sports teams. Over the years, cases involving gambling by baseball, basketball, and football players, both professional and collegiate, have been reported. The concern stems from the justifiable fear that players who gamble, particularly on their own sport, may not give their teams their best efforts in trying to win games. In addition, because of the control of so much gambling by elements of organized crime, an uneasy feeling exists with regard to the extent to which players may become beholden to or even under the control of organized crime figures. If those who attend sporting events begin to question a team's or a sport's integrity, there is the risk that they will discontinue their support. If this occurs, economic factors again are important.

GOVERNMENT OPERATIONS

In considering security in relation to government operations, it is necessary to look at the subject from two different perspectives: from the government's point of view in dealing with its contractors, and relating to the protection and conservation of government assets within various departments and agencies. The need for security is not confined to assets of the federal government; it exists at all levels.

Turning first to operations involving agreements between federal agencies and private contractors, the contract document from the awarding department or agency will set forth what the government expects in the way of security. As pointed out in Chapter 6, this is particularly true of the Department of Defense and the Nuclear Regulatory Commission. However, although private organizations benefit from government help in doing background investigations of employees who need clearances for access to secret or top secret information, and from direction in the form of a Department of Defense Industrial Security Manual which tells contractors what they must do to protect classified information, contractors must have someone who is responsible for overseeing implementation of the government's security requirements.

As an example, organizations doing work under contract to the Department of Defense are told about personnel security clearances; the receipt, storage, and mailing of classified documents; how they are to be marked; who may have access to them; whether they can be copied; and how they are to be destroyed when no longer needed. Procedures to ensure accountability are set forth. Although the specificity of the Department of Defense Industrial Security Manual makes program implementation relatively easy, contractors will have security officers whose job it is to oversee not implementation alone but also to ensure that it is carried out in strict accordance with the terms of the contract. The greatest incentive that government contractors have for adhering to the security provisions of their contracts is the knowledge that if there is a breach of security, the awarding agency may be in a position to cancel the agreement unilaterally. If this is done, it would mean an immediate loss of revenue, perhaps a long-term loss of business, and depending on the contractor's size and the nature of the breach, adverse publicity and a damaged reputation.

To assume that protecting information is the government's only security concern would be wrong. It would also be wrong to assume that because governments have investigative resources and the ability to prosecute, they have no real problems in the way of protecting and conserving assets, as evidenced by the theft of New York City assets cited earlier. The power of the government does not necessarily prevent losses or other types of security concerns from demanding attention.

Perhaps this is best illustrated with examples that reflect problems at both federal and state levels. An item in the *Boston Globe* of March 30, 1992, captioned "US Library Blocking its stacks" reports that hundreds of thousands of books have been mutilated or stolen from the Library of Congress, partially because of minimal security. It goes on to say that within only a few days in March 1992, 100 art folios had been stripped of their contents, representing a loss calculated in excess of $1 million. These losses prompted the Library to institute a number of changes to better protect its assets.[8]

Another story reported the theft of mail by postal workers. In the 1991 fiscal year a record number of 1297 postal workers and contractors were arrested for mail theft, destruction, and related crimes, and another 385 were charged with embezzlement or falsifying records. According to Postal Service records, although the number of arrests is but a minute segment of all U.S. Postal Service workers, the fact remains that the number of arrests for mail theft has jumped 54 percent since 1985. In addition, the news media occasionally have reported the deaths of postal workers at the hands of disgruntled co-workers or former employees. Serious though these killings have been, one can imagine public reaction if postal patrons also had been victimized.[9]

Even members of the judiciary, legal profession, and courthouses have not been immune from security concerns. From time to time the news media have reported the deaths of judges or attempts on their lives. In some cases they have received bombs sent through the mail; in others, shootings have occurred in the courtroom, with lawyers and bystanders also victimized. The matter of courtroom security became sufficiently critical in Massachusetts in 1992 for the court system to decide that it needed to employ a statewide security director. Among other things, over a three-year period there were 69 violent struggles or assaults on court officers at the district court level alone, and there were 42 instances where they were injured.[10]

By no means are the foregoing the only types of security concerns with which government agencies must cope. Recognizing the importance of protecting and conserving the federal government's assets, which would include among other things the supervision of "other activities for the purpose of promoting economy, efficiency and effectiveness" in administering programs or "preventing or detecting fraud and abuse" in programs, the U.S. Congress passed the Inspector General Act of 1978[11] and amended it in 1988.[12] As stated in Chapter 2 and as noted above, the role of inspector general in many ways parallels that of a private-sector corporate security director. At both the federal or state level, the mission is to prevent abuses and to effect recoveries when abuses are detected.

To further illustrate the role of inspector general and the parallel with private-sector corporate security, let's look at some of the work done by one such office. Among the many things contained in the "Semiannual Report, Office of Inspector General, U.S. Department of Labor, for the period October 1, 1990–March 31, 1991" are data on the inspector general's role in dealing with such varied issues as the defrauding of small employers and their employees in connection with health insurance premiums, losses to 22 states as a result of a 20-year unemployment insurance fraud scheme involving fraudulent claims on behalf of registered aliens living in Mexico, the vulnerability to fraud and abuse of the country's private pension and welfare plans, and the Department of Labor's financial management problems.[13]

Thus it is apparent that the resources and power of governments notwithstanding, they are no less vulnerable to security problems than is the private sector. Failure to protect and conserve government assets can affect the national economy. True, unlike private-sector organizations, government will not cease to exist should losses become excessive. Nevertheless, there will be an impact on every resident through an increase in taxes, a reduction in services, or a combination of the two.

COMPUTER OPERATIONS AND COMMUNICATIONS

Computer operations are now widespread. Computers are used to store data, as a way of communicating both externally and internally, for word processing, and to satisfy a number of other business needs. Computers are used to develop, process, store, and communicate

Courtesy of Data General Corporation

information, which, in any form, can be one of an organization's most valuable assets. Therefore, since computer operations and communications realistically involve information, and information needs to be protected, this is a type of activity that is of concern from a security viewpoint.

In addition, of course, is the fact that computers can be used to commit crimes, particularly of the white-collar variety. An example of criminal activity involving computer use was reported in the *New York Times* of July 9, 1992 under the heading, "5 Are Indicted in Computer Credit Theft." The five, calling themselves "Masters of Disaster" (MOD), operated for more than two years using their personal computers to intercept computer passwords and other access codes being transmitted. From this they not only broke into additional computer networks, but also reportedly devised programs that cracked passwords that had been scrambled into a special code for better security. According to the indictment, it cost Southwestern Bell Telephone Company $370,000 to reprogram its computers after the intrusion and to install new computer security devices.[14]

The problem of securing computer operations, and their use as a tool for purposes of communication, can pose some rather unique challenges. Organizations in general, and their security directors or managers in particular, know that a great deal more is required for secure operations than simply concern that employees not change their passwords. They are aware of the fact that the subject is complex, and if a problem is suspected or detected, a wide-ranging investigation may be necessary not only to isolate the problem but also to correct it so as to minimize the risk of repetition. They know that they should learn something about how employees can be made to change their passwords regularly, how computer programs are developed and made operative, how local and wide area networks (LANs and WANs) function, how important systems logs can be, what hackers and computer viruses can do to computer operations and communications, and what computer users can do with a modem. This does not mean that security directors or managers, unless employed exclusively as MIS (management information systems) security managers, need to understand the technical side of computers. Rather, they need to be able to identify trustworthy employees within the organization by which they are employed who can readily be available as resources to help them understand and deal with technical considerations.

The legitimacy of security concerns, which is unquestioned, is heightened by the fact that the very nature of much computer activity is such that an organization may be victimized for an extended period without even realizing what has occurred. Of course, this is no excuse for a failure to take steps, some of which are already available, to try to reduce the risks. However, it is no less important for security directors to understand that even though there are ways of coping with much illegitimate or questionable computer activity, implementing an effective security program depends primarily on all members of the organization by which they are employed, not just security personnel, cooperating in terms of program implementation. Taking the human factor into consideration is essential to a sound computer security undertaking. Therefore, security education for employees at all levels of the organization, and accountability for all aspects of computer operations, are critically important.

To illustrate, in the interest of security some organizations allow employees to select their own passwords. Since this should limit password exposure, it should also reduce the risk of compromise. On the other hand, when this is done it is not uncommon for employees to choose as their passwords words or numbers that can be identified rather easily. They may also fail to change their passwords at regular intervals. Furthermore, in a work environment where computer networking is so extensive that multiple "hosts" are used, there are employees who do not completely log off at day's end. When this occurs the terminal screen continues to display both the host and the user's names. This, of course, is helpful to anyone who wants to try to access that employee's computer files. In an effort to try to minimize these risks, many organizations now use software that randomly selects and distributes employee passwords, and will black out the screen if there is no activity for a predetermined period of time.

With major organizations using computers more and more as a way of communicating with other facilities and sites of the same company, as well as with vendors and customers, there is concern not only about the risk of the theft of services as noted in the Southwestern Bell Telephone Company case cited above, but also about the theft of information or sending of unauthorized communications. Consequently, securing electronic communications systems may necessitate using gateways or other means of controlling access to computer networks just as physical access to a corporate headquarters is controlled.

By no means is it unusual for some employees of an organization to have terminals and modems in their homes so they can do work from there. In addition, as portable or laptop computers have become easier to carry and use, it is not at all uncommon for people who travel on business to take a laptop and a modem with them so they can communicate with their offices from any location. This form of remote access can also pose a serious threat to organizations where these practices are allowed if not actually encouraged. Of course, if employees have terminals and modems at home, there are ways to minimize the risk by using some form of callback or other means to identify the person dialing into the system before allowing the person access. However, the same type of callback cannot be used when the person who wants access to a system is not dialing in from a regularly used or fixed location. Nevertheless, there are ways in which the risk of unauthorized access to computer files by persons using laptops and modems calling from transient locations can be minimized.

In addition, hardware and software must be protected. The importance of having, and properly storing, backup files in a suitably secure environment is critical. Access control to computer rooms, temperature and humidity controls, and suitable fire suppression systems cannot be ignored. Failure to have backup files off site, easy to recover in an emergency, under tight controls, and in a facility that is environmentally sound is inexcusable.

Computer size has changed over the years. The tendency is for less use of mainframes and more of mini and personal computers. The nature of what can be done with the smaller computers has grown with relative speed and so have the security concerns of organizations that rely on computers for much of their work. As additional changes occur in both the size and use of computers, there will be changes in what is needed to protect computer operations and use as an invaluable business tool.

SUMMARY

At this point two things should be apparent to the reader. First, security, or rather the protection and conservation of assets, consists of a great deal more than having security officers or guards control access to a facility, monitor its various alarm systems, make patrol rounds, and be responsible for placing and removing truck seals at shipping or receiving docks. Instead, security represents challenges to one's skills, creativity, and ability to work well with people at all levels both within and outside organizations. Regardless of which career opportunity in the field of security one is interested in, a good education is necessary to cope successfully with the multitude of security problems that have to be faced.

Second, where security problems are concerned, virtually no organization, whether private, such as a corporation or family-owned business, or public, such as a government agency, is immune. It is immaterial whether an organization is large, such as a multinational corporation, or small, such as one with a single location. Neither size nor location guarantees protection. Incidents can occur at suburban or rural locations as readily as at inner city or urban locations. While the nature of the activity may mean differences in some of the types of problems that have to be dealt with, problems exist nevertheless.

As noted in this chapter, some universal security concerns might be called generic. For instance, every organization needs to prevent losses caused by dishonest employees and to protect both its information and reputation. However, organizations with relatively little exposure to the general public, as might be the case with manufacturers, do not have the same risks as do retailers or hotels, for example. While hotels and medical centers have concerns that are quite similar, there are also differences. Easily distinguished are the differences between the transportation concerns of a manufacturer that ships product using its own fleet of trucks, and those of a carrier for hire that hauls passengers as well as cargo. Yet the thread that runs throughout is the continuing need that organizations have to protect and conserve their assets, whether tangible or intangible. If they are to survive in a highly competitive and complex environment, they must do this through employee participation and cooperation and through judicious use of proprietary or contract security personnel, technology, and operating systems and procedures.

REVIEW QUESTIONS

1. Why are some of the concerns regarding the protection of research and development in an academic environment different from those in connection with manufacturing operations?

2. What sorts of tangible assets need to be safeguarded in a manufacturing operation? Why is it necessary to protect everything needed for production?

3. As a practical matter, do customers or employees represent the greater risk of loss to retailers, and why?

4. What do hotels and medical centers have in common from a security viewpoint?

5. In what ways do hotel guests and hospital patients represent potential losses?

6. In terms of their security operations, what sets academic institutions apart from other organizations?

7. What is unique about some of the assets that public utilities need to protect?

8. What are some of the principal security concerns with which the entertainment field needs to deal?

9. In what way is the work of a government agency's inspector general comparable to that of a corporate security director?

10. Why is the protection of computer operations and computer use for communications purposes so critically important?

NOTES

[1]*Newsweek*, May 4, 1992, pp. 58–60.

[2]*The New York Times,* May 4, 1991, pp. 25–26.

[3]*The Boston Globe*, March 25, 1992, p. 37.

[4]Harvey Burstein, *Hospital Security Management* (New York: Praeger Publishers, 1977), p. 1.

[5]*The New York Times*, July 8, 1992, sec. B, p. 1.

[6]*The New York Times*, August 22, 1992, p. 35.

[7]*The New York Times*, March 25, 1992, sec. C, pp. 17, 19.

[8]*The Boston Globe*, March 30, 1992, p. 3.

[9]*The Boston Globe*, August 22, 1992, p. 3.

[10]*The Boston Globe*, September 10, 1992, pp. 31, 39.

[11]Public Law 95-452.

[12]Public Law 100-504.

[13]Information provided to the author under cover of a letter dated July 30, 1991, from Julian W. De La Rosa, Inspector General, U.S. Department of Labor.

[14]*The New York Times*, July 9, 1992, sec. A, p. 14.

Chapter 9

Security, Safety, and the Environment

With the passage of both time and legislation, the need to protect employees, and invitees where applicable, against injuries or illnesses resulting from unsafe conditions has become a matter of increasing concern to organizations. The same is true where the environment is concerned. Here, however, the obligation to avoid unhealthy or unsafe environmental conditions is not limited to consideration for employees and invitees; it extends to an organization's neighbors. To accomplish these objectives, state and federal laws have been passed that include both civil and criminal penalties for violations.

Since security is concerned with protecting and conserving an employer's assets, including all of its resources and reputation, it has a legitimate role to play in connection with an organization's safety and environmental programs. In some cases the role may be extensive, as where both the security and safety functions report to the same director or manager. In others, safety and environmental concerns each may be handled by separate departments, yet the security department cannot avoid involvement, even if only on a limited basis.

In this chapter we explore security's role in occupational safety and health matters, regardless of whether it is involved directly or indirectly. We also discuss the role of security in terms of environmental protection and how it can help those who are responsible for environmental matters.

SECURITY'S ROLE IN OCCUPATIONAL SAFETY AND HEALTH MATTERS

Employee injuries or deaths resulting from unsafe working conditions can affect morale adversely. Poor morale, in turn, can have a negative impact on virtually every aspect of an organization's operations, including its profits and reputation. If employees are unionized, the subject of safer working conditions is likely to be an issue when contract negotiations next come up; if they are not, the subject of safety may be the catalyst that brings about a union shop. If invitees are injured or killed as a result of unsafe premises where they are visiting or shopping, there will probably be both adverse publicity and litigation. These will also have a bearing on reputation and profits. With this in mind, one might presume that employee and visitor safety would have been a matter of real concern to all organizations. Unfortunately, this has not always been the case.

The issue of workplace safety, and of safety for invitees, was largely something to be decided upon by individual organizations. Programs might range from almost nonexistent to quite progressive, but there were no statutory or mandatory requirements. In some instances the primary impetus for developing and implementing safety programs was more a matter of economics based on recommendations made by insurance companies. If the latter saw what they considered to be safety deficiencies, they would suggest ways in which the insured could reduce its risks. If the insured elected to implement those recommendations, its reduced risks also reduced the amount of the premiums paid for coverage; if it did not, it got no premium reduction, and if an appreciable number of claims were filed, it actually could pay more for its insurance. Insurers also benefited by not having to pay as many claims.

Government did not interfere by passing laws designed to improve workplace safety and health, and despite a number of disasters in the mining industry, it was not until 1969 that the U.S. Congress enacted the Mine Safety Act, which it amended in 1977. This aside, it was not until Congress passed the Williams–Steiger Occupational Safety and Health Act of 1970[1] that any real effort was made at the federal level to provide a safe and healthful workplace for all employees, and for invitees where applicable. This, in turn, resulted in the development of standards for both general industry and the construction industry,[2] with oversight responsibility given to the Department of Labor. The act was amended in 1990. In the interim, Congress also enacted the Maritime Safety Act of 1984 for the protection of marine industry employees.

The Occupational Safety and Health Act also provides that individual states may, with Labor Department approval, establish their own safety programs. Generally speaking, if state programs submitted for approval are at least as stringent as the federal standards, they will be approved and are to be followed. Otherwise, the federal standards prevail. Although there may be political merit in this approach, it has its pitfalls. Under these conditions managers who are responsible for safety in organizations with facilities in more than one state cannot afford to assume that they only need to be familiar with the federal standards. Instead, they must determine whether each state in which the organization has operations has its own version of OSHA. If so, they must ascertain in what ways it may differ, however slightly, from the federal standards so that the employer's full compliance can be assured.

All organizations covered by OSHA, federal or state, are subject to inspection by compliance officers. While most inspections occur on the basis of random selection, any incident involving serious injuries or deaths will result in inspection. Inspections may be limited or broad in scope. For instance, one inspection may involve a particular part of a facility or a particular process; another may be "wall to wall" and cover the entire location. When inspections do occur, security, concerned about the possible exposure of proprietary information to the compliance officer, may recommend that the organization exercise its rights under the provisions of the Fourth Amendment to the Constitution and deny access to the facility. However, bearing in mind the fact that compliance officers rarely have a problem in obtaining ex parte administrative search warrants, and that the standards make provisions for protecting trade secret information[3] belonging to organizations under inspection, insisting on a search warrant may not serve any real purpose.

Regardless of whether security and safety are managed by the same person, in all likelihood security managers and the security staff will be among the first to know of a compliance officer's arrival for an inspection. Consequently, security directors or managers need to know more than that their employers can insist upon search warrants. They should also be somewhat familiar with what compliance officers can or cannot do in the course of an inspection. In this respect a question may arise relative to the taking of photographs by a compliance officer. Photographs might be every bit as revealing and risky to the employer as exposure of proprietary information. Security managers need to know that compliance officers are authorized to take environmental samples and to take or obtain photographs related to the purpose of an inspection.[4]

Recognizing that the foregoing are primarily reactive, it is equally important to understand security's proactive role where an organization's safety is at issue. Familiarization with OSHA standards is essential to provide a safe and healthful workplace. Therefore, security directors or managers should have more than a nodding acquaintance with them whether they are directly or indirectly responsible for the safety program. Perhaps this is best illustrated.

Even if security and safety are managed by the same person, there will be safety-related situations that require special knowledge or skills for proper disposition. By the same token, since security personnel are on duty around the clock and are in an excellent position to be alert for real and potential hazards, they should at least know what types of hazards may be encountered and to whom they should be reported for corrective action. On the other hand, if the departments are completely separate, the fact remains that both are obligated to protect the organization's best interests. Consequently, when real or potential safety hazards are observed by security personnel, they should know to whom they must be reported for proper disposition. To say that simply because security and safety are not joined and that safety matters are not part of the security function flies in the face of the logic upon which the security department's very existence is based.

Assume, for example, that a production area requires employees to wear safety glasses, a shipping area warrants wearing hardhats, or that during a winter storm there is ice on a walkway leading to and from a visitors' entrance and parking lot. Security officers on patrol see personnel not wearing safety glasses or hardhats, or see how slippery the walkway is, yet fail to report these conditions so that corrective action can be taken. Should employees or visitors suffer injuries as a result, and should the employer be found liable, it would be inexcusable for security personnel to say that because safety is not part of their function they were not obliged to do anything to correct a potentially dangerous situation. This is not to say that under such circumstances security personnel should go to department managers and direct them to have their employees put on their safety glasses or hardhats, or that they should be the ones to either sand and salt or shovel a slippery walkway. However, it does mean that their observations should be reported to the security director or manager immediately so that he or she can contact the proper persons and make certain that the problems are solved.

Perhaps an example of a proactive safety program adopted and implemented by a Fortune 500 company will be helpful. In this instance both security and safety reported directly to the corporate director of safety/security, who had a safety engineer on the department's staff. The program consisted of three main elements: direction, education, and implementation.

Direction came from the organization's safety policies and procedures, applicable corporate-wide. Even overseas facilities, some in countries with less strict standards than those in the United States, were obliged to adhere to the company's safety requirements, all of which were based on OSHA standards, unless local requirements were more stringent. In the latter event, the local standards prevailed.

Education consisted of presentations to employees in general, and to line managers and supervisors in particular, on various safety-related subjects. The subject matter for any given presentation was chosen with a particular facility's operations in mind. In addition, the corporate safety engineer was responsible for keeping abreast of all of the latest developments that might have an impact on the organization's activities, and for making certain that the information was forwarded to individual facility safety personnel for whatever action might be necessary.

As to implementation, the corporate safety engineer was required by policy to perform safety audits of all major facilities on a quarterly basis. In conducting these audits, the corporate safety engineer was accompanied by a safety engineer from a facility other than the one being audited. This brought a fresh approach to each audit; it also served as a valuable learning experience for both that person and the safety engineer of the site being audited.

Of course, regardless of whether the functions are separated or joined, there will be times when security managers will find themselves on the horns of a dilemma. They will feel torn between what they consider to be in the best interest of security on the one hand, and in the best interest of employee safety on the other. For instance, in theory it would be an ideal security situation if all doors other than the main entrance of a facility could be kept locked at all times. This certainly would reduce the risk of a number of security-related problems from arising, whether caused by employees or third parties. By the same token, if such a plan were in place, and an emergency arose that required the facility to be evacuated, but people could not escape, the cost to the organization might be far greater than the dollar value of what might be stolen because of multiple doors being accessible. Suppose that a security manager with a fixed budget, forced to choose between a sophisticated access control system and a state-of-the-art fire suppression system for an about-to-be-built facility, chose the former and after construction was completed, a major fire destroyed the building.

Although there was no evidence of security involvement as such, to illustrate just how tragic and costly such a situation might be, in September 3, 1991, a fire broke out at a chicken-processing plant, killing 25 employees, destroying the building, putting the surviving 215 people normally employed there out of work, and forcing the employer into a federal bankruptcy court. An investigation showed that the plant's doors had been locked and that the locks had to be broken for employees to escape, and that the plant had neither sprinklers nor fire alarms.[5] On September 14, 1992, the plant owner pleaded guilty to 25 counts of involuntary manslaughter and was sentenced to prison for 10 years on each count.[6]

In the foregoing case the failure to provide a safe working environment by having locked doors and no fire suppression system was not limited to the tragedy of 25 people dying. The plant's destruction had both a social and an economic impact on the community since the survivors' place of employment no longer existed. Forcing the business into bankruptcy also had an obvious economic impact on the owner/employer.

By no means are safety violations with serious consequences limited to small or relatively small businesses. Large businesses can be equally guilty even though they may be in a better position to absorb assessed penalties. In addition to employees who may be injured or killed because of inadequate or improper safety programs, stockholders of publicly held companies may be affected. Although there is no clear evidence of security involvement, examples of some of the types of cases and their impact on both organizations and individuals may be helpful in illustrating the scope and magnitude of some of the problems that may be encountered.

In 1984, an employee of Film Recovery Systems, Inc. died as a result of life-threatening dangers posed by the employer's plant operations, prompting the state of Illinois to charge the corporation with manslaughter and five of its executives with murder.[7] At about the same time the state of Michigan charged the General Dynamics Corporation with involuntary manslaughter and criminal violations of the state's occupational safety standards.[8] In December 1990, the USX Corporation, the biggest steelmaker in the United States, agreed to pay a $3.25 million fine for health and safety violations at two of its steel mills.[9] As a result of a 1991 fire at a Louisiana refinery that resulted in the death of six people, Citgo Petroleum Corporation agreed to pay $5.8 million to settle charges of worker safety violations in a case where the penalties could have been as high as $8.2 million.[10]

Although none of these stories make reference to the existence of security or safety departments, in both the chicken-processing plant and Film Recovery cases, the organizations may have had neither because of their size. However, this would not be true for General Dynamics, USX, and Citgo. They would have security and safety programs regardless of whether they were managed by a single manager or by two separate managers. The penalties levied against the corporations could not help but have an impact on both profits and stockholders' dividends for the years in which payment was made. This aside, the publicity generated by virtue of the charges and penalties did not reflect favorably on that major asset—an organization's reputation. And no penalties could compensate the families of those killed, or the injured parties, for their losses.

Based on the admittedly meager information found in the news items, one can only surmise that their safety programs failed either because they were deficient or because those responsible for their development, implementation, and oversight were too permissive or deferential. In matters of employee health and safety, ethics and morality, and their relationship to the way in which security managers discharge their responsibilities, as discussed in Chapter 6, should not be divorced from the need for efficient operations and the protection and conservation of the employer's assets.

On the other hand, there will be times when an incident results in injury to an employee even when the employer has an active safety program in place. Just as it is impossible to eliminate all security problems, it is impossible to eliminate all safety-related incidents. For example, the Fortune 500 organization mentioned earlier with the well-planned proactive safety program had a large metal fabrication plant where punch presses were used. The presses' safeguards were those provided by the equipment manufacturer. The equipment had been used for years without even a minor incident or injury. Nevertheless, one day an employee using a press had an accident and lost all the fingers of one hand.

The incident was reported to OSHA immediately, and all facilities at which punch presses were located were directed to stop using them pending further instructions from corporate headquarters. An OSHA investigation followed; a citation was issued indicating that a fine would be assessed against the employer. In response to an invitation to meet and discuss the matter with two OSHA compliance officers, the employer sent one of its lawyers and its safety and security director as its representatives. Upon the meeting's conclusion the latter were informed that the fine would be $500. They were told that a minimum penalty was being assessed not only because of the company's overall excellent safety program and record but because the compliance officers themselves were unaware of additional safety devices that could be installed on the presses to prevent a recurrence. Despite this, but consistent with the organization's proactive approach, members of the company's industrial engineering department were given the task of finding or developing more suitable guards for all the punch presses corporate-wide. No facility was allowed to use its punch presses until the industrial engineers succeeded in developing a solution to this safety problem.

SECURITY AND ENVIRONMENTAL PROTECTION MATTERS

The passage of various federal and state laws dealing with such diverse subjects as clean air, clean water, safe drinking water, toxic substance controls, emergency planning and a community's right-to-know, resource conservation and recovery, underground storage tanks, and water quality, all within a relatively short time, tends to convey the impression that concern with protecting the environment is a relatively recent phenomenon. In truth it is not.

In the 1850s there was a drive to install sanitary sewers. New York had a metropolitan health law in 1860, Massachusetts a state board of health in 1869, and 1872 saw the founding of the American Public Health Association. There was an antismoke campaign in the 1910s. A report issued in 1923 indicated that there were at least 248 water supplies throughout the United States and Canada that had been affected by industrial wastes. By the 1940s industrial wastes were seen as a problem that affected primarily water purity and complicated sewage treatment processes.[11] Understandably, water quality has been a major issue, but as the end of the twentieth century draws near there has been increased concern with such matters as acid rain and the quality of air.

An obvious question that needs to be answered for those who consider careers in security, particularly as security directors or managers, is: Where does security fit into the environmental protection picture? It is not uncommon to find security and safety under the umbrella of a single department; it is far less likely to find those responsible for environmental protection matters also reporting to a security director. This is not because the environment, unlike safety, concerns the community as well as employees. Rather, it is because some aspects of environmental protection almost require the person in charge of the program to have a background in or at least some understanding of a scientific or physical discipline. By no means is it inconceivable that an organization's environmental protection program would come under security, but when it does it tends to be the exception rather than the rule. However, one thing is certain—security must participate in the environment's protection whether it does so directly or indirectly.

An example of direct participation is the case where those responsible for an organization's environmental protection program report to the person in charge of its security department. When this occurs the environmental protection program can best be approached in a way similar to that outlined previously with regard to safety provided that persons with suitable professional qualifications are given the task of directly overseeing the program with emphasis on policies and procedures, implementation, and education. Policies and procedures are necessary so that all employees at all levels are fully aware of the employer's objectives, what it wants done, and how. Employees need to be kept informed of newly discovered hazards and kept abreast of the best ways in which to dispose of them. At the same time, the most detailed policies and procedures, coupled with the best informed employees, will not guarantee effective environmental protection programs. There must be effective policy implementation. One way of making certain that this is done is to employ an audit technique. Another is to make certain that the results of any required tests for which outside agencies might be used, as with underground storage tanks, are submitted directly to the department head rather than to the manager of the inspected site for forwarding.

However, recognizing that in many if not most cases an organization's environmental protection program will not be a security function, it is still important for security directors or managers to understand how they and their departments may be in a position to assist those whose job it is. To better understand this type of involvement it might be useful to look briefly at some of the environmental issues and the possible ways in which a security department might have been able to make a contribution. In other words, what about different ways in which security, by being proactive, might help those responsible for an organization's environmental protection program?

For instance, there have been times when companies licensed to transport hazardous waste from its point of origin to an authorized dump site have disposed of such material enroute. Once such unlawful dumping is discovered, the federal and/or state government would probably proceed against both the transporter and the generator. Where generators of hazardous material must have it transported off site, and transportation is by truck, occasional surveillance of the transporter's vehicle can be an effective deterrent to illegal disposal.

Another way in which security can make a significant contribution is in the execution of the federal government's Emergency Planning and Community Right-to-Know Act. While it is true that the nature of certain hazardous or toxic materials may be such that they require special treatment if accidentally spilled or otherwise discharged into the environment, the fact remains that efficient effective security departments, by their very nature, will have developed generalized plans for responding to emergencies. They will also have good relations with the public safety departments of the communities in which their facilities are located. Consequently, since basic emergency plans are already in place, and public safety departments are usually among those required to be informed of local operations that either generate or use toxic or hazardous materials, departments responsible for environmental protection programs would be well advised to avail themselves of the help that security can give. They can build on and refine security's emergency plans to incorporate an effective response in case of an environmental emergency, and they can also take advantage of security's contacts with public safety officials in terms of helping to keep the community informed.

Going beyond a more proactive role for security in connection with the environment, it is important to note—and to remember—that the liability of violators of environmental protection laws is not limited to civil actions; they can also be prosecuted in criminal court, a method being used by the U.S. government with increasing frequency. For instance, the number of federal indictments against polluters rose from 40 in 1983 to 134 in 1990.[12]

As further evidence of the trend, the pollution caused in Prince William Sound, Alaska, when the *Exxon Valdez* struck a reef on March 24, 1989, resulted in the Exxon Corporation, and its subsidiary Exxon Shipping Company, facing eight criminal charges.[13] A second-degree manslaughter charge was filed against a Rochester, New York, businessman who allegedly paid for the illegal dumping of chemical wastes that killed another man.[14] In 1991 the Aluminum Company of America (Alcoa) agreed to pay $7.5 million in fines, which could have been as high as $41 million, for violating an array of New York State's environmental laws, with both company officials and two plant supervisors pleading guilty to misdemeanor charges.[15]

A question that may have to be answered by some security directors and managers is what to do should they become aware of the fact that their employers may be in violation of federal or state environmental protection laws. There understandably will be concern about keeping one's job should the head of the security department dare to voice his or her thoughts on the subject. Of course, the situation may be further complicated if security directors find their employers unwilling to take corrective action and as a result the former go to the news media as "whistleblowers." In any case, just as with safety programs, the issues of moral and ethical behavior should not be ignored.

OSHA specifically provides protection against the termination of or other forms of punitive action against employees who report unsafe or unhealthful conditions. Similar protection may or may not exist for those who would express their concerns about environmental matters. This is despite the fact that if environmental problems do exist, the potential impact could be far greater since portions of the community at large, not merely employees, might be affected.

This being the case, one might ask if there is a trend toward letting employee whistleblowers in general, and security personnel in particular, twist slowly in the wind for reporting violations of environmental laws by their employing organizations. There appears to be some evidence to indicate that both the federal government and segments of private industry are aware of the dilemma that can confront those who know of or suspect someone of water, air, or noise pollution, yet hesitate to complain for fear of possible repercussions.

One encouraging sign reported in 1991 was the fact that some banks that make commercial loans would not finance business properties until they conducted an "environmental audit" to see if the real estate was clean of toxic or hazardous waste.[16] This would seem to emphasize the importance of protecting the environment and the possibility that those who report violations will be held in high esteem rather than being thought of as informers. Another sign, also in 1991, might be considered even more encouraging since it is indicative of the position of at least some members of the U.S. Congress regarding protection for those who report violations. In this instance the chairman of the House of Representatives Interior Committee, upon learning that a private security company had been hired by a consortium of oil companies in Alaska for the purpose of conducting a surveillance on environmental whistleblowers, stated that they may have violated both federal and state laws in doing so.[17]

As with safety standards, another challenge that must be met in the environmental protection area for organizations that have operations in multiple states is the need to be as familiar with state requirements as they are with those of the federal government. The latter has encouraged the states to pass their own environmental protection laws, and in some cases states have adopted requirements that are a good deal more stringent than the federal standards. Furthermore, an issue that must often be faced is the presumption, albeit a rebuttable one, that a particular organization is the potentially responsible party (PRP), a term used by both the federal and state environmental protection agencies.

The operative word under such circumstances obviously is *potentially*. For instance, if the air is polluted as a result of smokestack emissions, it may be possible to identify the polluter either because there is only one company with a smokestack, or because there is only one that emits the type of product that is causing the pollution. The same might be true when the problem is one of underground discharges of toxic or hazardous materials that work their way into water systems. However, identifying the responsible party may be infinitely more difficult when multiple organizations use the same types of materials in their work and no single source of pollution can be determined.

Two examples of the latter type of situation may be helpful. The first, and most publicized, is the acid rain problem. Pollutants discharged into the air are carried on air currents, with consequent mixing. It is impossible to say with precision that any one company, or even one locale, is the primary source and consequently the PRP. In such circumstances the presumption is that all businesses that emit certain types of pollutants into the atmosphere are equally responsible. Because air currents travel across state lines, remedial action must be imposed on the basis of clean air standards set by the federal government. In some cases the cost of cleaning smokestack or comparable emissions before they are discharged into the atmosphere can be quite expensive in monetary terms; the polluter's reputation can also be damaged.

A second illustration, involving the pollution of underground water sources, may be as complex but lends itself more easily to state regulation. For instance, a California manufacturer of computer parts, having stopped using two underground tanks in which certain toxic materials had been stored, arranged for their removal. When they were removed it became obvious that over the years some leakage had occurred. The company was located in an industrially zoned area, but only a main thoroughfare separated the plant from a residential area. Wells were dug to determine the direction in which the water table flowed and to test for the presence of carcinogens. The water flow was in the direction of the residential area; cancer-causing agents were identified. However, this plant had as its neighbors three competitors plus two more upstream. All used the same basic materials in their manufacturing processes. Despite constant testing it was impossible to say with any degree of certainty which company was primarily responsible for the pollutants. Consequently, the state required all possible contributors to take appropriate remedial action at a total cost that would eventually be in the millions of dollars. Unlike emissions into the air, the very nature of water pollution takes much more time before the water's purity can be reestablished.

Cleaning the environment is distinguishable from correcting safety problems in terms of the time and money that may be involved. Some safety issues can be disposed of in a reasonably short time without too much expense. Furthermore, once corrected, oversight may be required to ensure that there are no relapses. Unless the underlying problem is one directly related to employee behavior, such as wearing safety glasses, safety shoes, other forms of protective clothing, or using and cleaning respirators, rarely is the problem a continuing one.

Environmental problems can seldom be disposed of quickly and inexpensively. In addition, to avoid repetition, both constant oversight and a search for materials that are less likely to pollute the environment are needed. If, for example, noise pollution is a problem in the workplace, solutions may be as inexpensive as providing employees with earplugs, or at an admittedly higher cost, soundproofing a room. However, once done, time and expense are no longer factors. On the other hand, the water pollution problem illustrated previously not only made it necessary to buy and install equipment for cleanup, but after seven years the end was still not in sight since the water had not yet reached a level of purity acceptable to the state.

SUMMARY

With the passage of time and more than a little voter pressure on the political system, laws have been passed at the federal and state levels designed to ensure that employees work in safe and healthful places and that the environment is cleaned up and kept clean. It would be naive to ignore the fact that some organizations have tried to bring pressure to bear on the political system to minimize rather than maximize safety and environmental standards, alleging that the economic impact would be too costly and that indirectly, consumers would pay the costs of implementation. Nevertheless, the extent to which employees have been injured or killed during the course of their employment, and the degree to which the world's environment has been polluted, have prompted the federal and state governments to enact legislation that attempts to overcome many years of neglect in the fields of safety and environmental protection.

Like any other form of activity, safety and environmental protection programs serve no real purpose unless they are well thought out, carefully implemented, subject to constant scrutiny and supervision, and supported by the highest levels of management. Where senior management fully understands the role of security and appreciates what security can contribute to an organization's well-being, decisions have often been made to give responsibility for the safety program to the security director or manager; in others, separate safety departments have been established. Although admittedly rare, where safety is considered part of the security organization, some businesses have given security directors responsibility for their environmental protection programs as well. More often than not, environmental protection is assigned to an independent department not connected with either security or safety.

Regardless of whether safety and environmental matters are part of the security effort or separate from it, program effectiveness is largely dependent on certain factors. First, personnel directly involved must be professionally qualified. Well-meaning but otherwise unqualified employees are not persons to whom the responsibility for safety or environmental program development and supervision should be assigned. To follow this course may prove to be more than ineffective; in the final analysis it may prove costly.

Second, regardless of the extent to which security is directly involved, those in charge of the security department dare not lose sight of what their responsibility is: namely, to protect all of the employer's assets. Therefore, a failure to protect employees, or the organization's reputation, reflects adversely on the security function. To say that safety and environmental protection are to be ignored unless they are seen as security department functions is no different than having line managers say that security is not a part of their job simply because it is not specified in their job descriptions.

Third, for optimum effect, safety and environmental protection programs need to be proactive rather than reactive. In this regard, even though security may not be directly involved with either program, it can make a meaningful contribution by making itself available for whatever assistance it can provide. This is true whether security personnel merely report known or suspected safety violations or environmental problems to those who are in charge, or security's emergency plans and public safety contacts can be of help to them. The need to provide employees with a safe and healthful workplace, and to protect the environment, requires no less in the way of a team effort than is true of a successful security program.

REVIEW QUESTIONS

1. Should security departments also be given the responsibility for their organizations' safety programs? Why?

2. Should security departments have responsibility for environmental protection programs? Why?

3. Aside from legal or insurance requirements, why is it important to have effective safety programs?

4. What distinguishes safety from environmental protection?

5. What are some features that distinguish them insofar as program implementation and corrective action are concerned?

6. What problems can exist for multistate operations as a result of the existence of both federal and state safety standards and environmental protection requirements?

7. If both federal and state standards or requirements exist, upon which do local businesses rely in terms of program development and implementation?

8. Under what circumstances must OSHA compliance officers get administrative search warrants before they can make an inspection?

9. As a security director who is also responsible for your employer's safety and environmental protection programs, to what professional qualifications would you look in terms of hiring people to staff the safety and environmental jobs?

10. Must government choose between civil or criminal prosecutions for noncompliance with OSHA standards and environmental protection requirements, or can it elect to file both civil complaints and criminal charges?

NOTES

[1] 29 U.S.C. 657.

[2] 29 C.F.R. 1901.1 to end.

[3] 29 C.F.R. ch. XVII, § 1903.9(c).

[4] 29 C.F.R. ch. XVII, § 1903.7(b).

[5] *The Boston Globe*, September 3, 1992, p. 3.

[6] *The New York Times*, September 15, 1992, sec. A, p. 20.

[7] *Occupational Hazards*, December 1984, p. 43.

[8] *Occupational Hazards*, December 1984, p. 45.

[9] *The Boston Globe*, December 21, 1990, p. 78.

[10] *The New York Times*, August 30, 1991, sec. A, p. 17.

[11] See, generally, Martin V. Melosi, *Hazardous Waste and Environmental Liability: An Historical Perspective*, 25 Hous. L. Rev. 741 (1988).

[12] *The New York Times*, February 15, 1991, sec. B, p. 6.

[13] *The New York Times*, September 23, 1991, sec. A, p. 14.

[14] *The New York Times*, August 29, 1991, sec. B, p. 11.

[15] *The New York Times*, July 12, 1991, sec. B, p. 1.

[16] ROBERT J. SAMUELSON, "Who Cleans Up the Waste," *Newsweek*, May 20, 1991, p. 49.

[17] *The Boston Globe*, September 26, 1991, p. 10.

Appendix A

Sample contract
for security services

THIS AGREEMENT NO.   dated this   day of
        , 19   , by and between
a Corporation with its principal office at

(hereinafter referred to as Vendor), and DATA GENERAL CORPORATION, a Delaware Corporation located at 4400 Computer Drive, Westboro, Massachusetts (hereinafter referred to as DGC). WHEREAS VENDOR is in the business of providing guard services for industrial concerns and desires to supply such services to DGC; and WHEREAS DGC desires to utilize such services under the terms and conditions set forth herein;

NOW, THEREFORE, in consideration of the mutual covenants specified herein, the parties hereto agree as follows:

ARTICLE I - AGREEMENT TERM

The term of this Agreement will be twelve (12) months beginning on the date first written above and continuing thereafter in full force and effect unless and until either party gives the other ninety (90) days prior written notice of termination. Upon termination, both parties agree to continue honoring their respective obligations hereunder for the ninety (90)-day notice period or such shorter period of time as may be mutually agreed upon.

    In no event will DGC's liability for payment hereunder extend beyond the number of guard hours actually provided by Vendor under the terms of this agreement.

ARTICLE II - EMPLOYMENT

A. Vendor shall employ all persons necessary to perform its obligations hereunder according to the terms of this Agreement and DGC's requirements, which may be modified by DGC at any time, and Vendor will be solely and exclusively responsible for all acts or omission by its employees.

B. Vendor shall not discriminate against any applicant for employment or employee on the basis of race, creed, sex, color, country of national origin, or age, in violation of any federal or state laws or local ordinances.

C. No former DGC employees shall be assigned to DGC without DGC's prior written consent.

D. Guards will be solely the employees of Vendor and not DGC, and Vendor shall pay all of their salaries and related expenses, including but not necessarily limited to, all taxes and employees' contributions.

E. Vendor agrees that all services provided by it and through its employees under the terms of this Agreement will be performed by qualified, careful, efficient personnel in strict conformity with the best practices and according to standards that DGC may from time to time prescribe. Vendor also agrees that it will remove from service any employee(s) if asked to do so by DGC, with or without cause.

F. All personnel employed by Vendor will be covered by a fidelity bond, the amount and terms and conditions of which are acceptable to DGC, and a copy of said bond shall be provided to DGC prior to the effective date of this Agreement.

G. DGC agrees that it will not make an offer of employment to any employee(s) of Vendor without having first obtained written approval to do so.

ARTICLE III - GUARD QUALIFICATIONS

A. All guards assigned to DGC will meet the minimum standards set forth below, the only exception(s) being guards on temporary assignment. For the purpose of this Vendor, any assignment of less than one week's duration will be considered temporary. DGC reserves the right through its authorized agent(s) to waive any requirements set forth herein, but only in writing and in individual cases. In no event is any waiver in any particular case to be construed as revising that standard as it applies to other guards.

B. Before assigning any of its personnel to DGC, Vendor will do the following with respect to each such employee:

1. Conduct as complete a background investigation of that person as is legally permissible, complying with all laws relating to the making of investigative reports and the disclosure of their contents.

2. Verify that the person is a high school graduate or has the equivalent of a high school education.

3. Verify that the person has no record of criminal convictions, minor traffic violations excepted.

4. Determine that the person has not had any credit difficulties within the past three (3) years.

5. Certify the following for each employee:

   a. That the person is in good mental health, and has no physical defects or abnormalities which would interfere with complete performance of all guard duties.

   b. That the person has binocular vision correctable to 20/20, is able to discriminate standard colors, and has normal hearing without the use of hearing aids.

   c. That the person's weight is in proportion to his or her height.

   d. That the person is capable of performing duties that may require moderate to arduous physical exertion including, but not necessarily limited to, standing or walking for an entire tour of duty, climbing stairs and ladders, lifting and carrying objects weighing up to fifty (50) pounds, running, and acts of physical self-defense.

6. Provide DGC with a copy of the medical certification for each person as evidence of the fact that the person meets the prescribed minimum physical standards.

7. Certify to DGC in writing that a thorough background investigation of that person has been completed, and that the qualifications set forth herein have been complied with.

C. Vendor will maintain the employment applications, or copies thereof, of all of its personnel assigned to DGC under the terms of this Agreement. They will be maintained in Vendor's office located at _____ , and made available for review by DGC upon request for a period of three (3) years following the last appearance of that person at DGC whether permanent or temporary.

D. Vendor also will maintain at that office, or at some other location acceptable to DGC, records of all training and all disciplinary action provided or taken by it with respect to each of its employees assigned to DGC in the performance of this Agreement, and they will be made available for DGC's review upon request.

E. DGC reserves the right to review the employment application and/or résumé, and to interview, every person that Vendor proposes to assign to it. The final decision regarding an individual's acceptability for assignment to DGC will rest with DGC. Vendor understands that if the parties hereto agree to the assignment of supervisory personnel to DGC, those proposed for such assignment shall have had not less than three (3) years of increasingly responsible duties as guards.

F. Notwithstanding any of the foregoing, nothing in this Article or this Agreement is to be construed to imply employment of any guards by DGC and guards shall be solely the responsibility of Vendor.

ARTICLE IV - GUARD ASSIGNMENTS

A. Hours and Posts to be covered are as per Exhibit B which is attached hereto and made a part hereof. Vendor agrees that no guards assigned by it to DGC will be permitted to work in excess of twelve (12) hours in any given twenty-four (24)-hour period, or more than sixty (60) hours in any given week, and each guard will be off duty not less than twenty-four (24) consecutive hours in each workweek. For the purpose of this Agreement the workweek will begin at 12:01 A.M., Wednesday, and end at 12 midnight the following Tuesday. The provisions of this paragraph relative to time off may be waived only by DGC's authorized representative, and in writing.

B. A schedule of guard assignments in conformity with DGC's requirements will be submitted to DGC not less than seven (7) days before its implementation.

C. Inasmuch as certain guards assigned to DGC may have to get a United States Government Security Clearance, Vendor agrees that it will assign only personnel eligible for such clearances, and in the event that any guard assigned by it to DGC is denied clearance, that guard will be replaced immediately by one who can be cleared, at no cost to DGC.

D. Guards assigned to DGC will remain at DGC for a period of one (1) year or the remaining term of this Agreement, whichever first occurs, unless (1) the guard's employment is terminated, (2) DGC agrees to the guard's prior transfer, (3) the guard is promoted by Vendor and no such position exists at DGC, or (4) the guard requests transfer.

E. In no event will Vendor assign to any DGC facility a guard who has been removed for cause or discharged from another facility.

F. A guard assigned to one DGC facility will not be transferred to another without DGC's prior written approval. If a guard's transfer is approved, all training requirements hereinafter prescribed shall apply to the transferred guard as if that guard had not been assigned previously to a DGC facility.

G. If it becomes necessary at any time for Vendor to provide guards for special duty, it will be compensated for those special duty hours at the unit rates hereinafter set forth.

H. In an emergency, Vendor may be required to provide up to two times the number of guards normally assigned to DGC under the terms of this Agreement. In all such cases the unit rate hereinafter agreed upon will prevail, but DGC will reimburse Vendor for the actual cost of expenses incurred in providing such services that are in excess of those incurred in regularly furnishing guards to DGC under the terms of this Agreement, including premium wages, additional administration and overhead, provided, however, that the total payment to Vendor will not exceed 150 percent of the unit rate times the number of emergency guard hours actually worked.

ARTICLE V - UNIFORMS AND EQUIPMENT

A. Vendor will provide each of its guards with all uniforms, equipment, including flashlights, and related materials as specified by DGC necessary for the performance of their duties. DGC will furnish all firefighting equipment.

B. THE USE OR CARRYING OF WEAPONS, FIREARMS INCLUDED, ON DGC PREMISES IS PROHIBITED. Weapons may not be stored on DGC premises unless first approved in writing by DGC's Vice President and General Counsel, or his designee, which approval will state specifically the terms and conditions under which such storage will be allowed by Vendor's employees.

C. At all times while on duty each guard will wear or otherwise openly display identification badges provided by DGC.

D. Immediately upon termination of any guard assigned to DGC, regardless of reason, Vendor shall immediately notify DGC in writing of the termination and reasons therefore, and it also will immediately recover and return to DGC the identification originally issued to that guard. If for any reason the DGC-issued identification is not available, Vendor will submit in writing to DGC its explanation as to why the identification cannot be returned, and the efforts made by it for recovery.

ARTICLE VI - TRAINING AND SUPERVISION

A. In addition to whatever general training Vendor provides to all of its guards, it also will provide, prior to assignment to DGC, a minimum of eight (8) hours of training covering the subjects set forth below unless such requirement is waived in writing by DGC, or temporary guards as previously defined herein are used in unusual circumstances.

B. The subjects to be covered in training will include, but not necessarily be limited to, the following:

1. Legal restrictions on arrests, searches, and seizures.
2. Detection, reporting, and control of fires; the use of portable firefighting equipment; the control of sprinkler systems; and the use of emergency breathing apparatus.
3. Appearance, attitude, and conduct as may be set forth in DGC's Guard Manual, or otherwise prescribed by DGC's authorized representative(s).
4. General application of patrol routines (winds, rounds), activities, and reports.
5. Human, public, and employee relations.
6. Controlling entry to and exit from the premises.
7. Controlling the movement of DGC assets, and other property for whose protection DGC may be responsible, to, from, and between or among DGC facilities or premises.
8. Riot, strike, and emergency procedures.

9. Other topics selected from among those listed in DGC's Guard Manual or prescribed by DGC's authorized representatives.

C. Upon first reporting for duty at DGC, each newly assigned guard will be given a minimum of sixteen (16) hours of "on-the-job" training, and Vendor will not charge DGC for the services of any guard until all training required under the terms of this Agreement, including on the job training, has been completed to DGC's satisfaction.

D. Vendor also will give each guard assigned to DGC a minimum of eight (8) hours of refresher or in-service training once every six (6) months.

E. Vendor will provide at least twice weekly, at random times to cover all shifts on a regular basis, unannounced inspections of each post to which its guards are assigned, by one of its nonresident supervisors.

F. Vendor agrees to remove and replace any guard from assignment at DGC (a) if such employee is not properly performing his or her duties, or (b) upon request of DGC.

G. Vendor agrees that it will not knowingly hire, or assign to, any DGC facility any person who is or has been assigned, whether on a temporary or a permanent basis, to any entity that is a business competitor of DGC.

ARTICLE VII - GUARD RESPONSIBILITIES

A. Unless otherwise specifically instructed in writing by DGC's authorized representative, guards will be responsible for all aspects of protection, including but not necessarily limited to, the following: monitoring shipping and receiving dock activities; guarding the premises against fire, burglary, theft, breaking and entering, pilferage, acts of vandalism, damage to or the destruction of property; preventing malicious injury to persons; and allowing only authorized persons to enter the premises. They will make regular tours of the property, report immediately all violations of fire and safety regulations, and when instructed to do so they will control traffic on and in DGC-owned roadways and parking areas. Guards also will carry out such special written instructions as may from time to time be issued to them by DGC's authorized representative(s).

B. Upon completing a tour of duty, each guard will submit a written report to DGC's designated representative covering all activities, including details of all unusual or hazardous conditions encountered during such tour. Any guard who discovers an emergency condition will report it immediately, in person, by telephone, or by alarm, whichever is most appropriate, and will confirm both the discovery and action taken in response thereto in the written report submitted at the conclusion of his or her tour of duty.

C. Guards are prohibited from making arrests, detaining persons, or swearing out complaints on behalf of DGC without the express written consent of DGC's VicePresident and General Counsel or his designee. In the event that a guard witnesses a crime being committed in his or her presence, on DGC premises or in one of its facilities, it will be reported immediately to either the DGC Site Security Manager/Representative,

Supervisor, or Group Leader, if one is then on duty, and if not, to the guard's Contractor supervisor, and if the DGC representative or guard's supervisor, as the case may be, is of the opinion that immediate action is required, the DGC representative or guard's supervisor may notify the police directly, with notification immediately thereafter to both the DGC Site Security Manager/Representative and DGC's Vice President and General Counsel or his designee.

ARTICLE VIII - LIABILITY/INDEMNIFICATION

A. Vendor will indemnify and hold DGC, its directors, agents, employees, and representatives harmless against all loss and liability resulting from personal injury or death to its own employees or others, property damage, assault, false arrest and false imprisonment, slander, defamation of character, negligence, or any other cause arising out of or in connection with the services to be provided hereunder irrespective of whether performed on DGC's premises or elsewhere.

B. In the event that a claim is made against DGC, its directors, agents, employees, or representatives, for which Vendor has undertaken to indemnify DGC, DGC or its legal representative will promptly notify Vendor in writing of such claim or lawsuit arising out of or in connection with the services provided under the terms of this Agreement, will forward to Vendor all related documents, and Vendor then will defend the case at its own expense. However, DGC reserves the right to be represented by counsel of its own choice, and at its own expense, at any proceeding or settlement discussions related thereto.

C. Vendor will procure and maintain a minimum of the following insurance:

1. Worker's Compensation Insurance as prescribed by the laws of the Commonwealth of Massachusetts and Employer's Liability Insurance with a limit of $100,000.
2. Comprehensive Automobile Liability Insurance, including Automobile Nonownership Liability, with limits of $1,000,000 for bodily injury or death of each person; $1,000,000 for bodily injury or death for each occurrence, and $1,000,000 for property damage in each occurrence.
3. Comprehensive General Liability Insurance, including contractual liability, broad form property damage, and personal injury liability, with a combined $2,000,000 bodily injury and property damage limit in each occurrence.
4. Employee Dishonesty Insurance with a limit of $1,000,000 per loss.

D. Within two working days of this Agreement's execution Vendor will furnish DGC a Certificate of Insurance as evidence that the required coverage is in effect, and that DGC has been named as an additional insured under both the Comprehensive General Liability and Automobile Insurance policies.

E. Each of the insurance policies referred to above will include a provision that it may not be canceled without thirty (30) days' prior written notice to DGC of such cancellation.

F. Nothing in this Article will be deemed to limit Vendor's responsibility to the amounts stated above, or under any other provisions of this Agreement.

ARTICLE IX - PAYMENT

A. The services to be performed hereunder will be billable on an hourly basis at the rates shown on Exhibit A, attached hereto and made a part hereof (billable rate). All of the rates set forth in Exhibit A, with the sole exception described in paragraph B of this Article, will be in full force and effect for the duration of this Agreement, and they will include all of Vendor's profit, overhead, guard and supervisory salaries, administration expenses, and all other costs related to the performance of this Agreement. The billable rate will apply to all guard services provided, irrespective of the date or time of day when such services are to be performed. DGC will not be subject to any overtime or premium billings for additional hours or holiday rates except as provided for in paragraph B, below.

B. In the event that DGC, with less than twenty-four (24) hours' prior notice to Vendor requests additional hours of unscheduled service, Vendor will make every reasonable effort to provide such service to DGC without any charge for overtime. However, if the additional hours of service can be provided only with overtime, Vendor will advise DGC of that fact, the overtime rate that it will have to charge, and the number of hours to which it will apply.

C. Not until authorization has been received from DGC's Site Purchasing Manager, or his or her designee, will Vendor provide such additional hours of service, and the additional cost of the overtime will be paid by DGC within thirty (30) days from the receipt of a separate invoice referencing a DGC Purchase Order for the stated amount.

D. Vendor will maintain complete, clear, and accurate records of all guard assignments, hours of work performed by each, and actual direct labor hourly rates incurred in the performance of this Agreement. DGC reserves the right to inspect and audit, during regular business hours, Vendor's business records as they relate to the services rendered under this Agreement. Vendor agrees to make such records available either on site at the DGC facility where the guards are assigned, or in one (1) central location within a thirty-five (35)-mile radius of the DGC location where the services are being performed, and to retain all such records for a period of not less than three (3) years from the date of completion of this Agreement.

E. Vendor will submit for payment one (1) invoice supported by all documentation required by DGC for verification of the billing on a weekly basis for the preceding month, except that any overtime authorized by DGC, as set forth in this Article, will be invoiced separately against a DGC-authorized Purchase Order.

F. If DGC disputes the billing, in whole or in part, it will process promptly for payment the undisputed portion thereof, and it will confer with Vendor relative to the disputed portion. DGC is not obligated to make any payment until the billing and documentation therefor are submitted in a form acceptable to it.

G. Within thirty (30) days following the receipt of a valid invoice and its supporting documentation, DGC will remit payment.

H. The rates set forth in this Agreement are based on Vendor providing services to DGC's Westboro Corporate facility. However, if during the course of this Agreement DGC adds other locations under the same terms and conditions, Vendor then agrees to consider renegotiating downward of the billings set forth in Exhibit A.

I. Vendor will be responsible for all sales, use, or other taxes, if any, applicable to the work.

J. If, in DGC's opinion, guard rates should be reduced to conform to any reductions in minimum wages, Vendor agrees to renegotiate its billing rates.

K. Vendor warrants that the billable rate charged DGC hereunder is as low as the Vendor charges any client purchasing such services in the same or greater quantity under similar terms and conditions, and in the event that Vendor grants any other client a lower rate for the same quantity of services under similar terms and conditions during the term hereof, then DGC's price shall be adjusted for the balance of the term to reflect the lower rate.

ARTICLE X - DEFAULT

A. If Vendor fails to perform any of the services called for by this Agreement, or if any proceeding is filed by or against it in bankruptcy, insolvency, or an assignment is made by it for the benefit of its creditors, or if there is a transfer of proprietary interest, and such condition or conditions are not remedied to DGC's reasonable satisfaction within fourteen (14) calendar days following written notice thereof given by DGC, DGC may without any liability immediately terminate all or any part of this Agreement by written or telegraphic notice to Vendor and seek similar services elsewhere.

B. If, during the term of this Agreement, Vendor for any reason is unable or unwilling to furnish DGC the number of guards required for the protection of the site or sites covered thereby, DGC may contract with another guard service of its choice, at the then prevailing rate, for such additional or replacement services as it may require.

C. In such an event Vendor will be responsible for all damages and expenses incurred by DGC prior to the replacement of such services, as well as for all additional expenses incurred by DGC above and beyond the rates set forth in this Agreement for the protection of the site or sites covered thereby.

D. DGC agrees to make every reasonable effort to pay all properly submitted and documented Contractor's invoices within thirty (30) days of their receipt. In the event that

Vendor has not been paid within that time, provided Vendor has submitted correct and documented invoices and has otherwise complied with its obligations hereunder, it then may issue a written demand for payment to DGC, and if within fifteen (15) days of the receipt by DGC of such a demand Vendor still has not received payment, it may then notify DGC in writing of its intention to terminate this Agreement forty-five (45) days following DGC's receipt of such notice.

ARTICLE XI - CONFIDENTIALITY

A.   All information obtained by Vendor from DGC in connection with this Agreement, its performance, or for any other reason, is received by Vendor in confidence, remains the property of DGC, and will be used by Vendor only to the extent necessary for the performance of this Agreement and in accordance with DGC's Proprietary Rights and Nondisclosure Agreement, a copy of which Vendor has executed, and which is attached hereto as Exhibit C.

B.   All such DGC information and property will be returned to it upon the expiration, termination, or cancellation of this Agreement, or at any other time that DGC requests its return.

C.   Vendor agrees that it will not disclose to others, advertise, or publish the fact that it is performing or has performed any service or work for DGC, whether under the terms of this Agreement or otherwise, unless it is expressly authorized to do so in writing by DGC. It also agrees that all information, data, results, analyses, and reports received, collected, developed, prepared or written by it, its employees, representatives, or agents in the performance of this Agreement will be maintained in confidence without restriction as to time, that disclosure will be made only to DGC, and that no such information or material will be used by it for any purpose other than the completion of its obligations to DGC.

D.   Vendor agrees that the provisions of this Article XI will survive the expiration, termination, or cancellation of this Agreement.

ARTICLE XII - DGC-FURNISHED DOCUMENTATION

A.   DGC will prepare written instructions, including a Guard Manual where deemed appropriate, setting forth specifically the days and hours of the week when guards are to be on duty, the number of guards required and the duties that they are to perform, the location of guard rooms, and it will furnish guard logs. All materials provided by DGC, including but not necessarily limited to, Guard Manuals, post orders, and copies of DGC's Safety/Security Policies and Procedures and of DGC's telephone directory, will not be reproduced by Vendor or distributed to any of its personnel other than those guards working on site at the facility covered by the terms of this Agreement, and all such materials must be returned to DGC immediately upon the completion of this Agreement, its prior termination, or at any other time that DGC requests their return.

B. DGC may modify or revise these materials at any time upon twenty-four (24) hours' prior notification.

C. All guards will be required to sign in and out in the guard log provided by DGC.

D. If requested by DGC, Vendor agrees to assist with the preparation of written materials for guards, such as post orders, manuals, etc., at no additional charge to DGC.

ARTICLE XIII - GENERAL PROVISIONS

A. This Agreement and any amendments hereto will be governed by the laws of the DGC location where the services are provided. If any provision contravenes such law it will be deemed to have been deleted, but no such deletion will in any way affect any of the other portions of this Agreement.

B. This Agreement, and all exhibits referenced herein, or attached hereto and made a part hereof, constitute the entire understanding between Vendor and DGC and supersede all prior oral or written communications, agreements, representations, statements, negotiations, and undertakings relating to the subject matter hereof.

C. No representation, promise, waiver, modification, or amendment will be binding on either party unless made in writing and signed by an authorized representative of each.

D. DGC's failure to insist upon, or enforce in any instance, strict performance by Vendor of any part of this Agreement, or to exercise any of the rights herein conferred upon or reserved by it, will not be construed as a waiver or relinquishment by DGC to any extent of its right to assert or rely upon such terms or rights on any future occasion.

E. All notices required to be given by either party under the terms of this Agreement must be sent by Registered or Certified Mail, Return Receipt Requested, and addressed to:

> DATA GENERAL CORPORATION
> 4400 Computer Drive
> Westboro, MA. 01580
> ATTN: Corporate Purchasing Director

VENDOR :

> ATTN:

F. Neither this Agreement nor any interest hereunder may be assigned, in whole or in part, by either party without the prior written consent of the other, and any such attempted assignment will be null and void.

G. Vendor agrees that without having first obtained DGC's written consent it will neither disclose to any person or persons outside of its employ, nor use for any purpose other than the performance of this Agreement, any information pertaining to DGC or DGC's affairs, including the contents of this Agreement. Furthermore, without having first obtained DGC's written consent, Vendor will not in any way or to anyone disclose, advertise, or publish the fact that it has furnished or contracted to furnish any services to DGC.

IN WITNESS WHEREOF, the parties hereto have caused this Agreement to be executed in duplicate by their duly authorized representatives as of the day and year first written above.

ACCEPTED: ACCEPTED:

_____   DATA GENERAL CORPORATION

BY: _____   BY: _____

TITLE: _____   TITLE: _____

EXHIBIT A

The cost to Data General Corporation for security services is as follows:

$.   per hour for unarmed security officers and lead guard.

In the event that DGC, with less than twenty-four (24) hours' prior notice to vendor requests additional hours of unscheduled service, vendor will make every reasonable effort to provide such service to DGC without any charge for overtime. However, if the additional hours of service can be provided only with overtime, vendor will advise DGC of that fact, and the number of hours to which it will apply. The overtime rate will be charged at $.   an hour.

Appendix B

MANUFACTURING PLANT SECURITY AUDIT CHECKLIST

Facility Audited: _____   Audit Date(s): _____

Audited by: _____

I.   PHYSICAL SECURITY

A. Exterior

   1. Grounds

      a. Perimeter protection is _____ acceptable _____ unacceptable.
        If unacceptable, why? _____

        _____

      b. Lighting is _____ acceptable _____ unacceptable.
        If unacceptable, why? _____

        _____

      c. Parking lot protection is _____ acceptable _____ unacceptable.
        By what means, if any, is it provided? _____

        _____

2. Storage facilities

    a. Fuel

       Protection is   _____ acceptable   _____ unacceptable.

       By what means is it provided? _____

       _____

    b. Other (describe) _____

       Protection is   _____ acceptable   _____ unacceptable.

       How is it provided? _____

       _____

B. Buildings (total number on site) _____ If multiple buildings, are they physically connected or separated?

_____

1. Ingress and egress controls

    a. Total number of employee entrances? _____

    b. Total number of visitor entrances? _____

    c. Do employees and visitors use the same entrances? _____

    d. How is employee ingress and egress controlled?

       _____

    e. How is visitor ingress and egress controlled?

       _____

2. Doors generally

    a. Are perimeter doors, other than designated entrances and shipping/receiving doors, normally locked? _____ If yes, but there are any exceptions, explain.

       _____

       _____

    b. What means are used to secure perimeter doors?

       _____

       _____

    c. Are all key-operated door locks on the corporate system? _____ If not, explain.

       _____

       _____

    d. Describe the type(s) of shipping/receiving doors and how they are secured.

       _____

       _____

e. If shipping/receiving doors have automatic controls, how are the controls secured when not in use?

_____

_____

f. How are shipping/receiving docks protected when the doors are open?

_____

_____

3. Office area, office, computer room doors
   a. Are those with locks secured after hours? _____ If not, explain.

   _____

   _____

   b. If secured with combination locks, how often or under what circumstances are combinations changed, and by whom?

   _____

   _____

   c. How is computer room access controlled?

   _____

   _____

   d. Do computer rooms have door or window openings for the passage of work? _____ If not, how is this handled?

   _____

   _____

   e. Do computer rooms have security alarms? _____ If yes, describe.

   _____

   _____

4. Communications areas
   a. Are the mail and TLX/teletype rooms and copy centers consolidated into a single area? _____ If so, how is the space secured both during and after working hours?

   _____

   _____

   b. If not, describe how each separate area is protected both during and after normal working hours.
   Mail Room _____
   TLX/teletype _____
   Copy center _____

c. How is the telephone switchroom protected?

_____

_____

5. Stockrooms, tool cribs, warehouse space
   a. Is access to each controlled, and if so, how?

   _____

   _____

   b. If not, explain.

   _____

   _____

   c. Do those equipped with other than sliding doors have exposed hinges, and if so, how are the hinges secured?

   _____

   _____

   d. Is there overhead protection? _____ If not, is the security afforded the contents of each _____ acceptable or _____ unacceptable? Explain.

   _____

   _____

   _____

   e. Describe the physical protection, if any, provided for IOS materials.

   _____

   _____

6. Records and miscellaneous storage
   a. If in storerooms, do doors have locks, and are they secured after hours? _____
   b. If in file cabinets, how are the cabinets secured when not in use?

   _____

   _____

   The protection is _____ acceptable _____ unacceptable.
   c. If stored in locked file cabinets, how are the keys protected after hours?

   _____

   _____

   d. How is petty cash protected during the day and after hours?

   _____

   _____

e. How are travelers checks and blank check stock secured?

_____

_____

f. If the site has a check signing plate, how is it protected?

_____

_____

g. If any check stock and/or check signature plates are kept in a safe, how many people have the combination? _____ When and under what circumstances was the combination last changed, and by whom?

_____

_____

h. Where are computer backup tapes stored, and is their protection _____ acceptable or _____ unacceptable? Describe:

_____

_____

II. OPERATIONAL AND ADMINISTRATIVE SECURITY

A. Access control generally

  1. Employees
  a. Do photo ID badges conform to the corporate communications manual and corporate safety/security policies and procedures in *all* respects? _____ If not, explain.

_____

_____

  b. Are badge requests properly completed? _____ If not, explain.

_____

_____

  c. By whom are badges issued? _____ Recovered? _____ Do these conform to policy? _____ If not, explain.

_____

_____

  d. Do nonresident DG employees require escorts? _____ If so, explain.

_____

_____

e. How or by whom are employee IDs, resident and nonresident, verified at point of entry?

_____

_____

f. Are key authorization requests properly completed in *all* respects? _____ If not, explain. _____

_____

_____

g. By whom are keys issued, recovered, and records kept?

_____

_____

h. Are keys transferred from one employee to another without an actual recovery and reissue? _____

_____

_____

2. Contractors

   a. Are contractors issued identification badges, and if so, do they conform to the corporate communications manual and corporate safety/security policies and procedures? _____ If not, explain.

   _____

   _____

   b. By whom are they issued and recovered?

   _____

   _____

   c. Are written requests required for initial issue, renewal, or both? _____ If not, explain.

   _____

   _____

   d. Are keys issued to contractors? _____ If yes, explain.

   _____

   _____

3. Visitors

   a. Are visitors issued identification badges, and if so, do they conform to the corporate communications manual and corporate safety/security policies and procedures? _____ If not, explain. _____

   _____

   _____

b. By whom are they issued and recovered?

_____

_____

c. Are visitors required to sign in and out? _____

d. Do visitors require escorts? _____ If not, explain.

_____

_____

B. Access to sensitive areas (computer rooms, stockrooms/tool cribs, shipping/receiving docks, R&D areas, Marcom, etc.)

1. Are administrative as distinguished from physical security access controls used to protect sensitive areas? _____

2. If so, describe briefly the measures used for each such area.

_____

_____

_____

C. Protection of assets

1. Are all contractors required to execute DG's nondisclosure agreement before starting their work? _____ If not, explain.

2. If yes, where are copies filed?

_____

_____

3. What policy, if any, is followed regarding the use of cameras and picture-taking on site?

_____

_____

4. Does the site comply with *all* provisions of the corporate safety/security policy and procedure for the Protection of Assets in Transit, including those relating to property passes? _____ List deficiencies or evidence of noncompliance.

_____

_____

5. Is the site in compliance with the corporate safety/security policy and procedure for the loan, use, and recovery of Data General assets? _____ If not, explain.

_____

_____

6. Are personnel through whom property passes clear provided with current lists and sample signatures of authorized signatories? _____ How are sample signatures protected when not actually in use?

_____

_____

7. Have all managers and supervisors received copies of the corporate policy and procedure for the protection of Data General confidential information, and is the site in compliance? _____ If not, explain.

_____

_____

8. Describe how proprietary information is disposed of when not needed. Is destruction witnessed, and if so, by whom?

_____

_____

9. Are accountability records kept on engineering or similar notebooks? _____ If so, are they audited to ensure their preservation and need for retention by the employee to whom charged? _____ With what frequency?

_____

_____

10. Is the need to protect proprietary information discussed at the site manager's staff meetings? If so, how often? _____

_____

_____

11. If IOS materials are disposed of locally, what is done to ensure that those to be destroyed are in fact destroyed?

_____

_____

12. If truck drivers, other than DG employees, are not restricted to the immediate vicinity of shipping/receiving docks, how are their movements controlled?

_____

_____

13. Are they allowed to load their own vehicles other than under direct DG supervision? _____ If so, explain.

_____

_____

14. Are all quantities, whether being shipped or received, checked, counted, and/or weighed by DG personnel? _____ If not, explain.

_____

_____

III. EMERGENCIES

A. Bomb threats

1. Are switchboard operators and security personnel familiar with the procedure to be followed in the event of a bomb threat? _____ If not, explain.

_____

_____

2. Have they been made aware of the details of the call and about the caller for which they should be alert? _____ If yes, how? _____ If not, explain.

_____

_____

3. Does a local bomb search procedure exist? _____ If not, explain.

_____

_____

4. Have any bomb threats been received since the last (corporate or self) security audit? _____ If so, were they reported to corporate safety/security, and if not reported, explain.

_____

_____

B. Evacuations

1. Are evacuation routes posted conspicuously? _____ If not, explain.

_____

_____

2. Does a local evacuation procedure, including the designation of preselected departmental assembly points, exist? _____ Are all employees familiar with it? _____ When was it last reviewed with them?

_____

_____

3. If none exists, explain.

_____

_____

C. Fires

1. Are employees trained in the use of fire extinguishers? _____

_____

_____

2. If yes, by whom has training been provided, and with what frequency?

_____

_____

3. Have there been any fires, regardless of size or possible loss, since the last (corporate or self) security audit? _____

_____

_____

4. If yes, were they reported to corporate safety/security? _____

_____

_____

5. If there were, but they were not reported to corporate safety/security, explain.

_____

_____

IV. SECURITY ADMINISTRATION/OPERATIONS

A. Safety/security personnel

1. To whom does the site's safety/security manager, supervisor, or representative report directly?

_____

_____

2. Does the site's safety/security manager, supervisor, or representative attend the site manager's staff meetings? _____   If not, explain.

_____

_____

3. What percentage of his or her time does the site safety/security manager, supervisor, or representative devote exclusively to safety/security matters? _____

_____

_____

4. Does the site safety/security manager, supervisor, or representative regularly attend the scheduled corporate safety/security conferences? _____ If not, explain.

_____

_____

5. Are other safety/security personnel employed at the site? _____ If yes, for how many shifts per day, hours per shift, and hours per week?

_____

_____

6. If guards are employed at the site, are they proprietary or contract personnel, or a combination of the two? _____

_____

_____

7. Are guards uniformed? _____ Armed? _____ If armed, by virtue of whose authority?

_____

_____

8. How much training, both initial and refresher, is given to guards, and by whom?

_____

_____

9. If no training is provided for guards, explain.

_____

_____

B. Operations

1. Are patrol rounds regularly made both inside and outside the facility? _____ If yes, with what frequency?

_____

_____

2. Are rounds made using a Dextex or similar device? _____

_____

_____

3. Are patrols randomized both as to route and time? _____ If not, explain.

_____

_____

4. Are patrols made on foot, in a vehicle, or a combination of the two? _____

_____

_____

5. If no patrol rounds of any sort are made, explain.

_____

_____

C. Incidents and investigations

1. Are incidents reported to site safety/security recorded? _____

_____

_____

2. How are all reported incidents followed up? Describe the procedure.

_____

_____

3. Does the site comply with the corporate safety/security policy and procedure for security incident reporting? _____ If not, explain.

_____

_____

4. Has the site encountered any "reportable activities" as defined in the corporate safety/security policy and procedure on investigations since the last corporate security audit? _____

_____

_____

5. If so, have they been reported to corporate safety/security as required by and in conformity with that policy? _____ If not, explain.

_____

_____

D. Records and communications

1. Of what do security records consist?

_____

2. For what purpose(s) other than historical are they used? Describe.

_____

_____

3. Are security personnel duties and responsibilities in writing? _____ Are specific post instructions in writing? _____

_____

_____

4. Are security patrol personnel equipped with two-way radios? _____ If not, what means of communication are used to maintain contact?

_____

_____

E. Liaison

1. Is the site safety/security manager, supervisor, or representative personally acquainted with the locally appropriate ranking law enforcement and fire service officials? _____

_____

_____

2. Identify by title who those officials are for the audited site (e.g., police chief, sheriff, precinct commander, fire chief, fire battalion chief, etc.).

_____

_____

3. To what extent, if any, is contact maintained with the respective officials?

_____

_____

4. In the event of a bomb threat, how close is the nearest bomb disposal unit, and by what agency is it operated? _____

_____

_____

5. In the event of an accident or emergency, other than bomb threat or fire, how close is the nearest rescue squad or similar unit?

_____

_____

6. Is the local fire department a full-time paid or volunteer unit, or a combination of the two?

_____

_____

Appendix C

OFFICE SECURITY AUDIT CHECKLIST

Office/Remote Location Audited: _____

Audit Date(s): _____ Audited by: _____

I.   PHYSICAL SECURITY

    A.   Location

       1.   Urban or suburban _____

       2.   Structure

          a.   Office building _____

          b.   Office or industrial park _____

          c.   Type of construction _____

          d.   Sprinklered? _____

       3.   Floor(s) on which located _____

    B.   Exterior

       1.   Grounds landscaped? _____

---

2. Window/door exposure _____

3. Type(s) of door(s) and lock(s)

    a. Leading into space _____

    b. Within space _____

    c. If unacceptable, why? _____

4. Lighting is _____ acceptable _____ unacceptable.

    If unacceptable, why? _____

    _____

5. Parking protection is _____ acceptable _____ unacceptable.

    How is it provided? _____

6. Type(s) of window/door glass _____

C. Building security

  1. Ingress and egress controls

    a. Total number of entrances to space _____

    b. Do employees and visitors use the same entrances? _____

    c. How is employee ingress and egress controlled?

    _____

    d. How is visitor ingress and egress controlled?

    _____

    e. Are perimeter doors, other than designated entrances and shipping/receiving doors, normally locked? _____

    f. What means are used to secure perimeter doors? _____

    _____

    g. Describe the type(s) of shipping/receiving doors and how they are secured.

    _____

  2. Office area, office, computer room doors

    a. Are doors with locks secured after hours? _____ If not, explain. _____

    _____

    b. If secured with combination locks, how often or under what circumstances are combinations changed, and by whom?

    _____

    c. How is computer room access controlled? _____

    _____

    d. Do computer rooms have door or window openings for the passage of work? _____ If not, how is this handled? _____

    _____

e. Do computer rooms have security alarms? _____

   If yes, describe. _____

f. Are terminals and computers physically separated? _____

3. Communications areas

   a. Are the mail and TLX/teletype rooms and copy centers consolidated into a single area? _____ If so, how is the space secured both during and after working hours? _____

   b. If not, describe how each separate area is protected both during and after normal working hours.

      Mail room _____

      TLX/teletype _____

      Copy center _____

   c. How is the telephone switchroom protected?

      _____

4. Parts rooms

   a. Is access controlled? _____ If so, how? _____

      _____

   b. If not, explain. _____

      _____

   c. Do those equipped with other than sliding doors have exposed hinges?_____ If so, how are they secured? _____

   d. Is there overhead protection? _____ If not, is the security afforded the contents _____ acceptable or _____ unacceptable? Explain. _____

      _____

5. Miscellaneous storage

   a. If in storerooms, do doors have locks, and are they secured after hours? _____

   b. If in file cabinets, how are the cabinets secured when not in use? _____

      _____

      The protection is _____ acceptable _____ unacceptable.

   c. If stored in locked file cabinets, how are the keys protected after hours? _____

      _____

   d. How is petty cash protected during the day and after hours? _____

      _____

   e. How are traveler's checks and blank check stock secured? _____

      _____

   f. Where are computer backup tapes stored, and is their protection _____ acceptable or _____ unacceptable? Describe. _____

      _____

II. OPERATIONAL AND ADMINISTRATIVE SECURITY

A. Access control generally

1. Employees

   a. Is security discussed as part of new employees' orientation? _____ Is it ever discussed with employees generally at any time? _____ If so, at what intervals? _____ If not, why not? _____

   _____

   b. Do photo ID badges conform to the corporate communications manual and corporate safety/security policies and procedures in all respects? _____ if not, explain. _____

   _____

   c. Are badge requests properly completed? _____ If not, explain. _____

   _____

   d. By whom are badges issued? _____
   Recovered? _____ Do these conform to policy? _____
   If not, explain. _____

   e. Do nonresident DG employees require escorts? _____ If so, explain.

   _____

   f. How or by whom are employee IDs, resident and nonresident, verified at point of entry? _____

   _____

   g. Are key authorization requests properly completed in all respects? _____
   If not, explain. _____

   h. By whom are keys issued, recovered, and records kept? _____

   _____

   i. Are keys transferred from one employee to another without actual recovery and reissue? _____

2. Visitors

   a. Are visitors issued identification badges? _____ If so, do they conform to the corporate communications manual and corporate safety/security policies and procedures? _____ If not, explain. _____

   b. By whom are they issued and recovered? _____

   c. Are visitors required to sign in and out? _____

   d. Do visitors require escorts? _____ If not, explain. _____

   _____

B. Access to sensitive areas (computer rooms, store or parts rooms)

1. Are administrative as distinguished from physical security access controls used for protecting sensitive areas? _____
2. If so, describe briefly the measures used for each such area. _____

_____

_____

C. Protection of assets

1. What policy, if any, is followed regarding the use of cameras and picture-taking on site? _____

2. Does the site comply with the corporate safety/security policy and procedure for the loan, use, and recovery of Data General assets? _____ If not, explain. _____

_____

3. Have all managers and supervisors received copies of the corporate policy and procedure for the protection of Data General confidential information? _____ Is the site in compliance? _____ If not, explain. _____

_____

4. Describe how proprietary information is disposed of when no longer needed. Is destruction witnessed, and if so, by whom? _____

_____

5. Is the need to protect proprietary information discussed at managers' meetings? If so, how often? _____

6. Are all materials, whether being shipped or received, checked, counted, and/or weighed by DG personnel? _____ If not, explain. _____

_____

III. EMERGENCIES

A. Bomb threats

1. Are switchboard operators familiar with the procedure to be followed in the event of a bomb threat? _____ If not, explain. _____

_____

2. Have they been made aware of the details of the call and about the caller for which they should be alert? _____ If yes, how recently? _____ If not, explain.

_____

3. Does a local bomb search procedure exist? _____ If not, explain. _____

_____

4. Have any bomb threats been received? _____ If so, were they reported to corporate safety/security, and if not, explain. _____

_____

B. Evacuations

1. Are evacuation routes posted conspicuously? _____ If not, explain. _____

_____

2. Does a local evacuation procedure, including the designation of preselected functional assembly points, exist? _____ Are all employees familiar with it? _____ When was it last reviewed with them? _____

3. If none exists, explain. _____

C. Fires

1. Are employees trained in the use of fire extinguishers? _____

2. If yes, by whom has training been provided, and with what frequency? _____

_____

3. Have there been any fires, regardless of size or possible loss, since the last security audit? _____

4. If yes, were they reported to corporate safety/security? _____

5. If there were, but they were not reported to corporate safety/security, explain.

_____

IV. SECURITY INCIDENTS AND INVESTIGATIONS

A. Reporting procedures

1. Are incidents reported to local managers recorded? _____

2. How are all reported incidents followed up? _____ Describe the procedure.

_____

3. Does the site comply with the corporate safety/security policy and procedure for security incident reporting? _____ If not, explain. _____

_____

4. Has the site encountered any "reportable activities" as defined in the corporate safety/security policy and procedure on investigations since the last security audit? ____

5. If so, have they been reported to corporate safety/security as required by and in conformity with that policy? _____ If not, explain. _____

_____

B. Liaison

1. Are any of the local managers personally acquainted with the local law enforcement and fire service officials? _____

2. Identify by title who those officials are for the audited site (e.g., police chief, sheriff, precinct commander, fire chief, fire battalion chief, etc.).

_____

3. To what extent, if any, is contact maintained with the respective officials? _____

_____

4. In the event of a bomb threat, how close is the nearest bomb disposal unit, and by what agency is it operated?

5. In the event of an accident or emergency, other than bomb threat or fire, how close is the nearest rescue squad or similar unit? _____

6. Is the local fire department a full-time paid unit, a volunteer unit, or a combination of the two?_____

SELECTED BIBLIOGRAPHY

BLAIR, PETER M., and RICHARD A. SCHOENHERR, *The Structure of Organizations*. New York: Basic Books, 1971.

BURSTEIN, HARVEY, "Beyond Cops and Robbers: A Note on Corporate Security." *University of Michigan Business Review*, vol. 30, no. 2 (March 1978), pp. 30–32.

_____, *Hospital Security Management*. New York: Praeger, 1977.

_____, *Hotel Security Management*, 2nd ed. New York: Praeger, 1985.

_____, *Industrial Security Management*, 2nd ed. New York: Praeger, 1986.

_____, "The Law and Industrial Security." *Insurance Counsel Journal*, vol. 40 (April 1973), pp. 295–301.

_____, "Not So Petty Larceny." *Harvard Business Review*, vol. 37, no. 3. (May–June 1959), pp. 72–78.

_____, "Security Problems? It Could Be Your Attitude." *Journal of Applied Management*, vol. 5, no. 1 (January–February 1980), pp. 10–12.

"Check Your Management Costs." *Nation's Business*, January 1962, p. 36.

CLINARD, MARSHALL B., and PETER C. YEAGER, *Corporate Crime*. New York: Free Press, 1980.

CROWE, TIMOTHY D., *Crime Prevention through Environmental Design*. Stoneham, MA: Butterworth-Heinemann, 1991.

CUNNINGHAM, WILLIAM C., JOHN J. STRAUCHS, and CLIFFORD W. VAN METER, *The Hallcrest Report II, Private Security Trends 1970–2000*. Stoneham, MA: Butterworth-Heinemann, 1990.

JENKINS, BRIAN, M., ed. *Terrorism and Personal Protection*. Boston: Butterworth, 1985.

LAQUER, WALTER, *Terrorism*. Boston: Little, Brown, 1977.

"Managing Liability from Hazardous Waste." *Houston Law Review*, vol. 25, no. 4 (July 1988), pp.715–1003.

OSTERBURG, JAMES W., and RICHARD H. WARD, *Criminal Investigation*. Cincinnati, OH: Anderson, 1992.

PARKER, DONN B., *Crime by Computer*. New York: Charles Scribner's Sons, 1976.

RITZER, GEORGE, *Working Conflict and Change*, 2nd ed. Englewood Cliffs, NJ: Prentice Hall, 1977.

WHYTE, WILLIAM H., JR., *The Organization Man*. Garden City, NY: Doubleday Anchor Books, 1957.

INDEX

contract and insurance laws, 100–1
contractors, 181–82
controls and accountability, 79–81
copyrights, 104, 183
core training subjects, 47
counterfeiting, 143–44, 165–66
courtroom security, 187
credit cards, 165–66
crime prevention, 5
crimes and torts, 105–9
criminal and civil liability issues, 109–10
criminal histories, 119
crisis management, 133–34
  plan, 133–34
  team, 133

D

deductible clause, 86, 110
degree programs, 5
Department of Defense, contracts, 104–5, 186
  Industrial Security Manual, 4, 79, 104–5, 186
Department of Labor, 194
disasters, human–made, 65
discipline, 49
drugs, 183, 185
duties and responsibilities, security director or manager, 22–24

E

educational institutions, 169–74
  standards, 40
ego, 61, 64
emergencies and disasters, 64–66
  Emergency Planning and Community Right-to-Know Act, 199–200
employee attitudes, 150–51
  discounts, 151–52
  identification, 125–27
  orientation and education, 123–25
  parking, 127–28

terminations, 135–37
employees, protection against termination, 200
employer's legal right to protect assets, 55
employment applications, 120
entertainment, 183–85
environmental audits, 200–1
  protection programs, 199
espionage, 4
ethical behavior, 97–99
evaluating physical security proposals, 70
executive management support, 82–84
  protection, 131–134
exit interviews, 137
Exxon, 131, 134
  Shipping Corporation, 200
  Valdez, 200

F

false arrests, 107–8
FBI, 7, 16, 55, 119
felonies, 106
fences, 73
fidelity bonds, 120
fiduciary relationship, 8
Fifth Amendment, 12
Film Recovery Systems, Inc., 197
financial institutions, 163–69
finished goods, 143
fire suppression equipment, 75
food processors, 145–46
Fourth Amendment, 12, 98, 113
fraud, 151
fraudulent expense reports, 152

G

gambling, 183, 185
gateways, 189
General Accounting Office, 5
General Dynamics Corporation, 197
general legal principles, 98–105
geographic limitations on authority, 53

German-American Bund, 3
government contracts, 171–72
  operations, 186–87

H

health care, 159–63
hijacking, 155
Holmes, Edwin, 2, 5, 75
hospital patients, 160–61
  pharmacies, 161–62
  visitors, 160–61
hospitality, 155–59
hotel and motel guests, 156–58
human resources, 119, 135

I

identifying risks, 87
immigration law, 102
industrial espionage, 9, 62–63, 141
industrial wastes, 198
information, 9, 142
in-service training, 48
insider information, 167–68
inspectors general, 5, 31–32, 187
insurance, 111; claims, 111–12
  companies, 86, 110, 168–69
  considerations in security programming, 110–13
intangible assets, 9
intellectual property, 103–4
international law, 105
International Trade Commission, 7
interviews, 107–8
investigations, 107–8

J

Joint Economic Committee, 7

K

Kidnapping, 162
Kindsland, NJ, 3
"knock-offs," 143
Kostanoski, John, 5